Have you ever been asked to manage a group that was seeking creative solutions to a complex, ill-structured problem? If so, you may have found that it was one of the most frustrating experiences in your career. All too frequently group members muddle aimlessly through the process with little understanding of what they are looking for and even less of how to go about finding it. The result is often a low-quality solution that meets the minimal requirements of individual members but does not reflect the sum of their creative resources.

Human relations specialist Arthur B. VanGundy offers logical, well-researched techniques that will help you monitor, guide, and develop your group's synergistic creative potential. His unique modular approach to creative problem solving will help you break your problem down into workable segments. It will provide the structure needed to prevent your group from wandering off course, while at the same time allowing enough flexibility to facilitate the creative process. Dr. VanGundy takes you through your project step by step, anticipating common problems along the way and offering easily implemented solutions.

How will the composition of your group affect its chances for successfully solving the problem? How clearly do group members understand their roles? Is there a way to assess the quality of ideas your group comes up with? Throughout the book there are numerous questionnaires, rating forms, and flow charts that will enable you to answer these questions and many more. By scoring and evaluating your responses, you can tailor the problem-solving process to almost any complex situation your group may face.

Drawing on his extensive knowledge of human behavior and group dynamics, Dr. VanGundy shows you how to distinguish between ideas and solutions, how to deal with group members who are disruptive or nonproductive, and how to help a group discover new perspectives on problems. The book clearly describes dozens of intriguing techniques for generating, evaluating, and building on ideas — techniques that you will find invaluable for keeping group interaction both lively and constructive.

ARTHUR B. VANGUNDY is Associate Professor and Interim Chairperson of Human Relations at the University of Oklahoma, where he teaches courses on creative problem solving, organization development, managerial development, and research methods. He has previously served as an organization development consultant and as a college administrator. The author of *Techniques of Structured Problem Solving*, *Training Your Creative Mind*, and *108 Ways to Get a Bright Idea and Increase Your Creative Potential*, Dr. VanGundy has also published articles in various professional magazines and journals.

Managing Group Creativity

A Modular Approach to Problem Solving

Arthur B. VanGundy

90-2558

American Management Associations

Other books by Arthur B. VanGundy:

Techniques of Structured Problem Solving, Van Nostrand Reinhold, 1981
Training Your Creative Mind, Prentice-Hall, 1982
108 Ways to Get a Bright Idea and Increase Your Creative Potential, Prentice-Hall, 1983

This book is available at a special discount when ordered in bulk quantities.
For information, contact Special Sales Department, American Management Associations,
Publications Group, 135 West 50th Street, New York, NY 10020.

Library of Congress Cataloging in Publication Data

VanGundy, Arthur B.
    Managing group creativity.

    Includes index.
    1. Problem solving, Group. I. Title.
HD30.29.V35   1984   658.4'036   83-73035
ISBN 0-8144-5545-X

Printing number

10 9 8 7 6 5 4 3 2 1

To
Art and Lois Wilson

Preface

This book has been written for managers and facilitators of groups who must deal with complex, ambiguous, and ill-structured problems. Ill-structured problems require more creative solutions than do routine problems. Unfortunately, most managers have not received the training they need to tap the creative potential of their groups.

Even when individual group members demonstrate a high degree of creativity, this resource frequently goes unexploited because of managers' lack of awareness about the types of variables that need to be managed. Furthermore, many groups attempt to muddle through the creative problem-solving process, but with little awareness of what they are doing or why. Frequently, the results of such muddling are low satisfaction with the process and solutions with no creative sparkle.

It is my contention that group creativity can be managed, that it is an activity that will respond to basic principles of management and group behavior. I am not saying that managing group creativity will guarantee creative solutions. There can be no absolute predictability when it comes to managing most groups. Instead, by applying some basic principles and using a loose framework of concepts, a manager can increase the probability of success when dealing with ill-structured problems. That is, the introduction of some structure into ill-structured problem situations will increase the odds that creative solutions will result.

This book is built around a set of modules pertaining to different aspects of group creative problem solving. By analyzing the relevance of each module to a particular problem situation, a manager can develop an overall problem-solving strategy that is tailored to a specific group. In this manner, a group can use what works best for it rather than what works best for other groups.

Although it is not without its disadvantages, a modular approach has several apparent advantages over the seat-of-the-pants approach used in many groups. First, as mentioned, a modular approach provides the structure needed by groups to deal with ill-structured problems. Second, this structure helps group leaders manage the creative problem-solving process and increases the odds of producing creative solutions. Third, a modular approach reduces ambiguity and the stress often experienced by group members when dealing with ambiguous situations. By breaking down a complex process into discrete units of activity, the modular approach makes the problem-solving process more manageable and less stressful to group members. Fourth, a modular approach is especially suitable for training groups to use a creative problem-solving process. A group can proceed at its own pace and monitor its progress quite easily through the use of modules. Finally, the most important advantage of the modular approach is its flexibility. A problem-solving approach can be tailored to almost any ill-structured situation, in accordance with the needs, values, resources, and preferences of any given group. By deleting or modifying certain modules, a group can decide what will work best for it given the constraints of a particular situation.

The disadvantages of a modular approach also should not be overlooked. First, not all groups will benefit from such an approach. A group that is experienced in creative problem solving and has been successful in the past may not want to tamper with its problem-solving strategy. Even in this case, however, a group may be able to learn something to refine its overall approach. A second disadvantage of a modular approach is that a group may become overwhelmed by the number of variables and decisions involved. If the group perceives the approach as too complex, it may not be motivated to use it. In such a case, it helps to note that a little effort expended at the outset often results in a higher payoff in the long run. It takes time to learn a new approach, but the probable outcomes of higher group satisfaction and unique problem solutions are worth it. Finally, using a modular approach requires certain diagnostic skills that not all managers or group members may possess. If a situation is improperly diagnosed, the resulting approach may be inappropriate and produce more problems. However, this disadvantage should be offset somewhat by the overall amount of structure provided by using a combination of modules.

The modular approach used here is divided into six parts, loosely based on a general systems model. The first part (Chapters 1 to 4) discuss the context of group creative problem solving. Chapter 1 discusses broad issues in managing group creativity. Chapter 2 presents a researched-based comparison of individual versus group creativity. Chapter 3 describes the major variables involved in establishing a creative climate in groups. And Chapter 4 presents an overview of the modular approach used in the remaining chapters. The second part (Chapter 5) discusses some major inputs involved in group problem solving, such as problems, time, and people and physical resources. The third part (Chapters 6 and 7) looks at the content module. Chapter 6 discusses group composition, and Chapter 7 discusses group roles, tasks, and the physical environment. The fourth part (Chapters 8 to 11) focuses on the process module. Chapter 8 discusses redefining the problem. Chapter 9 deals with the generation of ideas. Chapter 10 focuses on idea evaluation and selection. And Chapter 11 discusses the implementation of ideas. The fifth part (Chapter 12) describes the product module. The outcomes module (Chapter 13) forms the sixth major part of the modular approach. The last chapter (Chapter 14) presents a "minimodular" approach, which is, in effect, an integrated summary of the overall modular approach. Figures are used extensively in this book and are often referred to either before or after they appear. To locate a particular figure you may wish to consult the List of Figures on pages ix–x.

I would like to make a couple of personal observations about conceptual models, such as the one represented by the modular approach described in this book.

I have long suspected that people who develop conceptual models of what is or what should be receive the primary benefits of such models. A model is a representation of reality as perceived by a model developer. While developing a model, the developer gains increased knowledge about and understanding of what is represented. Although others who study the same model may also benefit, I doubt that they will derive as much knowledge and understanding as the developer does. We each need to develop our own models of what is and what should be. In this regard, I hope that the model in this book acts as a stimulus for you to design your own model of how to manage group creativity.

The second observation I would like to make concerns the validity of the modular approach presented in this book. At present, no empirical research has been conducted to validate that the model is capable of doing what it was designed to do. The principles and concepts on which it is based, however, have been derived from numerous research studies on group dynamics and problem solving. Moreover, the specific variables in the model and the manner in which they have been related to one another are based on previous research on these variables and on my own personal experiences with the modular approach. Many differences of opinion exist within the scientific community as to how specific research results can be interpreted. Often, the variables used in the modular approach and their interrelationships represent my own interpretations of research results. Another person might have included other variables, eliminated some variables I included, and used other variable relationships. If the modular approach I designed can serve as a practical framework for practitioners and is capable of stimulating thinking among researchers, I will have accomplished what I set out to do. Neither I nor anyone else can design an all-encompassing model of group creative problem solving any more than anyone can develop an all-encompassing model of human behavior. I and others can only hope to capture bits and pieces of reality that are capable of being developed, over time, into better and more accurate descriptions of the way things are.

I would like to acknowledge the assistance provided by Candace Stockton-Bleakley, Donna Hogan, and Cheri Radford in typing the manuscript. Without their skills and helpful comments, this book would have taken much longer to produce.

Arthur B. VanGundy

Contents

List of Figures

List of Tables

1

Issues in Managing Group Creativity

An Example of Group Problem Solving

Jan shifted uncomfortably in her chair as she surveyed the other members in the group. She had never worked with any of them very closely and was a little apprehensive. From previous encounters, she had pegged Sally as being bright and a little domineering, Fred as being intense and unable to articulate his thoughts very well, and Joy as being slightly reserved and highly critical of the ideas of others.

In recent weeks, Jan had been under intense stress as director of personnel for the DHR Company. Due to the recession, her boss had directed her to fire 38 employees. Although DHR is committed to equal employment opportunities, it has a longstanding policy of "last hired, first fired." She and the other members of her committee must decide who will be let go.

Given the little she knows about the other members (who were assigned to her from other departments), Jan is unsure of whether the group will be able to reach much agreement. She has had several years of personnel experience, however, and is confident that she will be able to come up with some workable ideas.

Jan and Sally begin the meeting by proposing several ideas that are immediately criticized by Fred and Joy as being unworkable. Joy suggests a lottery system, but this idea is criticized by Sally. Joy then counters with a justification of her idea. With the group at an impasse, Jan proposes an idea involving development of an outplacement program. No one criticizes this idea or makes any other comments about it. Sally then suggests the use of job sharing, which is immediately criticized by Joy.

At this point, Fred suggests his first idea and it is met with silence. He mumbles, "Well, it was just a thought," crosses his arms, and leans back into his chair. Fred doesn't say anything else during the rest of the meeting.

Sally next proposes the idea of merit examinations, which is criticized by all except Fred, who remains silent. Joy recommends dropping the retirement age. Jan says she knows this is not feasible. Sally asks which departments contain the people who were last hired. Jan tells her and suggests rescinding all merit increases. She immediately criticizes her own idea, and the rest of the group agree with her.

Joy asks if they should be recording some of their ideas as they go along. Jan agrees and suggests that Joy become the recorder. Joy agrees and takes out a pen and a piece of paper.

Sally begins to get impatient and encourages the group to come to a decision, implying that they have been wasting time. Joy agrees with Sally and recommends that the merit exam idea be discussed again. The rest show little enthusiasm for discussing this idea again. Sally then proposes that the group brainstorm to develop new product ideas in order to turn the company around financially. That way, she states, they might be able to avoid firing anyone. Joy says that such an idea is not in the charge to their committee and they should get back on the track.

Eventually, the group manages to develop a list of 12 ideas and begins discussing ways of implementing them. During this discussion, the group criticizes several of the ideas as being unworkable. Fred begins making paper airplanes.

With time running out for their scheduled meeting, Jan asserts her expert knowledge about the personnel field and pushes the group to go along with her solution preferences. There are no objections, and Jan ends the meeting by thanking them all for their help and telling them she will let them know what her boss thinks of their ideas.

With some modifications, this discussion actually took place in a group I observed. You've probably been in similar groups many times. You are given a problem to solve, but you haven't had much, if any, experience working with the other people assigned to you. In addition, you have little idea of what resources the group possesses and of how best to develop some workable solutions. Typically, you flounder around until someone makes a suggestion that is minimally acceptable to most of the group. Then you explore this idea in some detail, usually with frequent criticisms. At this point, you might continue to accept and reject ideas, or it might become apparent that each group member has a different perception of what the problem is. You now have to go back to square 1.

If you have been in such groups, you most likely experienced considerable frustration. When problem-solving groups operate without any type of plan, group members frequently end up dissatisfied. Moreover, these groups frequently have trouble producing high-quality solutions; minimally acceptable solutions are often all that they can hope for.

Using Guidelines

Unfortunately, there are no simple behavioral recipes for dealing with all types of problem-solving groups. Every group is different, just as every individual is different. What will help one group manage its activities may be entirely inappropriate for another group.

Fortunately, there are rules of thumb that individual groups can use to guide their behavior in solving problems. Although these guidelines may not work for all groups, they have been found to be applicable to many different kinds of groups, so an individual group can have some confidence in them.

Whenever classes of events and activities can be observed frequently and in large numbers, predictability is possible if patterns of behavior emerge. The laws of probability dictate that linkages can be established between certain behaviors and outcomes within specified limits of confidence. However, the limits of confidence are meaningless if only a few observations are made on infrequent occasions. Thus the knowledge base used to guide group behavior must originate from established behavior patterns observed across many types of groups in many types of situations. Otherwise, there can be no predictability and any guidelines will be worthless.

Although the group problem-solving literature is not sufficiently well established to permit 100-percent-accurate predictions about group behavior, enough literature exists to allow tentative predictions. Used cautiously, these predictions can form enough of a base to allow most groups to improve their functioning; used incautiously, both the groups and the study of group problem solving will suffer. The uneasy alliance that has always been maintained between theory and practice can be disrupted at the slightest provocation.

If we can assume that valid and reliable guidelines do exist for structuring group behavior during problem solving, then managing group problem solving should be just a matter of applying the right prescriptions at the right time. It should be. The actual case, however, is that most guidelines have been developed in conjunction with a rather limited type of problem-solving situation.

Most available problem-solving guidelines apply to well-structured problems. These guidelines typically include enough information about the current state of the problem, the desired state, and how to close the gap, so that very little creative problem solving is required. When there is one "correct" solution, routine procedures generally work quite well. By comparison, unstructured or ill-structured problems can be solved only by using custom-made procedures, because of the lack of information and because any number of potential solutions may be capable of solving the problem.

When a group faces ill-structured problems, the issue of managing group creativity becomes quite messy. Guidelines for well-structured problems generally do not apply, and the group leader is faced with a choice among a variety of alternative approaches. Frequently the group leader falls back on a routine procedure that worked well in the past for routine problems—only in this case, the results may be disastrous.

Managing Groups

Before proceeding, we need to define the terms *group* and *managing*.

A group is, quite simply, a collection of two or more persons who interact for some common purpose. Not all group members may agree on this purpose, but the purpose exists nevertheless. A group's purpose may have been developed internally by consensus, mandated by the group's formal or informal leader, or imposed by conditions or an authority outside the group. Groups come in all sizes and generally can be distinguished by the diversity of resources and characteristics of their individual members. Although some groups may be either homogeneous or heterogeneous with respect to the characteristics of their members, all groups—like snowflakes—are unique. Each group develops its own identity and standards of behavior that make it unlike any other group.

One dictionary defines *managing* as "a dynamic, ongoing process that involves bringing something about, succeeding in accomplishment, and directing, governing, and controlling in action or use." In the context of managing groups, managing involves the activities of planning, organizing, directing, staffing, and controlling. Regardless of how the term is defined, however, managing is a process without a discrete beginning or end. People who manage groups cannot follow a linear schedule, with the steps all neatly laid out. Rather, managing groups usually involves cycles of activities that must be repeated over and over again, although not necessarily the same way each time. Furthermore, the process of managing a group involves the ability to exert some degree of control over how the group functions. Unless a group is controlled, it cannot be said to be managed.

It should be evident now that problem-solving groups need to be managed when they are dealing with ill-structured problems. But this is only part of the picture. Groups also need to be managed when (1) the group members lack experience, training, and task-relevant abilities, (2) essential resources are in short supply, (3) conflict exists among group members, (4) goals are unclear and motivation to achieve them is low, and (5) group cohesion works at cross-purposes to organizational objectives. Other conditions might also indicate the need for managing groups, but these five and the nature of the task seem to be the most important.

When group members lack experience, training, and the abilities needed to get the job done, the manager is usually responsible for rectifying the situation. Often the manager can have some say about the experience level of group members when selection decisions are made. The manager can also see that group members receive training and develop the skills they need to perform their jobs. The manager can obtain required resources to make up for a resource lack by acquiring or redefining time, using the boundary-spanning role to obtain vital information, or using formal channels to request additional personnel, supplies, or materials. When conflict arises within a group, it generally falls to the manager to resolve it. The manager can do this by acting as a referee, bringing in a third party to mediate the conflict, or referring the conflicting parties to some outside source of help. Most managers deal with lack of goal clarity and lack of motivation on a fairly regular basis. Managers often handle lack of goal clarity by using MBO and informal conferences, while they typically gloss over motivation problems, assuming they are taken care of by the use of external rewards or by referral to a counselor. Finally, the manager can counteract the negative aspects of group cohesion through the use of individual consultations with "key" group members, team building, or even structural changes in the workers' jobs.

Clearly, there are many areas in which managers can have an impact on their groups, either by using the authority of their position or by attempting to influence group members personally. However, having the potential to manage groups is not always the same as being able to manage them. There are many restraining forces that can make this task exceedingly difficult. For example, many managers do not have the power to control and administer certain types of rewards, time cannot always be manipulated, acquisition of resources can become bogged down in bureaucratic procedures, and managers themselves can lack the abilities needed to plan, direct, organize, and control a group effectively.

Note that the same factors that determine whether a group should be managed also determine whether a group should not be managed. A group handling a well-structured, clearly understood problem for which routine procedures are available will require little or no management. Similarly, management will not be needed when the group members possess adequate experience, training, and task-relevant abilities, sufficient resources are available, no major intragroup conflicts exist, goals are clear and the group members are motivated to achieve them, and the group's cohesiveness does not work at cross-purposes to organizational objectives.

Although such situations will arise, it is probably safe to say that group leaders will rarely be faced with ideal conditions. It is much more realistic to assume that all groups will require managing at one time or another.

Managing Group Creativity

Webster's defines *creativity* as "creative ability; artistic or intellectual ability." But for our purposes, we are defining creativity as a problem-solving process that involves bringing something new into existence. It is a set of activities by which custom-made solutions are developed to reduce or close a perceived gap between what is and what should be. For example, if you own a small business that sells computer hardware and your sales are not at the level you would like, you have a problem. Let's assume that you have the motivation and the resources to solve this problem. If there are no appropriate routine solutions, you would need to use creativity to solve it. You must develop tailor-made approaches to the problem—even if the approaches are identical to those used by others in your business. If you are not aware of these other solutions, you will have to develop your own. Creative products do not need to be new to the world; they need only be new to your own perceptual and cognitive world. If you create it, then it is creative.

Group creativity is a similar matter. What is created by a group and is new to it is creative. Thus, whenever a group uses creative problem-solving techniques to solve an ill-structured problem, it works through a creative process to produce a product that is unique to that group. It doesn't matter (from a definitional standpoint) whether other groups have produced similar or identical products. If a group-generated product is new to the group, it must be considered creative.

Managing group creativity is an altogether different matter. There are those who maintain that the term *group creativity* is a misnomer. They suggest that only individuals can be creative, since creativity is an individual matter. Consequently, it is inappropriate to talk about managing group creativity. If it doesn't exist, it can't be managed.

The fallacy of this argument stems from the fact that group creativity is more than the sum of the creative contributions of each group member. Groups possess a synergistic potential that allows them to operate beyond the capabilities of a given member on certain types of tasks. The interaction of each member's creative potential enables most groups to produce creative solutions of far greater quality than could be produced by an individual working alone.

This is not to say, however, that groups will always be more creative than individuals. The dynamics of group functioning often place considerable restraints on a group's ability to reach its potential. For instance, groups can be less efficient than individuals when time is diverted from a task to satisfy social interaction needs or when conflict develops among group members.

In order to maximize the potential of groups, groups must be managed. The fulfillment of the synergistic potential of a group is not something that should be left to chance. Group leaders can exert considerable control in helping groups to attain this potential, but a delicate balance must be maintained in meeting individual, group, and organizational needs and objectives.

Perhaps the most difficult aspect of managing group creativity is ensuring that the group achieves its potential while the individual members do not. For a group to be optimally effective, the creative potential achieved by each member has to mesh with the potential achieved by every other member. If all the members are left to their own devices and work toward maximizing their individual potentials, the group is not likely to reach its synergistic potential. Among other things, dysfunctional competition can develop. The parts of a group must fit together just as the parts of an engine must fit together. If the parts of a system do not mesh properly with each other, the system is not likely to work very well.

What, then, is involved in managing group creativity to ensure optimal group functioning? Although the research evidence doesn't lend itself to any definitive conclusions, enough information is available to allow at least a few tentative thoughts on the matter.

First, a group leader must be capable of assessing and using the resources possessed by the group members. A leader must learn about the creativity strengths and weaknesses of each member. And a leader must somehow decide how to use these strengths and weaknesses for the benefit of the entire group. For example, the leader must evaluate the creativity readiness or the attitudinal and cognitive disposition of members toward convergent and divergent thinking as well as the ability of the members to defer judgment. If some members are deficient or overly developed in one of these areas, the leader should take steps to make the necessary corrections.

Second, a group leader is responsible for establishing a creative climate within the group. A leader must ensure that the conditions that will predispose the group to produce creative solutions are present in the group. Among the important group conditions that a leader can control to some extent are openness to the ideas of others, willingness to take risks, perception of the internal environment as nonthreatening, feeling of freedom and spontaneity, and a general atmosphere of trust. (Other important conditions will be discussed in Chapter 3.)

A third area in which a group leader can manage group creativity involves the composition and roles of the group members. Although a leader cannot always control who is in the group, a leader can do several things to take advantage of the types of members who make up the group. For instance, recent research into brain hemispheric dominance has many implications for how group members can be used to produce creative ideas. More will be said on this in Chapter 5. The roles played by the group members are related to effective group outcomes and can be managed by a group leader. Some of the most important are the roles of task facilitator, maintenance facilitator, and internal process monitor.

Fourth, a leader can exert considerable control over the creative problem-solving process itself. A leader can structure the process to be used, coordinate its duration and timing, and suggest specific methods to bring out each member's creative contributions. Perhaps the most important element that a group leader can manage is the separation of the problem-solving process into relatively distinct stages. In particular, a group leader can make sure that idea getting and idea evaluating—activities fundamental to the development of creative solutions—are separated.

Finally, a group leader can manage the creative products produced by the group. A leader can clarify the group members' perceptions of different types of products, assist them in evaluating their products' uniqueness and feasibility, suggest criteria to use in deciding which idea(s) to select, help gain outside acceptance for the group's ideas, help "sell" the group's products, and work with the group in evaluating the outcomes of its products.

Being Motivated to Manage

These five elements—diagnosis of a group's resources, establishment of a creative climate, the content, the process, and the product—all can be managed by group leaders. However, not all group leaders have the skills, the motivation, and the time to manage groups, even though they may have the potential to do so. Of these, the motivation to manage is perhaps the most significant.

It is very easy to ignore development of the creative potential of groups and rely, instead, on the chance contributions of individual members. Many managers spend most of their time "putting out fires." It seems that there is always some minor crisis that requires their immediate attention. As a result, they have little time or desire to get involved in managing group creativity. Their priorities and rewards are pretty well established, and their motivation is not likely to change.

However, being unmotivated to manage group creativity is not a crime. Nowhere is it written that all managers must motivate themselves to manage group creativity. If it were, there probably would be a considerable loss in group and organizational productivity.

Not all groups need to be creative. Some groups may spend very little time on creative problem solving, some may spend a lot of time, and others may spend equal amounts of time on creative problem solving and on routine problem solving. A major determinant of the amount of time that any group spends on creative problem solving should be the nature of the problems it has to deal with. As already mentioned, only problems that are ill structured require creative problem solving.

When a group needs to deal with ill-structured problems, it is important that its leader be motivated to manage the problem-solving process. If group leaders facing such problems attempt to develop solutions on their own or leave the creative process in their groups to chance, the resulting solutions are not likely to be of high quality. Clearly, a group leader's motivation to manage group creativity can have a direct influence on the outcome of the creative problem-solving process.

Just as a leader needs to be motivated to manage group creativity, so also must group members be motivated to participate in the creative problem-solving process. If the group members lack this motivation, they will have a low readiness for creative problem solving and most of their efforts will be haphazard or halfhearted.

It is a major responsibility of a group leader to assess the members' motivation in this area and to take any necessary steps to improve it. For instance, a leader can often increase the members' motivation simply by showing them how they can benefit from using a creative approach. A leader can also increase motivation by working with the members to identify gaps between what is and what should be in the group. Once the group recognizes these gaps, the members are likely to want to reduce or close the gaps.

The motivation to manage is also important in a group's relations with its external environment. Very few, if any, groups exist in isolation. Most groups depend on their interactions with the larger system of which they are a part. Groups need a variety of resources from the larger system to perform, and the groups are needed by the larger system. In an insurance company, for example, the sales force needs information, training, personnel, money, and so forth. The sales force then uses these resources to help the larger organization achieve its objectives. Without this mutual dependency, neither the group nor the organization could survive.

When a group is engaged in creative problem solving, it is, therefore, essential that the leader both help the group obtain the resources it needs and clarify how the problem fits into the larger scheme of things. If the manager isn't motivated to do these things, the group won't be able to perform efficiently or effectively.

Self-Managing Versus Self-Perpetuating Groups

Groups, like most open systems, strive to maintain a balance between their inputs and their outputs. In general systems theory, this particular state is referred to as homeostasis or dynamic equilibrium; in the parlance of organizational life, the actions required to achieve this state are known as survival.

Most groups, especially those in bureaucratic systems, have a self-preservation need that they can fulfill only by maintaining a continuous flow of inputs, transforming these inputs into outputs, and then using feedback to make any necessary corrections. A group's efforts in these activities very often are motivated by its need to perpetuate its existence. In rare instances, a group's need to perpetuate itself can overshadow its need to achieve the objectives of the larger organization. And if a group successfully perpetuates itself, its members often develop feelings of insulation and invulnerability.

Although not all groups get carried away with justifying and perpetuating their existence, a group's need to achieve homeostasis can consume a considerable amount of the members' energy. Group leaders, in particular, can become unduly preoccupied with managing the flow of routine events, to the exclusion of other activities. When this occurs, leaders often find that they have little energy left for managing group creativity—typically a nonroutine activity. Routine matters are usually more immediate and much more noticeable. As a result, group creativity is quite frequently left to chance.

Leaving creativity to chance in this way produces a dilemma for a manager. On the one hand, the manager would be irresponsible to neglect the routine activities necessary to achieving the group's objectives. On the other hand, the manager is just as irresponsible in neglecting the management of the groups' creative activities when the creativity is needed to resolve problems related to the group's objectives.

It would be very easy to say that this dilemma can be resolved if managers would only seek a balance between their responsibilities for both routine and nonroutine activities. In fact, I just said it! Managers should seek such a balance. However, for a variety of reasons, this balance is not always very easy to achieve.

Another way out of this dilemma is for managers to work at making their groups self-managing in the area of group creativity. If managers did this, group creativity would not be left to chance and managers could direct more of their energies to routine activities and, especially, to long-range planning—another often-neglected managerial activity.

Self-managed group creativity can also provide group members with a greater sense of participation, assuming that they need it (testing this assumption would be a managerial responsibility). In addition, self-managed group creativity can increase group member satisfaction, identification with the group, and the quality of the product.

Achieving self-managed group creativity is a major responsibility of a group leader. This should be approached gradually by the manager, however, so that all group members can integrate the skills and behaviors needed for creative problem solving as they gain experience with them. Too rapid an approach could result in only superficial acceptance of the concept of self-managed creativity. In this regard, a group leader should reduce slowly the number of structuring behaviors used to manage the group as it becomes evident that the group is capable of assuming increased self-monitoring responsibilities.

Of course, self-managed group creativity is an ideal that is easier to aim at than it is to achieve. What is more important is for a group to develop a commitment to reaching a state of pure self-management. Whether or not this goal is actually achieved probably doesn't matter very much. The process of striving actively toward this ideal is what is important, since it is likely to increase the group's ability to manage its own creative efforts without draining the manager's energies.

Summary

Problem-solving groups that operate without the benefit of a plan often produce unhappy members and low-quality products. The use of guidelines can help groups better manage their problem-solving activities. And in most cases, there can be considerable predictability from using guidelines when they are based on frequent observations of large numbers of groups.

Most guidelines that now exist were developed to assist groups in resolving well-structured problems. These guidelines will be of little help to groups faced with ill-structured problems. For these problems, custom-made procedures involving creative problem-solving approaches are more appropriate.

The process of managing groups involves controlling and directing the activities of two or more persons who interact for some common purpose. Managing groups is not a single, discrete activity, but a process involving a cycle of activities that are performed over and over, possibly in a different way each time.

Most groups need to be managed when they are confronted with ill-structured problems. However, groups also need to be managed at certain other times, such as when the group members lack experience and when essential resources are in short supply. There are various measures that group leaders can apply to manage these conditions. Group leaders must also learn how to overcome certain external obstacles.

Creativity is defined here as a problem-solving process that involves bringing something new into existence. In order to be considered creative, the products generated by a group need only be new to the group.

Often, the process of managing group creativity is viewed as a contradiction in terms, since some maintain that creativity is strictly an individual matter. This position is weakened, however, by the fact that most groups are capable of synergistic functioning. That is, groups possess a potential that enables them to produce a product that can exceed in quality the sum of all the individual contributions. (In other words, the whole is greater than the sum of its parts.)

The achievement of group synergy in creative problem solving should not be left to chance. A group leader should seek to ensure that group members fulfill their maximum creative potential, but not necessarily their maximum individual potential. It is more important for the group members to work well together than for any one member to shine above the rest.

There are several specific actions that a group leader can take to manage group creativity; one of the most important pertains to motivation. A key element in managing group creativity is the ability of leaders to assess both their own motivation to manage and the motivation of group members to use the creative process. The motivation of leaders is also an important determinant of their ability to acquire resources for their groups.

Most groups attempt to maintain a steady state of functioning in performing their assigned routine tasks. In some cases, this steady state can develop into a group obsession to perpetuate itself. Furthermore, the regulation of routine group functions often diverts so much energy from a group that a dilemma is created for the group leader. It can become very difficult for a group leader to manage adequately all the routine and nonroutine tasks in his or her charge. Often, the result is that the group uses routine problem-solving procedures to handle both types of tasks, when, in fact, it should use creative procedures for the nonroutine tasks.

Resolving this dilemma is a matter of managers' working to achieve a balance in the energies devoted to routine and nonroutine activities. In addition, group leaders can improve the situation by striving to help their groups become self-managing in the area of creative problem solving. Any measures taken to move groups in this direction, however, must be introduced gradually. Although achieving a self-managed group might be more of an ideal than an actuality, it is important that groups strive toward this ideal.

2

Individual Versus Group Creativity

Justifying Group Creativity

Picture yourself sitting alone, trying to be creative. Think of the last problem you worked on that required the development of creative solutions. What did you think about? What approach did you take? Did you generate ideas serially and then reject each one until you found a satisfactory solution? Or did you examine all the ideas in detail without rejecting any until they all were generated? Did you find yourself daydreaming from time to time? In general, how successful do you consider yourself to be at individual creativity?

Now picture yourself in a group you have been in that tried to develop creative solutions to problems. Did the group approach the problem in a much different way than you would have alone? Were the quantity and quality of solutions generated higher or lower than you might produce on your own? Did the group use a formal, structured approach, or did it just ramble on? In general, how satisfied were you with the group experience?

When you analyze your individual and group creativity experiences, you may discover that you have a decided preference for one over the other. You may feel that you can be more creative when you are alone than when you are in a group, or vice versa. If you were to generalize this experience, you might conclude that either individuals or groups are more creative.

To a certain extent, comparison of individual versus group creativity may be irrelevant. The real question may be: In what situations and under what conditions will individuals or groups be more appropriate? Both individual and group creativity are valid ways to generate ideas, and both are needed. Using just one method and rejecting the other would be like throwing the baby out with the bath water.

Before proceeding, we need to distinguish between two types of individual creativity. In the first type, an individual generates ideas alone and selects one or more of these ideas to solve a problem. In the second type, a collection of individuals generates written ideas alone and pools the ideas (a so-called nominal group). The group then applies one or more ideas from this pool to a problem. For the remainder of the discussion on this topic, the first type of creativity will be referred to as individuals working alone and the second type will be referred to as nominal groups or a collection of individuals working alone.

Most of the time, a nominal group (or any other type of group) will outperform an individual working alone—at least in terms of idea quantity. The research literature is less clear on whether a nominal group will outperform a brainstorming group, in which individuals generate ideas in a face-to-face situation.

The lack of current research in this area and the comments of numerous individuals suggest that further investigations comparing nominal and brainstorming groups are not needed. Many people believe the matter is settled—at least in terms of idea quantity. (The common understanding is that nominal groups produce more ideas than brainstorming groups.) In fact, because of the complexity of the issues involved, reliability questions about measuring instruments, and the number and type of variables involved, the matter is far from settled.

Creativity research, like any other area in the behavioral and social sciences, is more an art than a science. Very few statements of fact can be made about most of the variables involved in the study of creativity. Instead, we often have to rely on intuitive statements that arise from a synthesis and interpretation of the existing literature. For example, it was noted in Chapter 1, that because of the synergistic potential of most groups, group creativity is not a misnomer. That is, groups are capable of producing creative products that exceed the sum of the individual contributions. Many other intuitive/research-based statements could be made about the relative superiority of groups over individuals. It could, for example, be said that groups have more knowledge and information than individuals working alone, make fewer errors, develop more unique problem perspectives, and use participation to increase acceptance and understanding of solutions (Maier, 1963; Huber, 1980), or that groups are more likely to make risky decisions and to produce higher-quality and more diverse ideas (Stein, 1975).

In addition, research has demonstrated that on certain types of problems, groups are superior to individuals working alone (Hoffman, 1965). For example, problems with many parts that can be solved through a division of labor are more likely to be resolved by groups than by individuals. And groups will outperform the average individual problem solver on problems with multiple stages and verifiable solutions.

The advantages of groups over individuals working alone have been discussed in the research literature for many years. For example, groups can reject incorrect solutions and check errors (Barnlund, 1959; Shaw, 1932), and group membership will arouse a greater interest in the task (Barnlund, 1959).

Groups also have certain negative aspects that must be weighed against their positive features. Groups consume more time than individuals working alone (Husband, 1940), use social pressure to push for conformity rather than for a high-quality solution (Maier, 1963), engage in conflict that can delay problem solving and create ill will among the members (Huber, 1980), make riskier decisions (Wallach, Kogan, and Bem, 1962), and are subject to interruptions among group members that can result in fewer ideas being generated (Stein, 1975).

In spite of this research and intuitive thinking about the positive aspects of group problem solving, it's important to remember that the general superiority of groups over a collection of individuals working alone has yet to be established conclusively. Research on group creativity has been rather narrowly focused on the idea-generation stage, using comparisons of brainstorming and nominal groups. Other aspects of group creativity and other techniques have been almost completely ignored.

There is, nevertheless, enough evidence to suggest tentatively that group creativity is a valid area of study for both researchers and practitioners. A manager cannot ignore the resources that groups can bring to bear on a problem (process losses notwithstanding) and the synergistic potential of groups when deciding whether or not to use groups over individuals working alone. Groups just have too much potential to do without them for solving many types of problems.

Types of Groups

A key element in managing any group is knowledge and awareness about the type of group needed to solve a problem. Under some conditions, one type of group may be more appropriate than another. If you don't choose the best type of group for a particular problem, the outcome may be a low-quality solution and group members who are dissatisfied with the problem-solving process. Furthermore, awareness about types of creative problem-solving groups will help you in understanding and interpreting the research literature on individual versus group creativity that will be discussed later in this chapter. For these reasons, the major categories of creative problem-solving groups are discussed next.

In general, creative problem-solving groups can be divided into two major types: brainstorming and brainwriting.

Brainstorming Groups

Brainstorming groups generate ideas orally and can be subdivided into structured and unstructured groups, depending on the type of procedure used. Structured brainstorming groups use an agreed-upon procedure to guide the activities involved in generating ideas; unstructured brainstorming groups (sometimes referred to in the research literature as interacting groups) use oral idea generation without the benefit of any agreed-upon procedure.

An example of structured brainstorming is Osborn's (1963) brainstorming procedure in which a preselected group generates ideas, guided by certain rules and principles—the most important of these being deferred judgment. Although the casual observer may not see a lot of structured activity during an Osborn brainstorming session, a close look usually reveals a highly orchestrated process conducted by an experienced group leader.

In stark contrast to structured brainstorming, unstructured brainstorming is usually characterized by little directed effort and a general lack of momentum. In the typical scenario for unstructured brainstorming, a group of individuals sit down and "brainstorm" about some problem, often without the benefit of a group leader to facilitate the process. Most ideas proposed are criticized, and dominant individuals can be observed exerting their influence. Such a group was described at the beginning of Chapter 1. Unfortunately, unstructured brainstorming gives a bad name to Osborn's method in particular and to creative problem solving in general.

Brainwriting Groups

Brainwriting groups generate ideas silently, in writing, and also can be subdivided into two categories: nominal and interacting. In nominal brainwriting groups, a collection of individuals generates ideas alone, and the ideas are then pooled and duplicates eliminated. Such groups are referred to as nominal, because they are groups in name only. That is, they generate ideas as if they were a group, but the ideas are not shared among the individuals. Interacting brainwriting groups, in contrast, share the ideas generated by the individuals. However, no discussion takes place about any of the ideas.

In nominal brainwriting groups, the participants write down their ideas on cards and then pass them to a group leader. One of the most popular nominal brainwriting methods is the nominal group technique (Delbecq, Van de Ven, and Gustafson, 1975). In using this method, the participants have an opportunity to see the ideas of others, but only after all ideas have been written down and passed in.

An example of interacting brainwriting is the brainwriting pool technique (Geschka, 1980; VanGundy, 1981), originally developed at the Battelle Institute in Frankfurt, Germany. A small group of individuals sit around a table, and each individual writes ideas on a sheet of paper, places the paper in the center of the table, exchanges it for someone else's paper, and then examines this paper for any new ideas or modifications that might be suggested. The process continues until an agreed-upon time limit is reached, when all the papers are collected; the ideas are evaluated at a later time.

Evaluating Brainstorming and Brainwriting

Like any other decision, the choice of one type of group over another involves certain tradeoffs. You just cannot always have your cake and eat it too. Creative problem-solving groups are no different, since each one comes with its own built-in advantages and disadvantages. Thus, once you have decided to use group creativity, you must then decide what type of group you want to use.

Your decision can be facilitated by looking at some of the criteria relevant to using brainstorming and brainwriting. Although there are many criteria that could be applied, an examination of the research literature and consideration of the techniques' practical aspects suggest eight major criteria: number of ideas, quality of ideas, time/money costs, interpersonal conflict potential, accommodation of social interaction needs, contribution to group cohesiveness, pressure to conform, and task orientation.

This listing is not presented in any particular order. The actual importance of any one criterion is relative and will depend on individual objectives and constraints. However, it is possible to rate brainstorming and brainwriting against these criteria. Such a rating should make the major advantages and disadvantages clearer as well as aid you in choosing from among the various group procedures. (The questionnaire in Figure 2-2 is provided as an additional aid. To locate Figure 2-2, as well as any other figures in the book, use the List of Figures on pages ix–x.)

In Table 2-1, structured and unstructured brainstorming and nominal and interacting brainwriting have been rated against the eight criteria on a scale of high to low. In addition, the quantitative rating (the numbers in parentheses) has been provided to help you make overall comparisons between the different procedures.

In the rating of the procedures, "high" is a positive rating for idea quantity and quality, accommodation of social interaction needs, contribution to group cohesiveness, and task orientation, and "low" is a positive rating for the other criteria. For example, a procedure's ability to produce a large number of ideas is an advantage, while a procedure's inability to control for conformity pressures is a disadvantage (it is for this reason that both a high and low rating may be quantified with either a 1 or a 3).

Also, it was assumed that the procedures would be used as they are intended. It often happens that a group will decide, for example, to "brainstorm" on a problem without following the rules and principles set forth by Osborn.

Before looking at Table 2-1 in more detail, note that all the ratings are fairly subjective. The rating for idea quantity and quality, interpersonal conflict potential, group cohesiveness, and pressure to conform are based partly on empirical evidence. The ratings of the other procedures are based primarily on my own knowledge of the procedures and experience in using them. Thus, not only are the ratings subjective, but they also reflect my own generalized perceptions. After you become more familiar with the procedures, you may want to rate them for your own use. You may also want to use additional criteria.

In examining Table 2-1, certain fairly obvious observations can be made. First, idea quantity and quality should be highest for interacting brainwriting, medium for nominal brainwriting and structured brainstorming, and lowest for unstructured brainstorming. The major reasons for these differences are

Table 2-1. Criteria for evaluating brainstorming and brainwriting procedures.

	Brainstorming		Brainwriting	
Criteria	Structured	Unstructured	Nominal	Interact-ing
Idea quantity	Medium (2)	Low (1)	Medium (2)	High (3)
Idea quality	Medium (2)	Low (1)	Medium (2)	High (3)
Time/money costs	Low (3)	Medium (2)	Low (3)	Low (3)
Interpersonal conflict potential	Medium (2)	High (1)	Low (3)	Low (3)
Accommodation of social interaction needs	High (3)	High (3)	Low (1)	Low (1)
Contribution to group cohesiveness	High (3)	High (3)	Low (1)	Low (1)
Pressure to conform	Medium (2)	High (1)	Low (3)	Low (3)
Task orientation	High (3)	Low (1)	High (3)	High (3)
Numerical Totals	20	13	18	20

related to some of the other criteria. For example, if a procedure minimizes or eliminates interpersonal conflict and pressures to conform while maximizing task orientation, it should be easier for a group to generate more high-quality ideas than when these conditions do not exist. Thus brainwriting procedures restrict the participants to written idea generation and circumvent social problems within groups. (Incidentally, interacting brainwriting was rated higher than nominal brainwriting because the former uses other people's ideas to help stimulate ideas.)

Second, with the exception of unstructured brainstorming, all the procedures are relatively low in time and money costs. The low time and money costs can be attributed to the time limits and specified and reasonably efficient processes used for structured brainstorming and nominal and interacting brainwriting. Since unstructured brainstorming usually involves no time limit and no specified processes, the time and money costs are generally higher than for the other group procedures.

Third, brainwriting has a clear-cut advantage in eliminating the potential for interpersonal conflict. The silent, written generation of ideas used in brainwriting makes it impossible for individuals to engage in conflictual behaviors. Although the conflict potential for structured brainstorming was rated medium, the actual amount of observable conflict will be determined largely by the group leader's ability to control the discussion and mediate differences of opinion. Of course, not all conflict is detrimental to group creativity, and in some cases, it can heighten and sharpen the members' creative abilities. However, it is probably best to eliminate the possibility of conflict whenever a group leader lacks the skills to manage it.

Fourth, the major strength of brainstorming lies in its ability to accommodate social interaction needs and contribute to group cohesiveness. Because some people have stronger needs than others to interact in a social setting, brainstorming is the method of choice when such interactions are desired and not seen as having a negative effect on a group's ability to develop creative solutions. If the majority of the group members are *task*-oriented, brainwriting is more appropriate—at least in terms of this single criterion. The evidence is also fairly strong in indicating that brainstorming contributes to group cohesiveness. The very nature of the close interpersonal contacts that take place in brainstorming groups predisposes such groups to developing cohesiveness. Of course, brainwriting has no provision for interpersonal contact, and as a result, it will have little or no impact on group cohesiveness. This is especially true in nominal brainwriting groups, where there is no opportunity for interaction.

Fifth, brainwriting has a decided advantage in eliminating all pressures toward group conformity. Either because of the influence of a dominant member or general consensus, groups frequently can exert pressure on members to adhere to a particular norm or standard of behavior. When this conformity is accepted without questioning, the group climate is not likely to be conducive to freedom of thought and risk taking. And creativity in such groups may suffer accordingly. This phenomenon, known in the research literature as "groupthink" (Janis, 1972), often occurs in groups that are highly cohesive. Like interpersonal conflict, cohesiveness can be a plus or a minus for a group, depending on how it is handled by the group leader.

Sixth, all the group procedures except unstructured brainstorming have a relatively high task orientation. This emphasis is due solely to the structured procedures used in most formal brainstorming and brainwriting. In addition, group leaders may have some influence on a group's task orientation. The importance of this criterion is especially great for groups operating under significant time constraints. In this situation, excessive social interaction may prevent a group from accomplishing its tasks and goals. A heavy task emphasis will enable a group to be more successful and, in some instances, will even help a group to produce a larger number of ideas.

Finally, the quantitative ratings in Table 2-1 illustrate the overall utility of the four procedures. According to the numerical totals, structured brainstorming and interacting brainwriting appear to be the best procedures when all the criteria are considered together. Nominal brainwriting is a close second, but unstructured brainstorming is a distant third.

In general, it might be concluded that when social factors are important to a group, structured brainstorming should be used. When social factors are not important or certain social dysfunctions need to be controlled, either of the two brainwriting procedures should be used. In any event, both brainstorming and brainwriting procedures involve certain tradeoffs that suggest the need to use both whenever possible.

Research on Individual Versus Group Creativity

The need to examine the issue of individual versus group creativity is, foremost, a practical one. The investment in resources required to use groups dictates that groups be used only when necessary. If an individual or a collection of individuals working alone can produce equal or better results with a smaller resource investment (most notably, of time and money), it makes little sense to use group problem solving. Conversely, it would be foolish to rely on individual creativity when more successful outcomes could be achieved with a group. Like any other endeavor, creative problem solving should be both effective and efficient.

The discussion on individual and group creativity that follows centers on idea quantity and quality. Other issues could also have been included but were not in order to keep this review relatively brief. This discussion is not intended to be exhaustive and all-encompassing for the issues that are dealt with. Its primary purpose is to highlight the complexity of the issues involved in researching individual and group creativity and to demonstrate that the research findings are far from conclusive. The reader interested in a more in-depth examination of these issues, as well as many others, is advised to consult Stein's *Stimulating Creativity* (Vol. 2, 1975). In it, Stein provides a detailed and incisive look at group creativity research, especially as it pertains to nominal brainwriting and structured brainstorming.

Idea Quantity and Quality

Idea quantity and quality are separate issues that have been combined here because they have often been researched jointly. Of all the issues involved in comparing individual and group creativity, these two are the most heavily researched. Unfortunately, all this research has not led to many definitive statements about idea quantity and quality. Although some tentative statements are indicated, the failure to control for several key variables makes much of this research suspect. More will be said on this matter later on.

As noted earlier in this chapter, nominal brainwriting groups appear to be capable of producing more ideas than structured brainstorming groups. The research supporting this finding is fairly extensive (e.g., Bouchard, 1969; Bouchard, 1972b; Dunnette, Campbell, and Jaastad, 1963; Madsen and Finger, 1978; Street, 1974; Taylor, Berry, and Block, 1958). Research also appears to support the contention that nominal brainwriting groups outperform structured brainstorming groups in terms of idea quality (e.g., Bouchard, 1969; Bouchard, 1972b; Campbell, 1968).

However, there is some research that suggests contradictory results. For example, in a secondary data analysis, Taylor, Berry, and Block (1958) found that adjusting for the total number of responses made (using covariance procedures) produced results suggesting the superiority of structured brainstorming groups over nominal brainwriting groups in terms of idea uniqueness. However, this finding held for only one of the three types of problems studied. Parnes and Meadow (1963) also obtained similar results, although it must be noted that the participants in their study (who used structured brainstorming) were instructed to defer judgment, whereas those in the Taylor et al. study were not.

Other research in this area has dealt with comparisons of structured brainstorming and synectics; nominal brainwriting and unstructured brainstorming; unstructured brainstorming and structured brainstorming; and structured brainstorming, nominal brainwriting, and interacting brainwriting. The results of these studies indicate the following: (1) Synectics (a brainstorming variation that relies heavily on different types of analogies) produces more unique ideas than structured brainstorming (Bouchard, 1972a). (2) Nominal brainwriting groups produce more ideas than unstructured brainstorming groups (Van de Ven and Delbecq, 1974). (3) Structured brainstorming groups produce higher-quality solutions than unstructured brainstorming groups (Meadow, Parnes, and Reese, 1959). And (4) nominal and interacting brainwriting groups produce more ideas than structured brainstorming groups (Madsen and Finger, 1978). In the Madsen and Finger study, the interacting brainwriting groups generated 20 percent more solutions than the nominal brainwriting groups, although the difference was not statistically significant (i.e., it may have been a chance difference). More research is needed on interacting brainwriting groups; they have been more or less neglected in comparison with the research done on nominal brainwriting and structured brainstorming groups.

Although it would not be appropriate here to launch into a detailed examination of these different group procedures in regard to idea quantity and quality, it can be concluded (based on a superficial examination) that nominal brainwriting groups produce more ideas than structured brainstorming groups. The evidence in regard to idea quality is more equivocal. Sometimes nominal brainwriting groups produce higher-quality ideas and sometimes structured brainstorming groups do. As far as other types of group comparisons go, evidence thus far is insufficient to draw even a tentative conclusion.

Alternative Explanations

Although most of the research literature supports the superiority of nominal groups over brainstorming groups (at least with respect to idea quantity), no discussion of this area would be complete without some mention of alternative factors that might account for the relatively low performance of brainstorming groups. Examination of some of the original studies reveals several factors that could "wash out" any observed differences between nominal and brainstorming groups. The most important of these factors seem to be types of responses, types of problems, and validity of experimental instructions.

Types of Responses

In previous research that found that nominal brainwriting groups produce more ideas than structured brainstorming groups, Bouchard observed that there was more variance in responses between the nominal groups than between the brainstorming groups. As an example, Bouchard (1969) notes that nominal groups in one of his studies produced an average of 39.3

responses while those in the Taylor et al. study had an average of 68.3 responses for the same problem. However, the brainstorming groups produced an average of 35.3 responses in Bouchard's study and 38.4 in the Taylor et al. study.

Among the reasons that Bouchard (1969) puts forth to account for these differences is the fact that participants in his study used written responses in the brainwriting condition and oral, tape-recorded responses in the brainstorming condition. In the Taylor et al. study, the responses from both nominal and brainstorming groups were oral and tape-recorded. The similar number of responses recorded for the brainstorming groups in these two studies may be directly attributable to the recording method, since identical group procedures were used.

Parnes and Meadow (1963) provide additional reinforcement for this view. Their study found that brainstorming groups outperform nominal groups. All participants recorded their ideas in writing as they spoke them. Thus only a small difference or no difference at all may be observed between nominal and brainstorming groups when responses are written.

Bouchard, citing a study by Horowitz and Newman (1964), provides a simple explanation for the effects of response type on number of ideas produced. This study found that a response requiring ten minutes when written requires only two minutes when spoken. Horowitz and Newman also speculate on other possible factors. For example, some group members may speak a lot to fill a silence, and writing down responses may represent a commitment to their ideas that some people are unwilling to make. In any event, the method of recording ideas may determine differences in idea quantity more than the type of group procedure used.

Types of Problems Used

Research has used both real and unreal problems. An example of a real problem is one in which participants are asked to think of ways to increase the number of European tourists who visit the United States; an example of an unreal problem is one in which participants are asked to consider the consequences of having an extra thumb.

Most of the research using these types of problems has shown that people are able to generate more ideas for unreal problems than for real problems (e.g., Harari and Graham, 1975; Maginn and Harris, 1980). This rather surprising result might be due to the tendency of participants to react in a silly manner and have fun with, say, the thumbs problem. As a result, their motivation is increased and they produce more ideas.

Nevertheless, both the real and the unreal problems used in the research are very dissimilar to the types of problems most groups encounter in "real life." The problems groups in organizations face usually have more significance to them than problems contrived by an experimenter. Consequently, research is needed in which individuals and groups are compared on problems that the participants perceive to have some direct effect on them—that is, problems in which a solution would have more practical implications.

Validity of Experimental Instructions

Another factor that may provide an alternative explanation for the superiority of nominal groups is the experimental instructions given to study participants. In research methodology, the question is one of internal validity. That is, did the experimental manipulations really affect the variables being measured? In regard to experimental instructions, the question is: Does telling people to follow the rules of structured brainstorming mean that they will behave in the intended way?

At present, few attempts have been made to determine whether study participants used brainstorming as it was intended to be used. Instead, most researchers have simply assumed that they were comparing the effects of structured brainstorming and nominal brainwriting. However, it is possible that what they really were comparing are the effects of *unstructured* brainstorming and nominal brainwriting. If this is true, all the conclusions and inferences that have been made about nominal and structured brainstorming groups may have been derived from what is really an experimental artifact.

Solution Acceptance

Despite the controversial nature of the research on different types of group creativity, it must be remembered that groups—in general—will be superior to a single individual working alone. This superiority stems from the practical implications involved when comparing a group with an individual. These implications will be most significant when a manager needs to decide whether to attempt to solve a problem alone or involve a group in the process.

One of the most important of these implications is solution acceptance. Because of the dynamics involved in participating in problem solving, groups have the potential to increase the group members' acceptance of a solution. And if solution acceptance is increased, group member satisfaction and involvement in solution implementation may also increase. Understanding the nature of these variables will help managers choose between individual and group problem solving. More will be said on this matter in the next section.

Acceptance of a solution by group members is a fundamental group problem-solving principle. Groups do not need or want to have input into every problem that comes up, but evidence indicates that groups want to participate in decisions that affect them directly. The best solution in the world will be of little value if it is not supported by those who are affected by it or by those who must implement it. And acceptance is not likely if one person (such as a group leader) solves a problem alone when others should have been involved. As a result, if group members have an opportunity to interact and discuss a problem, often the dynamics of the process can ensure solution acceptance and implementation.

One of the spin-offs of participation in problem solving is greater member satisfaction with the final solution. Group members who participate in a decision generally will be more satisfied than group members who are handed a decision made by one individual (e.g., Coch and French, 1948; Carey, 1972). Note, however, that satisfaction does not always guarantee follow-through to implementation (Powell and Schlacter, 1971).

Although the research literature is much less conclusive on implementation than it is on satisfaction, there is some evidence to suggest that group participation also increases effective implementation of a solution. People will often help carry through to completion what they have helped create. Nevertheless, there may be many instances in which such behaviors are not observed. For example, someone who helps produce a group solution but who does not believe it to be the best possible solution may not be highly motivated to implement it. Of course, the fact that some people may be more motivated to implement a solution when they have participated in developing it must be kept in mind as a positive feature of using groups.

Choosing Between Individual and Group Problem Solving

From the preceding discussion, it should be evident that there is a major difference between individual creativity and nominal or interacting brainwriting creativity. Individual creativity involves the generation of ideas by a single individual, and the ideas are not shared with others as part of the idea-generation process. Brainwriting also uses individual creativity, but either the ideas are simply pooled (nominal brainwriting) or written feedback is shared with others and then the ideas are pooled (interacting brainwriting).

As a result of this difference, there will be two decisions involved in choosing between individual and group creativity. First, you must decide whether you wish to generate ideas alone or to use a group. Second, if you decide to use a group, you must then decide whether to use brainstorming or brainwriting.

In making the first decision, the factors you will need to consider are (1) the amount of time available, (2) subordinate acceptance, (3) desired solution originality and uniqueness, (4) subordinate needs for social interaction, (5) the amount of information you possess about the problem, (6) the need to increase group cohesion, (7) the personal development needs of subordinates, and (8) the conflict potential within the group.

The individual versus group decision-making questionnaire in Figure 2-1 will help you use these factors in your decision making. In using this questionnaire, you can rate the relative importance of each factor, given a particular problem. Keep in mind that not all situations are alike. At times, it may be better to use individual problem solving, and at other times, group problem solving may be more appropriate. For example, in some situations, you may feel that the need to increase group cohesiveness outweighs your own need to produce a quick solution.

Note that this questionnaire does not qualify as a valid and reliable scientific instrument. No research has been conducted on its ability to predict the appropriateness of individual or group problem solving for different types of situations. Nevertheless, it should serve as a rough guide in helping you sift through the various factors involved in deciding whether to use individual or group problem solving.

Figure 2-1. Individual versus group decision-making questionnaire.

Instructions: Read each question carefully and place an X above the one response to each question that best describes your general reaction. Do not spend too much time on any one question; your first reaction is likely to be the most accurate one.

1. How much time do you have to solve this problem?

Very little	Some	Just enough	More than needed	Much more than needed

2. How likely is it that you could obtain more time to solve this problem?

Unlikely	Somewhat unlikely	About 50/50	Somewhat likely	Likely

3. How likely is it that your subordinates will accept the solution if you try to solve this problem by yourself?

Unlikely	Somewhat unlikely	About 50/50	Somewhat likely	Likely

4. How important to your subordinates is acceptance of the solution to this problem?

Unimportant	Somewhat unimportant	Hard to tell	Somewhat important	Important

5. How reluctant would your subordinates be to implement a solution to this problem if they did not participate in solving it?

Completely	Somewhat	Hard to tell	A little	Not at all

6. How much do the advantages of solving the problem by yourself outweigh the need to obtain acceptance of the solution by your subordinates?

Completely	Somewhat	Hard to tell	A little	Not at all

7. How likely is it that solution uniqueness and originality would be decreased if you tried to solve this problem by yourself?

Unlikely	Somewhat unlikely	About 50/50	Somewhat likely	Likely

8. How much do the advantages of solving the problem by yourself outweigh the need for unique and original solutions?

Completely	Somewhat	Hard to tell	A little	Not at all

9. How important is it for your subordinates to interact with one another while solving this problem?

Unimportant	Somewhat unimportant	Hard to tell	Somewhat important	Important

10. How much do the advantages of solving this problem by yourself outweigh your subordinates' need to interact with one another in solving this problem?

Completely	Somewhat	Hard to tell	A little	Not at all

11. How much information do you have about this problem?

Very little	Some	A moderate amount	Quite a bit	A lot

12. How useful is the information you have about this problem (with respect to its ability to help you solve this problem alone)?

Not very useful	Slightly useful	Moderately useful	Useful	Very useful

13. How important is it that your subordinates become more cohesive?

Unimportant	Somewhat unimportant	Hard to tell	Somewhat important	Important

14. How much do the advantages of solving this problem by yourself outweigh the need for your subordinates to become more cohesive?

Completely	Somewhat	Hard to tell	A little	Not at all

15. How important is it for your subordinates to develop their creative problem-solving skills?

Unimportant	Somewhat unimportant	Hard to tell	Somewhat important	Important

16. How much do the advantages of solving this problem by yourself outweigh the need for your subordinates to develop their creative problem-solving skills?

Completely	Somewhat	Hard to tell	A little	Not at all

17. How likely is it that interpersonal conflict will develop among your subordinates if you attempt to solve this problem as a group?

Unlikely	Somewhat unlikely	About 50/50	Somewhat likely	Likely

18. How much do the advantages of solving the problem by yourself outweigh taking a chance on interpersonal conflict developing among your subordinates?

Completely	Somewhat	Hard to tell	A little	Not at all

Scoring and Interpretation: Change each of your responses for questions 1, 2, 4, 6–10, 13–16, and 18 to a numerical score between 1 and 5, going from left to right. For example, if you placed an X over the response "more than needed" for question 1, you would score it as a 4. For questions 3, 5, 11, 12, and 17, assign a "reverse" score to each of your responses. That is, score these questions by going from right to left. Thus, if you placed an X over the response "somewhat likely" for question 3, it would be scored as a 2. Once you have scored all 18 questions, add up the scores to determine your total score.

As a rough guide to interpreting your total score, you probably should involve your subordinates if your score is between 70 and 90. If your score is between 40 and 69, give serious consideration to using group problem solving. Your ratings on the time factor (questions 1 and 2) may help you to make this decision. For example, if you have little time and are unlikely to be able to obtain additional time, you probably will want to attempt to solve the problem by yourself. In this situation, time constraints will outweigh most of the other factors. If your score is between 18 and 39, however, you will be better off solving the problem yourself, regardless of your ratings on the time factor.

If you decide to use group problem solving, you next have to choose between brainstorming and brainwriting. Although some of the factors involved in choosing between individuals and groups also apply in this situation, there is enough of a difference to justify using a separate approach.

The factors involved in choosing between brainstorming and brainwriting are those already discussed and presented in Table 2-1. These factors are (1) idea quantity, (2) idea quality, (3) time/money costs, (4) interpersonal conflict potential, (5) accommodation of social interaction needs, (6) contribution to group cohesiveness, (7) pressure to conform, and (8) task orientation.

A questionnaire has also been constructed to help you to use these factors in choosing between brainstorming and brainwriting (see Figure 2-2). As with the previous questionnaire, this questionnaire is not scientifically valid and must be used and interpreted with caution. However, it should greatly simplify your decision making in this area. Before completing this question-naire, you might find it helpful to review the material on the different criteria discussed earlier.

Figure 2-2.   Brainstorming versus brainwriting decision-making questionnaire.

Instructions: Read each question carefully and place an X above the one response that best describes your general reaction. Do not spend too much time on any one question; your first reaction is likely to be the most accurate one.

1. How important to you is the number of ideas you produce to help solve this problem?

Unimportant	Somewhat unimportant	Hard to tell	Somewhat important	Important

2. How important to you is the quality of ideas you produce to help solve this problem?

Unimportant	Somewhat unimportant	Hard to tell	Somewhat important	Important

3. How much time is available for solving this problem as a group?

Much more than needed	More than needed	Somewhat more than needed	A little more than needed	Just enough

4. How task-oriented do your subordinates tend to be when working together as a group?

Completely	Somewhat	Hard to tell	A little	Not at all

5. How important to your subordinates is it for them to interact with one another while solving this problem?

Important	Somewhat important	Hard to tell	Somewhat unimportant	Unimportant

6. How important is it for your subordinates to become more cohesive as a group?

Important	Somewhat important	Hard to tell	Somewhat unimportant	Unimportant

7. How likely is it that interpersonal conflict will develop among your subordinates if they discuss this problem as a group?

Unlikely	Somewhat unlikely	About 50/50	Somewhat likely	Likely

8. How likely is it that your subordinates will exert pressure on each other to conform if they discuss this problem as a group?

Unlikely	Somewhat unlikely	About 50/50	Somewhat likely	Likely

Scoring and Interpretation: Change each of your responses to a numerical score between 1 and 5, going from left to right. For example, if you placed an X over the response "unimportant" for question 1, score it as a 1. After you have changed each X to a numerical score, determine the totals for question pairs 1 and 2, 3 and 4, 5 and 6, and 7 and 8. When you have added together the responses for each pair, you should have four separate sets of scores, each ranging between 2 and 10.

To interpret your scores, use the scoring guide presented in Table 2-2. Under each column of question pairs are possible score ranges, from 2 to 6 and from 7 to 10. Read across all the columns and locate the row in which all your response totals fall within the available score ranges for each question pair in the row. Thus, if your score totals for the four question pairs were (in order) 3, 7, 4, and 8, you would find them in row 11. Next, read across this row to the Procedures portion of the table and determine which procedures are most appropriate for your score totals. The procedures are presented in order of appropriateness, going from left to right. Thus, if your score totals for the question pairs were all in row 11, the most appropriate procedure would be interacting brainwriting, followed by structured brainstorming, nominal brainwriting, and unstructured brainstorming.

Table 2-2. **Scoring guide for selecting brainstorming and brainwriting procedures.**

	Question Pairs				Procedures
	1 & 2	*3 & 4*	*5 & 6*	*7 & 8*	
1.	2–6	2–6	2–6	2–6	UBS, SBS, IBW, NBW
2.	2–6	2–6	2–6	7–10	IBW, NBW, SBS, UBS
3.	2–6	2–6	7–10	7–10	NBW, IBW, SBS, UBS
4.	2–6	7–10	7–10	7–10	NBW, IBW, SBS, UBS
5.	7–10	7–10	7–10	7–10	IBW, NBW, SBS, UBS
6.	7–10	7–10	7–10	2–6	NBW, IBW, SBS, UBS
7.	7–10	7–10	2–6	2–6	SBS, IBW, NBW, UBS
8.	7 10	2–6	2–6	2–6	SBS, IBW, UBS, NBW
9.	2–6	7–10	7–10	2–6	NBW, IBW, SBS, UBS
10.	2–6	7–10	2–6	2–6	SBS, IBW, NBW, UBS
11.	2–6	7–10	2–6	7–10	IBW, SBS, NBW, UBS
12.	7–10	2–6	2–6	7–10	SBS, IBW, NBW, UBS
13.	7–10	2–6	7–10	7–10	IBW, NBW, SBS, UBS
14.	7–10	2–6	7–10	2–6	NBW, IBW, SBS, UBS
15.	7–10	7–10	2–6	7–10	IBW, NBW, SBS, UBS
16.	2–6	2–6	7–10	2–6	IBW, SBS, UBS, NBW

SBS = structured brainstorming; UBS = unstructured brainstorming; NBW = nominal brainwriting; IBW = interacting brainwriting.

In most cases, you should use the first procedure listed. However, there may be situations in which you will not be able to use the first procedure listed and will have to use an alternative procedure. For instance, you may not have the right materials or physical facilities. If this occurs, choose the next procedure in the row you are using.

Keep in mind that this approach to selecting brainstorming and brainwriting procedures is intended to serve only as a rough guide. Your experience in using the different procedures may prove to be more valuable to you if you have the opportunity to use all four of them. In addition, the scoring guide in Table 2-2 assumes that the procedures will be used as they are intended. To do otherwise would invalidate the selection process.

Summary

From our personal experiences, most of us have developed preferences for using creativity alone or in groups. In actual practice, however, the issue may not be whether one approach is better than another. Both individual and group approaches are needed, depending on various situational factors.

Individual creativity can be divided into two types. The first type involves individuals working alone and not sharing or pooling their ideas. The second type is similar to the first except that the ideas are pooled after being generated by individuals working alone.

Group creativity also consists of two types: brainstorming and brainwriting. In brainstorming, individuals generate ideas orally in a face-to-face setting; in brainwriting, a collection of individuals generate ideas alone in writing, without any oral interaction (a nominal group). The ideas are then shared and pooled or pooled without sharing. In general, a nominal group will outperform a brainstorming group in terms of idea quantity and sometimes idea quality, although the research results are far from conclusive on these issues.

Groups seem to have certain advantages over individuals working alone without pooling their ideas. For example, groups have an advantage in the amount of information and knowledge they can bring to bear on a problem, in making fewer errors, in developing more unique solutions, and in increasing solution acceptance and understanding. The disadvantages of groups include the amount of time they consume relative to individuals, the social pressure often used to force conformity, the internal conflict that can delay problem solving and create ill will, and the interruptions that can reduce idea quantity. In spite of these disadvantages, groups have a definite edge over individuals working alone. The real issue seems to be whether brainstorming procedures or nominal procedures are best for creative problem solving.

Of the four major types of groups (structured brainstorming—oral idea generation using an agreed-upon procedure; unstructured brainstorming—oral idea generation using no agreed-upon procedure; nominal brainwriting—individual idea generation without face-to-face interaction and pooling of ideas; and interacting brainwriting—individual idea generation with sharing and pooling of written ideas), structured brainstorming has received the most attention in the research literature. Nominal brainwriting and unstructured brainstorming have also received a fair amount of attention. Very little research has been conducted on interacting brainwriting methods.

In choosing between brainstorming and brainwriting procedures, eight criteria can be used: idea quantity, idea quality, time/money costs, interpersonal conflict potential, accommodation of social interaction needs, contribution to group cohesiveness, pressure to conform, and task orientation.

When rated against these criteria, structured brainstorming and interacting brainwriting are tied as the highest-rated procedures. Nominal brainwriting is a close second, and unstructured brainstorming is a distant third. However, these ratings reflect overall capabilities of the procedures. In actual use, there are certain tradeoffs involved with any procedure. For example, the brainstorming procedures rate high or medium in interpersonal conflict potential, accommodation of social interaction needs, contribution to group cohesiveness, and pressure to conform. The brainwriting procedures rate low on all these criteria. Because of these tradeoffs, both types of procedures might be used whenever it is feasible to do so.

In surveying the literature on studies comparing structured brainstorming and nominal brainwriting groups, the evidence suggests that nominal brainwriting groups produce more and higher-quality ideas than structured brainstorming groups. However, a secondary analysis of one research study indicates that adjusting for the total number of responses made produces opposite results for idea quality. Research on other types and variations of brainstorming and brainwriting procedures has resulted in mixed findings. More research on these procedures is needed.

Several explanations have been offered to explain the superiority of nominal brainwriting over structured brainstorming. First, written versus oral recording of responses in generating ideas may account for some of the differences. When brainstorming groups use oral recording procedures and brainwriting groups use written procedures, fewer ideas may be produced in the brainwriting groups due to the commitment involved in written recording, among other factors. Second, the problems used in experimental research on group creativity often are so unlike the problems encountered in real life that any observed differences in group procedures may be meaningless. Until more studies are conducted that use problems directly affecting the participants, any conclusions about the superiority of one procedure over another must be tentative at best. Finally, differences in group procedures may be explained by examining the validity of the experimental instructions used. In most cases, researchers have failed to determine whether telling study participants to use a particular procedure actually results in the intended behaviors.

Aside from all the research attempting to account for differences between individual and group creativity, it must be remembered that groups have certain practical advantages over individuals. When compared to a single individual solving a problem alone, groups have a major advantage in being able to ensure acceptance of a solution and, to some extent, group member satisfaction and commitment to solution implementation. When a manager needs to choose between individual and group procedures, these factors should be major considerations.

When a manager must choose between individual and group creativity, two decisions are involved. The first is whether to generate ideas alone or in a group. Some of the factors involved in making this decision are the amount of time available, subordinate acceptance, desired solution originality and uniqueness, subordinate needs for social interaction, the amount of information you possess about the problem, the need to increase group cohesion, the personal development needs of your subordinates, and the interpersonal conflict potential. A manager who decides to use a group must next decide what type of brainstorming or brainwriting procedure to use. Factors involved in making this decision include idea quantity, idea quality, time/money costs, interpersonal conflict potential, accommodation of social interaction needs, contribution to group cohesiveness, pressure to conform, and task orientation. Questionnaires are provided to assist in making both of these decisions, but they must be used with caution because their validity has not been scientifically established.

3

Establishing a Creative Group Climate

Nature of a Group Climate

I happen to live in the southwest part of the country, where the sun shines almost every day. Since I had lived most of my life in the northeastern United States, it was a welcome change to move here several years ago and find that there was very little cloudy and overcast weather. However, after a few summers of months without a cloud in the sky, I began longing for a place where the skies were cloudy all day.

When I shared this feeling with people native to the southwest, I found that most of them did not feel the same way. They felt that cloudy skies were depressing—even if they lasted only a day or two. I like one type of climate and they like another.

There is no doubt that climate can affect our moods. Some of us are affected more than others, and we all are affected differently. I like a balance of sun and clouds, while others may prefer more of one than the other. Like perceptions of beauty, weather preferences are an individual matter. What affects my behavior and attitudes may not affect yours.

Climate has several different features, including temperature, precipitation, and wind. Each of these features can affect life in both constructive and destructive ways. Temperature, precipitation, and wind all affect the growth and nurturing of plants and trees. When just the right amount of each climatic feature is provided, growth will be maximal. Too little or too much of any feature may be destructive. Thus, if the temperature is too hot, there is too little rain, and the wind is inadequate for pollination, the growth of many living things will be retarded if they cannot adapt to such conditions.

Similar types of effects can be observed in groups if an analogy is made between meteorological and psychological climates. Unless the conditions in a group are optimal, the group will not be able to grow and to nurture its creative potential. If, for example, a group is given too much freedom, encouragement to take risks, and encouragement to produce divergent ideas, it may not be able to generate workable ideas. On the other hand, too little freedom, risk taking, and a norm against divergent ideas may stifle creativity and result in mundane solutions. A balance in climatic factors within a group must be achieved for a group to grow and develop in proportion to its creative potential.

Of course, not all groups want or need to have a well-developed creative climate. Groups that are concerned primarily with the processing of routine tasks need to have a climate that emphasizes the efficient achievement of objectives. Conformity and control are essential in such groups. A well-developed creative climate would only disrupt the group's functioning and retard its development as an efficient processor of routine activities.

However, even when a group needs to have a creative climate, there will be situations where development of such a climate will be exceedingly difficult if not impossible. A major factor that determines whether a group will have a creative climate is the skill level and ability of the group leader. The group leader is usually the person most responsible for setting the tone in a group. If this individual does not have the ability and/or motivation to do this, it is very unlikely that the group will ever be able to develop a creative climate.

Furthermore, the larger organization of which most groups are a part may present another, sometimes insurmountable, obstacle. Unless the organization itself has a creative climate and is supportive of creative group climates, even the most skilled group manager will find it very difficult to establish a creative climate in a group. Groups in organizations exist as interrelated subsystems in which the effects of a climate in one subsystem can influence the climate in one or more other subsystems. If the managerial subsystem at higher organizational levels does not have a creative climate, the other subsystems in an organization are not likely to have one either.

Creativity in organizations and groups is not something that can be mandated like work hours, production schedules, or personnel policies. Ordering or telling people to be more creative is usually not very effective, especially in organizations with repressive climates. Creative climates must be carefully developed and nurtured in order to maintain a free and open environment in which innovation is encouraged and not discouraged.

In an organization in which a creative climate is desired, a primary concern of management will be to arrange the conditions that are conducive to the development of such a climate. Groups cannot develop an optimal amount of creativity unless the appropriate conditions exist. Without a creative climate, there can be no creativity enhancement.

A creative climate is also essential to groups that must deal with unstructured problems. Whereas structured problems can be solved by applying a recipe that will virtually guarantee an effective solution, unstructured problems, for which there is no routine way of proceeding, require creative solutions. The ambiguous nature of unstructured problems requires that a creative climate exist to foster the development of many different kinds of solutions.

Some groups are faced primarily with structured problems, some with unstructured problems, and some with a fairly equal mixture of both. As a result, it is not always easy to say that one group should have a creative climate and another should not. It depends on the amount of time a group must devote to dealing with unstructured problems requiring creative solutions. A group that spends a majority of its time dealing with unstructured problems has a very clear need to develop and maintain a creative atmosphere. The situation is a little more difficult to manage in groups that spend only a moderate amount of time on unstructured problems. In these groups, the group leaders will have to take special care to ensure that a creative climate is maintained, but also see that it does not interfere with the efficient accomplishment of routine tasks. Of course, groups that deal primarily with structured problems do not have a great need to work on fostering a creative climate. However, managers of such groups must be alert to the possibility that creativity could be stifled completely. New ideas for accomplishing even routine tasks should always be welcome in any group. The primary issue is one of maintaining the proper balance between efficiency and creativity.

Determinants of a Creative Group Climate

Developing and maintaining the proper amount of creativity within a group can be accomplished much more effectively if the factors responsible for producing a creative climate can be identified. Just knowing that a creative climate is or is not needed in a particular situation at a particular time is not enough. A group leader and group members also need to know the specific characteristics that make up a creative climate. Once these characteristics are identified, a group and its leader may be able to take actions to control them or at least to exert some influence over the type of climate desired.

In general, the factors that determine a group's creative climate can be grouped into three categories: the external environment, the internal creative climate of the individuals within a group, and the quality of the interpersonal relationships among the group members. There undoubtedly will be considerable overlap among these categories, as is often the case when categories are relatively interdependent. However, dividing these factors into separate categories can help clarify the interrelationships that exist among the factors and make it easier to conceptualize the nature of a creative climate.

The External Environment

This category includes all the things in a group's larger environment that can have an impact on how conducive to creativity a group perceives its climate to be. Such factors as management controls, communications, reward systems, attitudes, feedback, information, energy, supplies, materials, and values are all parts of an external environment that can have a direct impact on a group's internal environment.

Some of these factors are essential to a group's functioning and others are more discretionary, depending on the personal preferences of higher management or others in the external environment. For instance, most supplies and materials are essential, while values and attitudes are usually based on personal preferences. If a group perceives that it is receiving essential supplies and equipment and believes that attitudes and values outside the group are supportive of creativity, it will be much more likely to function creatively than if these variables are not seen as being positive.

Most environmental factors associated with a creative climate focus on two primary areas: the task and the people. Each one affects the other, and both are affected by the external environment. In most cases, this environment is the immediate system of which a group is a part. In some cases, however, the environment extends well beyond a group's immediate boundaries and has a much less direct influence on a group. Nevertheless, all environmentally influenced group creativity arises from a combination of the people and the tasks that make up a particular group.

Note also that the people and the tasks that exist in a group's environment (including other groups) may affect either the people or the tasks within a group. For example, a higher-level manager may dictate the way tasks are to be performed in a group, or the way tasks are performed in the immediate environment may affect how people feel about their jobs and lead to changes in their attitudes and behaviors. In other words, the variables of task and people are interrelated at both the intragroup, and the intergroup levels. The dynamics of a group's creative climate are fairly complex when environmental factors are considered.

The external environment should help to develop and maintain a creative climate, supporting task factors by:

1. *Providing freedom to try new ways of performing tasks.* A group's larger environment should build in mechanisms to encourage its employees to experiment without fear of reprimand. Of course, some controls have to be used, since everyone cannot do things the way they want to. This is especially true for highly interdependent tasks. However, the general atmosphere should be one in which managed change is seen as a desirable activity.

2. *Maintaining a moderate amount of work pressure.* If people are pushed too hard or hardly at all, they are not likely to perform very creatively. In order to be creative, a group must feel that it is under optimal pressure to get the job done. If all the group ever hears is how they need to turn out more widgets, they will have little time or motivation to be creative. Too little work pressure can also be a problem. Creativity usually works best when there is some felt need to achieve a goal. When there is very little emphasis on doing work, the only creativity observed may be employees thinking up ways to avoid work altogether.

3. *Providing challenging, yet realistic, work goals.* This factor is similar to the preceding one. The motivation to be creative is highly dependent on how work goals are perceived. If the majority of the group members believe that their work is challenging, they are more likely to apply creative means to achieve the goals. However, it is very important that the group members see the established goals as ones that they can attain with their skills and abilities. If a group believes that its reach exceeds its grasp, it probably will become discouraged and fail to apply its creative abilities.

4. *Emphasizing a low level of supervision in performing tasks.* Most people who have maximized their creative potential resent too much supervision. If at all possible, supervisory efforts should be focused on self-guided work, with only occasional supervisory controls used. Creativity requires a certain amount of independence and individual judgment, which can be stifled if too much control is exerted.

5. *Delegating responsibilities.* Establishing a norm for pushing down task functions to the lowest possible level will greatly expand the opportunities for workers to exercise their creative abilities. Too many workers, and especially managers, fail to use all their creative powers because they have allowed themselves to become overburdened by the minute details of their jobs. Groups operating at organizational levels where creativity is essential to organizational growth and survival should not

have to spend the majority of their time putting out small fires. It takes a courageous manager to delegate tasks, since delegation is often seen as an abdication of responsibility. However, without it, no real progress can be made.

6. *Encouraging participation in decision making and goal setting.* As noted in Chapter 2, group participation can increase the acceptance of solutions as well as ensure their successful implementation. When people feel that they have some ownership in the decisions affecting them, they usually are more motivated to use creative approaches in making the decisions. If they know that they stand to lose or gain by a decision, they may want to ensure that the highest-quality decision is made. Furthermore, just knowing that their opinions are valued can provide people with the self-confidence that they need to open up their creative thought channels.

7. *Encouraging use of the creative problem-solving process to solve unstructured problems.* Many groups must solve unstructured problems. For unstructured problems, the only appropriate process is creative problem solving, since it encourages the development of many different types of solutions—any of which may be capable of solving the problem. A routine problem-solving strategy (based on a rational and logical approach) would be inappropriate, since such an approach assumes the existence of one "correct" solution. Also, routine problem solving requires very little creative thinking and, for that reason alone, is inappropriate for developing a creative group climate. Consequently, using the creative problem-solving process at the appropriate time can do much to develop a climate conducive to creativity.

8. *Providing immediate and timely feedback on task performance.* It is probably safe to say that most people appreciate receiving feedback about their performance at a time when they can use it constructively to alter their performance if required. Performance feedback that is provided too late to make adjustments is of little constructive value and can even be destructive because of its potential negative effect on job satisfaction and morale. To be useful, feedback must be provided when it is needed most. The timing of feedback is especially important to people who are using creative problem solving, since new information can alter substantially the way a problem is approached. People who feel frustrated by a lack of feedback may experience a diminished capacity in their creative functioning. It is hard for people to be creative when they have an unmet need hanging over their heads.

9. *Providing the resources and support needed to get the job done.* Problem-solving groups require a certain minimum of time, money, people, information, supplies, and other resources. Without these resources,

they cannot perform to the maximum of their abilities. Although a perceived resource shortage may allow people to exercise creative skills in overcoming the shortage, such use of creativity only diverts creative energy from the tasks that are central to the group's existence. As a result, a creative climate cannot be sustained unless a minimum of required resources are provided. By making these resources available, higher management indicates its support and demonstrates its willingness to provide the conditions essential to creative problem solving.

The external environment should help to develop and maintain a creative climate, supporting people factors by:

1. *Encouraging open expression of ideas.* This action is essential in nurturing and sustaining a creative group climate. A repressive atmosphere in an organization is sure to foster a repressive climate within work units. If open expression of ideas is not encouraged organizationwide, it cannot be expected to occur at the group level. Upper management must set the tone for the rest of the organization. However, the encouragement of the open expression of ideas should be more than just lip service. Upper management's sincere commitment to new ideas must be evident in both its speech and its actions.

2. *Accepting divergent ideas and points of view.* Basic to encouraging expression of ideas is acceptance of different types of ideas and ways of looking at things. An organization that respects the differences among individuals is much more likely to receive original ideas than is one that values homogeneity in its employees. Conformity is fine in certain situations, but it is of little value for generating unique solutions to problems. A fundamental precept of creative problem solving is development of different viewpoints. And unless such viewpoints are encouraged, a creative group climate is very unlikely to occur.

3. *Providing assistance in developing ideas.* Most ideas come as rough stones that need to be polished before their full potential can be realized. However, an idea's proposer often lacks the information, abilities, or technical skills to develop an idea to a workable quality. Getting an idea and refining it frequently involve two entirely separate abilities. When the originator of an idea is unable (or unmotivated) to develop it to the extent needed to produce a workable solution, other people can take over this responsibility. If this is done, the net result may be a dramatic increase in the creative climate of a group. Idea originators are likely to feel supported in their efforts, and perhaps more significant, they are likely to feel rewarded enough to produce other

ideas. Consequently, a self-reinforcing cycle can be engendered that encourages creativity and provides the assurance that worthy ideas can be developed and refined. Of course, not all ideas are worthy of development. But working on those that are is preferable to automatically rejecting every initial idea simply because it is unworkable in its initial state.

4. *Encouraging risk taking and buffering resisting forces.* Being creative in a group or organization involves a certain amount of risk. If the overall organizational climate is not conducive to creativity, groups that exhibit creative behavior risk bucking a norm that may discourage creativity. And taking such risks can jeopardize performance ratings, promotion opportunities, and even careers. However, creativity by its very nature requires that risks be taken. Proposing a new idea or a new way of doing something old must be encouraged and facilitated for group and organizational creativity and innovation to flourish. People who know they are expected to take an occasional risk and that the potential consequences of such risks will be buffered by management are much more likely to exercise their creative abilities. In this regard, higher management must play a critical role in holding back the organizational pessimists and "naysayers," who always seem to pop out of the woodwork whenever something new is proposed. It is very easy to say that an idea won't work; it is much more difficult to help break the ground, beat back the opposing forces, and allow the worth of an idea to be given a fair hearing.

5. *Providing time for individual efforts.* Although the stimulation provided by other people in a group setting can be beneficial to creativity, too much group interaction can be a negative force. We all need some time that we can call our own and use to contemplate the mysteries of our existence. When we do this on the job, it often appears that we are loafing or goldbricking. Individual creative efforts, however, can be just as valuable as group creative efforts. When individuals have the time to work on a problem requiring creative solutions, they can use incubation to their advantage and not worry about what others may think of their ideas. Working alone on a problem is a time to commune with one's self as well as with the problem. And when organizational members are given this time, the climate of the entire organization will be more conducive to creative thinking.

6. *Providing opportunities for professional growth and development.* Much of the knowledge gained by professionals during their formal education becomes obsolete a few years after they have begun to apply it. As a result they need to be "reborn" every few years to acquire new knowledge. People in nonprofessional jobs can also benefit from being

"reborn" if for no other reason than that in this way they break out of the routine and monotony of their jobs. For both professionals and nonprofessionals, creative growth and development related to job performance will not occur unless the proper conditions for them exist. For many organizations, such conditions come in the form of workshops, seminars, refresher courses at universities, and even sabbaticals and leaves of absence. The creativity of all working persons needs recharging. One of the best ways an organization can provide this recharging is to create opportunities for employees to break away from familiar environments and experience something new—even if it is only for a short while.

7. *Encouraging interaction with others outside the group.* Groups obviously represent a very powerful force in their potential to harness the combined talents of several individuals. In some situations, however, the dynamics operating within groups can bring about very negative outcomes. One of the most notable of these outcomes is when a group develops a feeling of invulnerability and begins to function with perceptual blinders. This is especially noticeable in very cohesive groups and in groups that are relatively isolated from outside influences. After a while, they start thinking that they can do no wrong and that what they do and how they do it are the only ways of getting the job done. They may think they are being creative, but to a disinterested outside observer, it is usually apparent that they are only reinforcing a standard of conformity. When an organization makes it possible (through formal or informal means)—and perhaps even necessary—for group members to have regular contact with people outside their group, new ideas can be introduced to the group thinking process and help eliminate any tendencies toward group conformity.

8. *Promoting constructive intragroup and intergroup competition.* Competition, in general, can be a motivating force. When individuals or groups desire a common goal, the strength of their desire will be intensified if they are striving for the goal at the same time. Increased motivation can be a positive force within groups whenever the group members are competing among themselves or with one or more other groups. Motivation to succeed fosters the development of creative solutions by establishing a climate that encourages problem-solving behaviors needed to achieve a goal. The more difficult and complex the goal and the more intense the competition is perceived to be, the greater will be the efforts at creative problem solving. However, competition can also be dysfunctional in a group. When an entire group or certain individuals within a group become overly competitive, they may lose sight of the goal they are trying to achieve. As a

result, they may compete only for the sake of competing. When such destructive competition occurs, the outcome is usually a no-win, zero-sum situation. Everybody loses, because the goal is not achieved (or at least not in a timely and effective manner). Creativity requires some sense of competition but not too much.

9. *Recognizing the value of worthy ideas.* Most people like to be recognized for their ideas. They want to know that their efforts are valued and have not been expended in vain. Although some people derive enough satisfaction from internal recognition of their own task accomplishment, others are more dependent on external recognition. It's just nice for people to know that others think highly of their ideas. And receiving recognition can stimulate people to produce more ideas. Giving recognition is a low-cost activity that, surprisingly, is overlooked by many managers. A group is much more likely to sustain a climate conducive to creativity if its members receive recognition that is in proportion to the amount of effort made and the value of the ideas produced. Sometimes this recognition can take the form of a pat on the back and a simple, "Well done." At other times, more tangible rewards may be appropriate, such as cash bonuses or merchandise. In any event, all worthy ideas must receive some type of recognition for a creative climate to flourish.

10. *Exhibiting confidence in the workers.* This last of the people-related environmental factors is to some extent a more general form of all the other people factors. For example, encouraging open expression of ideas and providing assistance in developing ideas both demonstrate that management has confidence in the workers' abilities. In fact, working at establishing creative climates within groups is an expression of confidence of sorts. Management logically would not provide conditions conducive to creativity if it did not believe that both workers and the organization would benefit. At a more specific level, demonstrating confidence in people is another way of rewarding them for their efforts. When management shows that it feels positive about workers, the workers are encouraged to develop the belief that they are creative and can be counted on to produce unique ideas. The more that management reinforces a belief in the creative abilities of the workers, the more the workers will believe they are creative and act accordingly.

It should be apparent that most of the task and people actions that contribute to a creative group climate can be performed directly by managers at almost any level. Managers usually function as the link or boundary spanner between a group and its environment. They are responsible for obtaining resources, interpreting and implementing policies, buffering the group by absorbing risks, directly supervising the performance of tasks, and maintaining a balance between a group's task and people considerations. In short, managers often represent the external environment and are a determining factor in how creative a group's climate will be.

Individual Internal Creative Climates

A second factor involved in determining a group's creative climate is the creative climate of each individual. Just as groups and organizations can be characterized by specific types of climates, so can individuals be characterized this way. Each one of us possesses internal attitudes and perceptions that determine the extent to which we can develop our own creative potential. The more open and receptive we are to creative thinking, the more creative we can become. Individuals with well-developed internal creative climates are usually more proficient at viewing problems from many different perspectives, at generating unique ideas, and at generating many different kinds of ideas.

However, simply putting together a group of individuals with highly developed internal creative climates will not guarantee that the climate of a group will be conducive to creativity. As discussed previously, groups are more than the sum of their parts. Groups have the potential for synergy, which means that the performance of the entire group depends on the interaction of its individual members. In relation to a group's creative climate, the individual creative climates must mesh in such a way that an overall creative climate is produced. More important, however, each member of a group must perceive the climate of the entire group to be conducive to creativity. These perceptions are the cognitive and psychological cement that binds individual creative climates into a synergistic whole. Without these individual perceptions, there can be no creative group climate.

Many of the characteristics and qualities that make up an individual's internal creative climate are described next. There may be others, and the ones to be described will probably overlap to some extent. Nevertheless, these 19 characteristics should be fairly representative of the factors involved, and any finer discriminations most likely would be redundant.

Curiosity. Creative individuals are inquisitive and always searching for explanations. Such individuals usually will not accept the obvious and are constantly asking: "Why?" Much like young children who ask a continual stream of questions, creative people are not satisfied with tradition or answers that do not go beyond: "Because I told you so." Creative individuals need to discover answers by themselves.

Independence. Creative people are free thinkers. They are not overly influenced by others, and they maintain a strong sense of their own identity. When told how they should do something, they usually will resist—if only at a covert level. They want to do things their way. Their freedom from convention enables them to break away from the traditional constraints imposed on problems and view things with new eyes.

Ability to defer judgment. Many people have become conditioned by their educational backgrounds and other experiences to analyze and judge ideas, concepts, and opinions. They seem to react instinctively and attack new ideas with their most negatively critical opinions. They go right for the jugular vein and relent for only the most highly polished ideas. In contrast, people who have developed their creative potential have learned to give new ideas a chance to breathe and grow. They recognize judgment as an important part of the problem-solving process but exercise it only after all possible ideas have been proposed and developed. Creative people have learned that the most unique ideas usually emerge when judgment of all proposed ideas is deferred.

Willingness to test assumptions. Creative problem solving, in large part, involves the testing of many different assumptions. Perhaps the most important of these assumptions concerns the nature of the problem itself. A common mistake of problem solvers is failing to solve the correct problem. They think they are solving the correct problem, but after all the information is in, they may find that they were dealing with only a symptom or a subproblem. Adept creative problem solvers know that the most important phase of the process is defining the problem by testing all possible assumptions about the problem situation. Once they have done this, they are more likely to solve the correct problem.

Optimism. Creative people view the world with bright, positive eyes. This does not mean that they see everything through rose-colored glasses. On the contrary, creative people are realistic in their assessments. However, they tend to maintain a positive attitude that things can be done, that the problem can be solved. With such an attitude, they are, in fact, much more likely to achieve positive results than if their attitude were negative.

Humor. An individual with a sense of humor knows how to make connections between apparently unrelated events. Humorous people are capable of taking life and twisting it around to produce new ways of looking at themselves and others. These traits of humorous people are invaluable to creativity. Creativity also involves making unexpected connections and developing new twists on the way things are normally seen. Moreover, humor acts as a catalyst to creativity by helping to unleash subconscious information useful for making connections and producing creative insights. Humor and creativity go hand in hand.

Self-confidence. Being creative requires a certain amount of belief in oneself. Creative people believe that they have the abilities needed to produce unique problem solutions. If they didn't, they wouldn't be able to attack unstructured problems from many different perspectives. In fact, believing in one's ability to solve a problem can often be much more valuable than any actual abilities a person may have.

Openness to ideas. Most creative people are willing and even eager to listen to the ideas of other people. To a creative person, shutting out new ideas would be like going blind and not being able to hear. The ideas of others are rich sources of stimulation that creative people thrive on and grow from. In their awareness that being creative is not a static condition but a dynamic, ongoing process of growth and development, most creative people are constantly vigilant for any new ideas they might use or build on.

Persistence. Creative individuals do not give up easily. Most of them have a dogged determination that drives them to reach a solution. Thomas Edison is probably the most vivid example of such a person, in his search for just the right light bulb filament. Creative problem solving isn't easy. And luck doesn't help very much either. Persistence can do much to ensure that a solution will be achieved.

Concentration. Because of the hard-to-solve nature of most unstructured problems, intense periods of concentration are required to deal with them. This usually isn't hard for most creative people, since they become so immersed in the problems they must solve that little else is able to disturb them. However, complete and absolute concentration on a problem can also be counterproductive. Being too absorbed in a problem can prevent people from developing fresh perspectives and make it difficult for them to make remote connections. As a result, most creative people have learned to switch occasionally to another problem or some other, unrelated activity. Then, when they return to the original problem, they can resume their intense concentration with fresh energy.

Tolerance for ambiguity. People with a relatively poor internal creative climate usually have trouble dealing with ambiguity, which characterizes most unstructured problems. Such people tend to categorize other people and situations in either black or white terms. It is their way of dealing with ambiguity. Creative people, in contrast, tend to view people and situations in different shades of gray. Rarely will a creative person stereotype either people or situations. To deal with unstructured problems, a person must be able to tolerate ambiguity. A person who finds ambiguous situations extremely stressful is not likely to be very successful at creative problem solving.

Self-awareness. To be creative is to know who you are, where you have been, and where you are going. To be creative is also to recognize your strengths and weaknesses; to know what you can and cannot do. Before you can expect to develop awareness about a problem, you first must become aware of who you are. Most problems are portions of situations onto which we project a little of ourselves. Thus it is important to know what about yourself you are projecting when you attempt to define and solve a problem. As an extension of yourself, a problem situation will be easier to solve if you know why you are perceiving it in a particular way. Self-awareness is also important to creativity because of the information it provides you in knowing which of your personal skills will be best able to deal with different aspects of a problem situation.

Commitment. The total involvement needed to solve unstructured problems requires a commitment to developing solutions. Because unstructured problems do not bring with them any easy recipes that will guarantee a solution, solvers of such problems must commit themselves to working toward a solution. They must develop an attitude that nothing can deter them, that this is their problem and they have dedicated themselves to developing a workable solution. Without such an attitude, they are likely to take many shortcuts or settle for any solution that appears to be minimally acceptable.

Flexibility. Creative problem solvers have to hang loose. Becoming rigid in one's thinking is a sure sign that no creative solutions will be forthcoming. When mental inflexibility sets in, the senses are dulled and the production of most original problem insights ceases. Mental flexibility is a basic prerequisite of all creative problem solvers. A person needs it to develop new problem perspectives when defining a problem as well as to generate many different types of potential solutions. And it is one quality of an internal creative climate that cannot be compensated for by trying harder. Mental flexibility requires a controlled looseness of thought that trying harder will only cause to degenerate into more rigid thinking.

Willingness to take risks. Creative problem solving is an ambiguous, uncertain, and unpredictable process in which the outcomes are never known at the outset. People who engage in such an activity must be prepared to assume certain risks in their quest for solutions. Otherwise, they may not be able to view the problem in a way that makes creative solutions possible. That is, people who are not willing to take risks may inappropriately redefine a problem so that it is more structured and involves fewer risks or at least less overall risk. Creative individuals working in groups must also be willing to expose a little bit of themselves and risk the negative consequences that might arise from group opinion. A conservative course of action works only when people are dealing with known variables; creative problem solving involves unknown variables and, therefore, people must approach it with a willingness to take a certain amount of calculated risk.

Discipline. Contrary to what a lot of people might think, creative people exercise discipline in their approach to unstructured problems. They have trained themselves to follow a very specific procedure, even though at times it may seem chaotic and random to an observer. However, it is not the correctness of the approach that distinguishes creative problem solvers from other types of problem solvers. There is no such thing as a "correct" approach in creative problem solving. Rather, the essential factor is the extent to which progress is made in working toward a solution—regardless of the approach used. And making progress requires discipline to stick with a problem and approach it from many different angles.

Ability to use imagery. Everyone is capable of developing visual images of problems. Unfortunately, many fail to use imagery when it would be most helpful. By developing mental images of problems at the appropriate times, a person can often produce unique solutions with less effort than might be required using a more analytical procedure. Imaging, which has been the key to many great scientific discoveries (e.g., Einstein's theory of relativity), can be a better source of problem solutions than more conventional methods. Images provide new problem viewpoints and are a central ingredient of an internal creative climate.

Ability to toy with problems and ideas. Another hallmark of a creative person is the ability to toy with ideas. Think of very young children and how they will examine some new object, exploring all its features in great detail. Playing with an object like this helps children to understand it better. The same can be true when we are dealing with ideas. Creative people play with problems and ideas for some time before taking any action. They look at all aspects of a problem or idea and then perhaps decide that they need a new problem definition or a new form of the idea. By comparison, less creative people usually ride roughshod over a problem or idea in their quest to produce a quick solution. However, it is only by playing with problems and ideas that people can truly understand and deal with them.

Impulsiveness. Being impulsive can be a bad thing in some situations. For example, impulsively jumping up during a church service and loudly proclaiming yourself to be Napoleon probably would be frowned upon and not earn you much respect. In other situations, however, impulsiveness might be extremely effective. Creativity, for instance, usually benefits from intuitive and impulsive leaps of the subconscious. Considering the first thought that pops into your mind can frequently result in a remote association that you wouldn't have made if you had been more deliberate in your approach. Thus people who impulsively jump to conclusions quite often have a fertile internal creative climate.

Quality of Interpersonal Relationships

The third and last element of a group's creative climate concerns the quality of interpersonal relationships that exist among the group members. Unless these relationships are of a relatively high quality, creativity is not likely to flourish. The members of a group must be able to work with and relate to one another on a personal level in a way that is conducive to creativity. For example, if group members bicker constantly, they will have little energy left for creative pursuits related to the task at hand. Good interpersonal relationships and group creativity go hand in hand.

However, good interpersonal relationships can also work to the detriment of group creativity. If the members of a group relate to one another too well, the lack of tension or overemphasis on conformity may stifle creativity. The quality of interpersonal relationships in any group should be neither too low nor too high. Examination of the following ten factors can aid you in knowing when the interpersonal relationships in a group are optimal.

Interpersonal trust. Members of a group should feel comfortable working with one another and not harbor excessive suspicions about the others' motives. Individual group members should have faith in the abilities and skills of other members and should demonstrate this faith in their words and actions. Such trust can do a great deal to eliminate misunderstandings and interpersonal conflict. In fact, a high trust level is one of the most important ingredients of a creative group climate. If group members do not trust each other, they will have trouble cooperating on problem-solving tasks that require their interaction. Furthermore, a low level of trust may prevent development of a group's synergistic potential.

Acceptance of deviant behaviors and ideas. Many behaviors that charactertize a creative group might be considered deviant in a less creative, more traditional group. When members of a group engage in deviant behaviors and propose deviant ideas, the other members should be willing to accept such behaviors and ideas without undue criticism. Being deviant and being creative are often closely associated behaviors. Of course, extreme deviation in a group can be counterproductive and must be monitored by the other group members, including the group leader.

Willingness to listen. Interpersonal relationships within a group are based on the verbal and nonverbal communications of the group members. To be effective, these communications must be attended to; otherwise, there will be no real communication, and the quality of the interpersonal relationships will be extremely low. However, just listening is not enough. Communications must be understood, and perceptions and meanings must be checked if they are to be effective. Communication without checking for understanding can be as useless as no communication at all. Even the best forms of communication will be useless unless the other parties are willing to listen actively to what is being said. In groups whose members are willing and effective listeners, there will be evidence of attentive behaviors and paraphrasing of comments such as, "What I think I hear you saying is . . ." Without such behaviors and comments, high quality interpersonal relationships will never have a chance to develop.

Friendliness toward one another. Group members with effective interpersonal relationships will be outwardly friendly toward one another. This does not mean that they will agree with each other's opinions all the time or that there never will be any interpersonal conflicts. Rather, these group members will maintain an atmosphere of friendship that is optimally conducive to performing their tasks. They may not be "best" friends, but they are able to work together without undue strain.

A *spirit of cooperation.* Cooperation involves the group members' putting aside individual differences and working together toward some common goal. When a group is cooperating, it is using each member's resources in such a way that individuals almost tend to lose their identities as the identity of the total group takes over and moves the group forward. In this regard, a spirit of cooperation will usually precede and accompany a group as it begins to function synergistically. Group synergism is next to impossible unless the group members have learned to work together for the good of the entire group. And once a group has developed the ability to cooperate, it can unleash its creative potential for solving the problems it faces.

Encouragement for expression of ideas. When one group member proposes an idea, the other members should react to it in a positive way and encourage the proposer to elaborate on it. Very few ideas are initially proposed in the form of a workable solution. Therefore, it is imperative that a norm be developed within a group that makes it okay and even rewarding to propose new ideas. As each idea is proposed, the other group members should encourage the proposer by asking for additional information and by building on it with ideas of their own. Everyone has ideas, and silence during an idea-generation session should not be allowed for very long. The primary reason most people keep quiet during idea generation is that they fear ridicule or are intimidated by one or more other members. Every group member should view every other group member as a source of valuable ideas. The best way to benefit from this is by actively encouraging the open expression of ideas by all group members. To do otherwise is to risk missing the one idea that might be the germ of a final solution.

Open confrontation of conflicts. It is usually not socially acceptable to engage in interpersonal conflicts. Heated discussions, especially when they are conducted in the presence of people who are not involved in the conflict, basically are considered tacky and undesirable. In many groups, a basic norm is to repress conflicts and withdraw from any head-to-head encounters. At the very most, the majority of groups probably encourage compromise as the primary conflict resolution strategy. In spite of what most groups actually do in this area, however, what they should do is often avoided. According to a considerable body of research literature, open confrontation of interpersonal conflicts is the best resolution strategy to use. Anything less than this frequently results in a dormant conflict that will be triggered whenever the conflicting parties interact. Unless there is a group consensus that conflicts are to be dealt with by open confrontation, there can be little hope of cooperative behavior. And without cooperative behavior, synergy and the creative potential of a group that goes with this synergy are not likely to develop.

Respect for each other's feelings. Members of creative groups with high-quality interpersonal relationships are sensitive to the feelings of others. When interacting with one another, they make a special effort to consider how their words and behaviors might affect others. This does not mean that their words are sugarcoated or that their behaviors are cushioned by velvet gloves. There is a big difference between tiptoeing around someone's feelings and being forthright and demonstrating respect for the person's feelings. Most people need to express their opinions about others, and such expressions should not be repressed. Otherwise, the long-range effect may be development of serious interpersonal conflicts. Opinions about others should be expressed—but with a tact and sensitivity that show consideration for feelings. Hurt feelings can seriously damage a group's creative climate and should be avoided whenever possible. Of course, it will not always be possible to avoid hurting someone's feelings, and the costs always must be weighed against the benefits. In many instances, risking a personal hurt could actually improve a group's creative climate in the long run. When there is open confrontation of feelings in a group, the group's overall climate is more likely to be open and thus more conducive to creativity.

Lack of defensiveness. Many of us come ready-made with very fragile egos. For whatever reasons, we are sensitive about the comments others make to us and often interpret them in a negative light. We take things personally when the actual content of a comment may have been entirely objective and constructive. Defensive individuals typically respond to negative comments as attacks on themselves as people rather than as observations about their behaviors or opinions. For example, a defensive person who receives a negative comment about his eating habits may perceive the comment as a personal attack instead of as a comment on his behavior. In doing this, he shifts the focus from what he does to who he is. A fairly high degree of defensiveness in a group can have a disastrous effect on creativity. In order to stimulate group creativity, the members of a group must be able to perceive accurately the negative comments of others and react constructively. Instead of thinking, "You don't like me," people receiving the comments should exercise a certain amount of selective perception. By attempting to see the intent and meaning of a negative comment, a person's understanding will be increased and something new might even be learned. Whenever possible, people who recognize themselves as defensive should request additional feedback when they receive a negative comment and then sort out the good from the bad, the relevant from the irrelevant, and the useful from the unuseful. Group members whose interpersonal relationships are characterized by a lack of defensiveness are likely to have a more positive mental attitude that can aid them in their search for the positive values in all ideas proposed.

Attempts to include all group members. A group with a well-developed creative climate usually works as a team. All members are fully aware of their roles and know exactly what is expected of them. Such groups interact as a whole and with a sense of purpose that requires balanced participation from all group members. Recognizing that each person in a group is a rich resource for analyzing problems and generating ideas, creative groups actively encourage all members to participate to the full extent of their ability. Intentionally excluding or ignoring the comments and ideas of any group member could result in overlooking or missing out on the one idea that might lead to a unique and workable problem solution. Therefore, it is imperative that creative problem-solving groups continually work at drawing out the contributions of their shy or noncontributing members. Not attempting to include all group members in the problem-solving process would drastically lessen the chances of achieving group synergy and producing the creative ideas desired.

Although some factors from the three categories will affect development or maintenance of a creative climate more than others, the sum total of all the factors should be the major consideration when reviewing a group's creativity readiness. No single factor alone is likely to determine how creative a group will or can be in its creative problem solving.

In the next section, an instrument is provided for using these factors to assess your group's creative climate. After you have completed this instrument, you should be in a much better position to know which factors in your group need to receive more emphasis.

Assessing a Group's Creative Climate

Although reading and thinking about the factors that influence the development and maintenance of a creative climate can help you to understand these factors, reading and thinking are not a very systematic way to actually assess the factors for a particular group. A better alternative is to incorporate the factors into an assessment instrument that can yield quantitative ratings. Subjective as such ratings may be, they are still preferable to the more diffuse assessment likely to result from trying to assimilate and consider all the factors simultaneously. Used cautiously, the questionnaire presented in Figure 3-1 should guide you in determining how conducive your current group climate is to creativity and in pinpointing specific factors needing improvement.

This questionnaire is designed to help you to better understand the specific factors in your group's internal and external environment that contribute toward the development and maintenance of a climate conducive to creativity. It is not intended to tell you how creative your group is. Rather, it will provide you with some idea of how likely it is that your group can foster and sustain its creative potential while working on creative problem-solving tasks.

If the group climate is relatively open, you might consider completing the questionnaire as a group. However, all group members (including the leader) should participate equally. If you have the time available (or can make it available), try to achieve consensus in your ratings. Use voting or averaging only as a last resort. If you judge the group climate to be somewhat closed and characterized by defensiveness, the questionnaire should be completed individually. The results can be averaged and then discussed by the group.

Figure 3-1. Group creative climate questionnaire.

Instructions: For each of the following items, circle the one number that describes best the extent to which you agree or disagree with the item. Even though you may have trouble deciding among responses for a statement, circle only one number. Work as fast as you can, and do not spend too much time on any one statement. Your first reaction is likely to be your most accurate one.

1 = Disagree	4 = Slightly agree
2 = Slightly disagree	5 = Agree
3 = Neutral or undecided	

The External Group Environment
Overall, this organization:

1. Makes it easy to try new ways of performing tasks.   1 2 3 4 5
2. Maintains a moderate amount of pressure to "get the job done."   1 2 3 4 5
3. Provides challenging yet realistic work goals.   1 2 3 4 5
4. Emphasizes a low level of supervision in performing tasks.   1 2 3 4 5
5. Encourages managers to delegate responsibilities.   1 2 3 4 5
6. Encourages participation in decision making and goal setting.   1 2 3 4 5
7. Encourages use of the creative problem-solving process to solve unstructured problems.   1 2 3 4 5
8. Provides immediate and timely feedback in regard to task performance.   1 2 3 4 5
9. Provides the resources and support needed to "get the job done."   1 2 3 4 5

Total task score: _____

10. Encourages open expression of ideas.   1 2 3 4 5
11. Accepts divergent ideas and points of view.   1 2 3 4 5
12. Encourages risk taking and buffers resisting forces.   1 2 3 4 5
13. Provides time for individual creative thinking.   1 2 3 4 5
14. Provides opportunities for professional growth and development.   1 2 3 4 5
15. Encourages people to interact with others outside their primary work group.   1 2 3 4 5
16. Promotes constructive intragroup and intergroup competition.   1 2 3 4 5
17. Recognizes worthy ideas.   1 2 3 4 5
18. Demonstrates confidence in the workers.   1 2 3 4 5

Total people score: _____

Total environmental (task plus people) score: _____

Individual Creative Climates of Group Members
In general, the members of this group can be described as:
1. Curious.   1 2 3 4 5
2. Independent.   1 2 3 4 5
3. Able to defer judgment.   1 2 3 4 5
4. Able to test assumptions.   1 2 3 4 5
5. Optimistic.   1 2 3 4 5
6. Humorous.   1 2 3 4 5
7. Self-confident.   1 2 3 4 5
8. Open to new ideas.   1 2 3 4 5
9. Persistent when problem solving.   1 2 3 4 5
10. Able to concentrate.   1 2 3 4 5
11. Tolerant of ambiguity.   1 2 3 4 5
12. Self-aware.   1 2 3 4 5
13. Committed.   1 2 3 4 5
14. Flexible.   1 2 3 4 5
15. Willing to take risks.   1 2 3 4 5
16. Disciplined.   1 2 3 4 5
17. Able to use imagery to help solve problems. 1 2 3 4 5
18. Able to toy with ideas.   1 2 3 4 5
19. Impulsive.   1 2 3 4 5

Total individual climates score: _____

Quality of Group Member Interpersonal Relationships
When interacting with one another, the members of this group usually exhibit:
1. A high degree of interpersonal trust.   1 2 3 4 5
2. Acceptance of deviant behaviors.   1 2 3 4 5
3. A willingness to listen for understanding.   1 2 3 4 5
4. Friendliness toward one another.   1 2 3 4 5

5. A spirit of cooperation.   1 2 3 4 5
6. Open confrontation of interpersonal conflicts.   1 2 3 4 5
7. Respect for each other's feelings.   1 2 3 4 5
8. A lack of defensiveness.   1 2 3 4 5
9. Very definite attempts at including all members in group
   discussions.   1 2 3 4 5

Total interpersonal relationships score: _____

Scoring and Interpretation: Add up the numbers circled for each of the three major categories and obtain a total score for each. (Note: Subtotal scores for the task and people factors of the external environment category are provided for supplemental interpretation purposes only. Use the total environmental score to compute the group's overall creative climate score.) Next, compute an average score for each category. Then multiply the three average category scores together to obtain your group's overall creative climate score (CCS). Thus, the formula for computing CCS would be:

$$CCS = \left[\frac{External}{environment} \div 18\right] \times \left[\frac{Individual}{climates} \div 19\right] \times \left[\frac{Interpersonal}{relationships} \div 9\right]$$

Because the three category scores are multiplied together, a low score on any one of the categories will result in an overall low CCS for the group. This procedure reflects the synergistic aspects of a creative climate that could not be evidenced by summing the three scores. All three categories must interact at a relatively high level to produce a creative group climate—it can be produced only if a group is fulfilling its synergistic potential.

Possible average scores for all three categories range from a low of 1 to a high of 5. For the overall CCS score, the range of possible average scores is from 1 to 125. In general, the higher the score, the more conducive a group's climate is to creative problem solving.

As a rough guide to interpreting your group's actual scores, you can use the table at the top of page 57.

These scoring guides are only approximate, and you will have to use your own best judgment in interpreting the scores for your group. However, a low score in any area indicates that the group could benefit from special training in creative thinking before engaging in many creative problem-solving activities. Of course, a low score on the external environment probably could be increased only by actions that may be outside the control of an individual group. If this is the case, you will have to decide to what extent a nonconducive external environment would affect your group's ability to exercise its creative potential (assuming it has moderate to high scores on the other two category scores).

Category	Average Score	Interpretation
External environment	1–2	Low
	3	Moderate
	4–5	High
Individual climates	1–2	Low
	3	Moderate
	4–5	High
Interpersonal relationships	1–2	Low
	3	Moderate
	4–5	High
Overall creative climate score (CCS)	1–41	Low
	42–84	Moderate
	85–125	High

Finally, note that scores obtained from assessment instruments such as this one are rarely static. Groups and their environments are usually in a constant state of flux. The way a group is described one month or even one week may be entirely different from the way it would be described the next month or week. People leave and join groups, higher management changes in both personnel and policy, technology changes, the environment outside the organization is dynamic and can affect groups indirectly, and people themselves change over time.

To benefit the most from a creative climate self-assessment, a group needs to conduct periodic audits of its creative performance and to attempt to make adjustments whenever possible. As a rough rule of thumb, a group that spends a lot of time on creative problem solving should conduct an assessment every three or four months; a group that spends very little or only a moderate amount of time on creative tasks can probably get by with a creative audit every 10 or 12 months. The frequency of such audits, however, is much less important than the group's simply recognizing the need to evaluate its creative climate on a regular basis.

Summary

Just as the weather can have a psychological effect on individuals, so can the climate within a group have an effect on the creative potential of a group. For a group to be creative, it must possess certain characteristics for nurturing and maintaining creative thinking.

Not all groups need to have a creative climate, but for those that do, a leader is needed who is capable of setting the right tone and arranging the conditions conducive to such a climate. Creativity cannot be mandated. It can be provided for only by facilitating the processes, events, and resources needed for creative problem solving. Once a creative climate is established, a group will be in a much better position to deal with the unstructured problems that require creative approaches.

Knowledge about the need for a creative climate in groups is rarely sufficient for establishing such a climate. It is also necessary to identify the specific factors that determine whether or not a group's climate will be creative. In general, these factors can be divided into three categories: the external environment, the internal creative climates of the individuals within a group, and the quality of the interpersonal relationships among the group members.

The external environmental factors include actions that can affect either tasks or people. Task-related actions include providing freedom to try new ways of doing things, maintaining a moderate amount of work pressure, encouraging participation in decision making and goal setting, and providing immediate and timely feedback. People-related actions involve encouraging the open expression of ideas, accepting divergent ideas and points of view, encouraging risk taking, and buffering resisting forces.

Because groups are more than the sum of their individual parts, their creative climates will be more than the sum of the individual climates of the group members. The climates of all the people in a group must mesh in such a way that the group can express its synergistic potential in becoming more creative or in maintaining its current level of creativity. The individual factors that contribute to group creativity include curiosity, independence, ability to defer judgment, willingness to test assumptions, and optimism.

The third category involved in a group's creative climate concerns the quality of interpersonal relationships among the group members. Because most group problem-solving activities require group members to interact with one another, it is essential that their interpersonal relationships be of high enough quality to sustain and encourage creative thinking. Groups that are characterized by high-quality interpersonal relationships usually have such features as high interpersonal trust, acceptance of deviant behaviors and ideas, a willingness to listen for understanding, and an overall friendliness toward one another.

4

The Modular Approach

Introduction

The first three chapters presented basic background information on managing group creativity. Chapter 1 looked at the basic concept of group creativity and the issue and importance of managing group creativity. Chapter 2 reviewed some of the literature pertaining to individual and group problem solving as well as the different categories of group creative problem-solving procedures. And Chapter 3 examined the importance of and need for a creative group climate and the factors that make up such a climate. This chapter forms the bridge between the introductory background chapters and the chapters that describe the modular components involved in managing group creativity.

As shown in Figure 4-1, the modular components have been grouped into six major categories. Inputs, the first major category, includes problems, time, people resources, and physical resources. All these factors influence the content and process categories that make up the core components of managing group creativity. The combination of these core components then determines the creative products that result. The products, in turn, lead to certain outcomes, such as effects on the original problem, group member satisfactions, required adjustments in previous modules, and new problems that might be created by solving the original one.

The basic premise underlying the modular approach is that group creativity can be managed more effectively and efficiently by breaking down the major variables involved into more manageable units. When confronted with a task as formidable as managing group creativity, managers often feel overwhelmed by both the size and the complexity of the task. When managers deal with discrete units of the factors involved, the task at least can appear to be more manageable. Smaller units are much more reasonable and realistic to deal with than large amorphous masses.

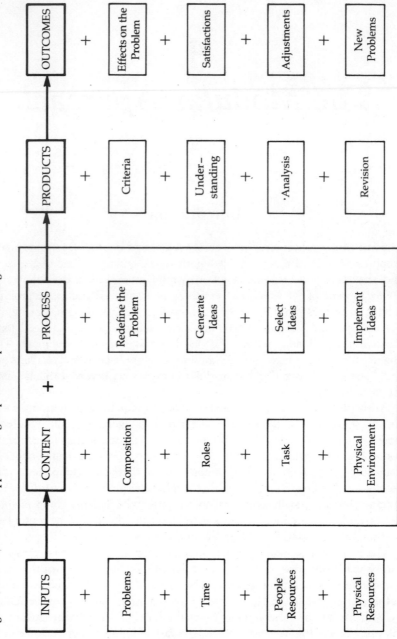

Figure 4-1. The modular approach to group creative problem solving.

INPUTS	+	CONTENT	+	PROCESS	+	PRODUCTS	+	OUTCOMES
Problems	+	Composition	+	Redefine the Problem	+	Criteria	+	Effects on the Problem
Time	+	Roles	+	Generate Ideas	+	Under-standing	+	Satisfactions
People Resources	+	Task	+	Select Ideas	+	Analysis	+	Adjustments
Physical Resources		Physical Environment		Implement Ideas		Revision		New Problems

A related advantage of the modular approach pertains more directly to how group creativity can be managed. Dealing with only small units permits managers greater flexibility in how the overall creative process can be controlled and directed. More specifically, most of the modules shown in Figure 4-1 can be rearranged (at least within categories) and even joined and used in different ways. For example, it may not always be necessary for group leaders to pay as much attention to some modules as to others. Or one module might be combined with another when appropriate. More specific information on using the modules appears in the section, "Using the Modular Approach," later in this chapter. However, before turning to this section, it will be necessary to examine one of the underlying dynamics of the modular approach.

Of the various dynamics involved, perhaps the most important one deals with diagnosing groups. The manager's ability to diagnose is essential to group management. And without group management, there can be no creativity—at least, no creativity that maximizes the synergistic potential arising from the interactions of the different group members. Thus, it is important to examine how group diagnosis is related to and can be incorporated with the modular model.

Diagnosing Groups

Diagnosing groups is very much like reading a "whodunit" novel. You read all the information, decide what information is relevant and what is not, try to understand the characters and their motivations, make inferences and draw conclusions, and make your choice for the guilty party. However, in diagnosing groups, your primary objective is not to identify who did it. Instead, your objective is to determine how a particular group might be managed best given a particular set of people, circumstances, resources, and so forth.

To diagnose is to delve into something, investigate pertinent information, and determine its nature or essence. When working with a group, you must understand what kind of group it is, where the group is in terms of variables related to creativity (e.g., climate, skills, experience), and where it should be or would like to be in its ability to function creatively. You will also need to decide whether where a group is will enable it to deal effectively with the different types of problems it faces. Furthermore, diagnosing a group requires an assessment of group products and the group itself after it has worked on a problem. Diagnosis is a dynamic, ongoing process that cannot be performed once and then ignored.

Obviously, groups must be diagnosed if they are to be managed and are to generate creative products. When applied to the modular approach, group diagnosis is necessary because of the fluid nature of the different modules. As represented in Figure 4-1, the various module categories are in a constant state of flux. Inputs, for example, change fairly frequently as factors such as the amount of available time and group member expectations (people resources) vary over time and across different types of problem situations.

Knowing when these factors and others will vary and how much they will vary across different problems is essential to using the modular approach. You must be able to determine where the group should be with respect to creative problem solving and all the variables pertaining to its implementation.

You can obtain this information only by making a thorough diagnosis of your group in relation to the modular approach. When you note deficiencies, they must be corrected if possible or accepted as unalterable—at least for a particular set of circumstances. Failure to identify and deal with these deficiencies will reduce a group's chances of producing a creative solution and could lead to decreased group member satisfaction and morale.

Diagnosis is fundamental to all problem solving. No problem can be solved without some form of diagnosis. If you visit a doctor for a pain in your back, you probably would not be very happy if he or she made no diagnosis and immediately prescribed surgery to remove your toenails. Such an action would involve putting the cart before the horse, the solution before the problem. A problem must be understood before it can be solved. And understanding cannot be achieved without diagnosis. You cannot get there if you do not know where you are now.

Although many managers and others involved in creative problem solving are aware of the importance of diagnosis to problem solving, it may be fair to say that they are much less aware of the need to use diagnosis before they begin problem solving. Before you can begin diagnosing a problem, you first need to diagnose the context in which you will be doing your problem solving. That is, you need to diagnose the inputs, content, process, product, and outcomes before you start working on a particular problem. Then you need to take whatever actions are required prior to dealing with the focal problem.

Another way of stating all this is that you must first solve the problem of where you are in terms of problem-solving readiness before you can begin dealing with the problem of primary concern. This first set of activities might be referred to as contextual problem solving, while the second set might be referred to as focal problem solving. When you are doing contextual problem solving, you are assessing your inputs, evaluating group understanding of the process to be used, identifying and understanding the significance of content variables, understanding and analyzing product variables, and anticipating the effects and consequences of outcome variables. In focal problem solving, you use the information gained from contextual problem solving as a guide to dealing with the problem situation that originally set into motion the need to resolve a gap between what is and what should be. It is the process that is applied directly to the problem that is creating a "pain" of some sort.

This distinction between these two types of problem solving should make the need for diagnosis more evident. Both types require diagnosis, but contextual problem solving is often overlooked. Use of the modular approach should help you to avoid this oversight, since with it you focus directly on the contextual variables that must be dealt with before you begin focal problem solving.

Using the Modular Approach

The discussion that follows is divided into: (1) a general description and overview of the approach and (2) a discussion of the procedure involved in using the approach. Although there is nothing sacred about the different steps described, you should give some consideration to them before developing your own approach. You may want to make alterations in the approach, depending on your perceptions of your circumstances. However, you should follow some sort of systematic procedure if you decide to deviate from the one suggested. There is no sense in using an ill-conceived approach to implement a well-conceived plan.

Description and Overview

Using the modular approach involves four elements: the group leader, the group members, assessment questionnaires for the different modules, and flow charts for guiding both focal and contextual problem-solving efforts.

The group leader generally is the person who initiates the modular approach and monitors its completion and evaluation. Although it would be helpful if this individual were proficient at facilitating groups and dealing with various aspects of group dynamics, this is not an essential requirement of the modular approach. Rather, group leaders should be aware of their strengths and weaknesses in these areas and adjust their approaches accordingly. For example, if a group leader does not feel skilled or comfortable in facilitating idea-generation sessions, the leader should recognize this feeling and use methods that do not require a highly skilled leader.

One of the most important functions of group leaders is to familiarize themselves with the procedures involved in using the modular approach. You must feel reasonably comfortable with the approach before attempting to use it. However, although a lot of knowledge can be gained from reading about the approach, there is no substitute for actually using it and experimenting with different variations until you find one that is comfortable for both you and your group.

When you apply the modular approach, it is best to use groups of five people. If you are a group leader supervising more than five people, divide the group up as well as you can. If necessary, use a group with seven people, but don't use more than seven or fewer than five people. In exceptional circumstances, where it would be inappropriate to divide a large group, the large group can be used. However, you then will have to consider carefully the techniques used during the process module. Most group techniques work best with five to seven people, although there are a few that can be used quite well with relatively large groups. For more information on this matter, refer to the material in Chapter 6.

Beyond consideration of group size, the major factors pertaining to group members using the modular approach revolve around their understanding of the approach and their motivation. Although the group leader is responsible for facilitating the use of the approach, the approach will work much more smoothly if the group members have a good understanding of it and how it is used. As a result, you should set aside time for training group members to use the approach. Before you attempt to use the modular approach, you will need to assess the group members' motivation to use the approach. New approaches to doing anything often meet with fairly strong resistance, and you will need to be overcome this resistance before taking any further actions.

If the group members appear to be resistant to the approach, you should explain its major benefits and suggest that they give it a try to see how they like it. The major advantages to be stressed in using the approach are: (1) It is a way to provide group member input and participation for problems affecting the group. (2) It is a way to achieve personal development in learning new skills. And (3) it has the potential to structure the problem-solving process, reduce inefficiency, and make problem-solving meetings more effective and productive.

The assessment questionnaires involved in using the different modules are tools that can simplify greatly the decisions that need to be made in using the overall approach. In addition to the questionnaires already presented for choosing between individual and group approaches, choosing between brainstorming and brainwriting techniques (Chapter 2), and evaluating a group's creative climate (Chapter 3). Others are provided in the chapters dealing with the individual modules. These questionnaires should help you make the decisions required at various points throughout the flow charts shown in Figures 4-2 through 4-8. In addition to the individual questionnaires, a summary questionnaire, covering the major variables assessed in the individual questionnaires and the flow charts, is presented in Figure 4-9.

Although these questionnaires will help you structure and simplify modular activities, they are not a substitute for the broader-based analytical and intuitive skills possessed by most group leaders and members. Quantitative scores are fine as long as they are interpreted correctly. However, if too much weight is placed on such scores, a group's basic analytical and intuitive abilities may be overridden inappropriately. View the questionnaires as rough indicators suggesting approximate interpretations of situations and behaviors and not as precise, absolute indexes of what actually is. Exercise caution in using and interpreting all the questionnaires in this book.

The final major element pertaining to the modular approach is the use of flow charts to structure and guide your problem-solving activities. These charts (Figures 4-2 to 4-8) describe activities and decision points incorporating both focal and contextual problem solving. Like the questionnaires, the flow charts will help to simplify the overall process. However, they also must be used with caution to avoid the problem of overrelying on the charts. They are intended to serve only as guides and not as precise steps to be followed to the letter. Again, you must consider your own and the group members' analytical and intuitive skills when you use such charts.

Procedure

The procedure for implementing the modular approach in a group that has never used it consists of six major stages. The first two stages focus on the manager's willingness to use the approach and on learning about it if interest exists. The next three stages focus on the group and its willingness to use the approach and on providing training in using it if the members are willing to give it a try. The last stage involves the direct application of the approach by the manager and the group to an actual problem of some concern to all. If you and your group decide to use the modular approach on a fairly regular basis, you will need to focus your attention only on this last stage. If you use the approach infrequently, however, some form of review may be required before beginning the process each time.

The following description and discussion of the six procedural stages are directed to the group manager/leader, on the assumption that this is the individual who will be responsible for initiating the overall approach and seeing that it is carried through to completion. Note, however, that the flexibility inherent in the modular approach makes it possible for a single person to use it for individual problem solving, with only a few modifications. In this case, stages 3, 4, and 5 would not be used, and the group composition and role variables in the content module would not need to be analyzed. Otherwise the procedure would be identical to that used by a group.

1. *Decide whether you want to use the modular approach.* The first activity of this stage involves becoming familiar with the approach. Before deciding whether or not to use it, you first need to understand what it is. To do this, you can read the entire book; briefly skim over the first three chapters, but read the remaining chapters a little more closely; or just read this chapter and examine the summaries and questionnaires presented in all the other chapters. Whatever you do, however, you will need to decide whether you have enough information to make the decision.

The next activity in this stage involves examining the advantages and disadvantages of using the approach. For example, advantages might include such things as: provides for group participation, helps to structure a basically ill-structured process, provides flexibility in putting together the approach, and helps to ensure that all major factors and activities are considered. Disadvantages might include such things as: is relatively time-consuming, requires that group members be motivated to learn and use the procedures, does not guarantee that a solution will be any more creative than one produced by an individual or a group using a less systematic procedure, and may be used unnecessarily if applied to an inappropriate problem situation.

After examining these and other advantages and disadvantages you might think of, you then need to decide whether the potential benefits of the approach outweigh the potential costs. You are the one who will have the major responsibility for seeing that the approach is used properly, and you must be willing to devote your time and efforts to using it.

2. *Study the approach in depth.* If you decide that you would like to try to use the approach with your group, you will need to develop a strong working knowledge of it. The ideal way to achieve this knowledge would be to skim the whole book and then read it again more closely for understanding. Next, select a practice problem and work through the flow charts and questionnaires as if you were working on the problem with your group. If you encounter any difficulties while doing this, you can refer to the appropriate chapters in the book. Once you have gone completely through the various procedures, the final step is to check yourself for understanding. This check is particularly important for areas that you found difficult to understand or difficult to do. If you cannot find the answers you need in the book, you will have to develop your own solutions. The important thing, however, is to try to anticipate any obstacles that might arise in actually using the approach and then to devise means for overcoming these obstacles. If you know other group leaders who might be interested in using the approach, you might consider studying the approach with them or at least practicing on a problem with them. Learning and understanding often can be accelerated and integrated better in a group setting.

3. *Describe the approach to the group members.* Once you believe that you

understand the approach, determine whether the group members are interested in using it. Before you can do this, you must give them some basic information. Begin by providing a brief overview of the approach, using the model depicted in Figure 4-1. Then move to the flow charts (Figures 4-2 to 4-8) and briefly review them with the group members. Avoid going into much detail, so the group does not become overloaded with information and reject the approach outright as being too complex. Instead, focus just on the key aspects of each module represented by the flow charts. Next, detail the advantages and disadvantages of the approach and ask whether the group members can add any to your list. Finally, ask the group members if they have any questions about the approach. If possible, you should have anticipated the questions you might receive at this point and developed answers to them.

4. *Determine the amount of interest in using the approach.* If you are strongly committed to using the approach but do not believe that the group members are (or you are uncertain of their interest), consider having the group defer making a decision on it. In the event that you decide to do this, tell the group to think about it for a period of time. Then consult with each group member individually to assess reactions and clarify any misconceptions. After conducting these interviews, meet again as a group and decide whether the approach is worth trying. Of course, if the group seems to be enthusiastic at the outset, a decision can be made at that time. Although you may not want to use this strategy because it seems manipulative, keep in mind that your purpose in using it is to make sure that all group members understand the approach and have enough information to permit them to make a well-informed decison.

5. *Provide group training in using the approach.* If the group members are willing to try the approach, you will need to provide some type of training to increase their understanding about how to use it. In general, this training can begin in much the same manner that you used to familiarize yourself with the approach. Have the group members individually skim this book and then read it in some depth. Next, have them work through the flow charts and questionnaires using a problem (either real or hypothetical) selected in advance by all the group members (each group member should work on the same problem). After they have done this, encourage them to develop a list of potential obstacles that might arise in using the approach and ways these obstacles might be overcome.

When the group members have completed their individual study of the approach, hold a group training session. At this session, the first thing to do is ask for any questions. Defer evaluative comments at this time, and focus instead on gaining understanding and clearing up any misconceptions. When the group seems to be clear on the approach and how to use it, ask for evaluative comments. These comments may deal with "gut" reactions or with more cognitive types of reactions. In either case, the objective at this point is to vent feelings and thoughts about the approach in order to ensure that no hidden agendas will arise while the approach is being applied.

When all these considerations have been dealt with, have the group begin working together on the practice problem they used as individuals. Your role will be critical now, since this is also your opportunity to practice facilitating the approach. Work with the group in discussing results from all the questionnaires and in dealing with the decision points in the flow charts. While doing this, place particular emphasis on the outcomes module, since this is where the group will evaluate the overall training process.

6. *Apply the approach to a real problem.* The primary difference between this step and the preceding one is that in this step practice time is over and it's time to get on with the business of solving a problem the group feels it needs to solve. Although the group may have practiced with a so-called real problem in Step 5, the common understanding should have been that the problem was being worked on primarily to provide practice. In this step, the primary objective is to solve the problem.

This distinction, while subtle, is an important one. Practicing on a problem requires a climate that encourages and accepts failure, since understanding of the approach is a prime objective. Working on a problem that involves a certain amount of "hurt" also requires a climate that encourages and accepts failure. However, the group members should experience a greater need to develop a workable solution when they have problem ownership and feel that they must reduce the amount of "hurt." Thus the motivation of the group members should be higher during this stage of the procedure.

After the group has selected a problem it wants to work on, it can begin using the flow charts presented in Figures 4-2 through 4-8. The charts have been designed to correspond with the five major modules depicted in Figure 4-1. Each chart describes a series of events and activities that can be used to guide application of the modular approach. Figure 4-2 presents decision points that must be dealt with before entering the five basic modules. The input module is dealt with in Figure 4-3, the content module in Figure 4-4, the process module in Figures 4-5 and 4-6, the product module in Figure 4-7 and the outcome module in Figure 4-8.

Remember that these flow charts are to be used only as general guides for working through the different modules. Only major events, activities, and decisions are represented in the charts. Thus what is actually involved is simplified to some extent in the charts. Do not feel that you have to follow these charts exactly. Depending on a given situation, you may want to deviate from the sequence of events or from the alternate paths suggested. The charts can help to guide and structure your use of the modules; they cannot replace the analytical and intuitive skills that often must be applied to adjust to changing situations.

a. *Begin the modular approach.* Some of the considerations involved in beginning the modular approach are shown in the flow chart depicted in Figure 4-2. The chart begins with the notion that you think you have a problem. Either you or you and your group have been feeling some need to change a situation. To better understand this situation, you have implicitly or explicitly placed boundaries around a portion of the situation and called it a problem.

To test out your feelings about the situation, you first need to determine whether a gap exists between what is and what should be. If you are involved in processing insurance claims and have an error rate of 9 percent but believe it should be under 3 percent, a gap exists. If no gap exists, you would terminate the process, since you do not have a problem; if a gap does exist, you would continue to the next point, which states you have a problem.

What you need to decide after you have recognized that you have a problem is whether or not you will need group input to solve it. To help you make this decision, you could complete the individual versus group decision-making questionnaire (Figure 2-1). If you decide that the problem does not need group input, you might decide to use individual procedures instead of the group modular approach. If you decide that group input can help to solve the problem (or is necessary), continue to the next decision point in the flow chart.

At this point, you need to assess the group's creative climate to determine whether it is conducive to using the modular approach. The group creative climate questionnaire (Figure 3-1) can help you make this decision. On the basis of the results of this questionnaire, you might decide that the group's climate is not conducive to creative thinking. If this is the case, you should provide training (assuming you have the time, money, motivation, and other resources) to improve the group's climate, or you could decide to eliminate training altogether and redefine or rethink the problem. If you rethink the problem, return to the point at which you have awareness of a problem situation; if you redefine the problem, return to the "Gap exists?" decision point. In either case, the outcome will be to terminate the process or proceed again through the remainder of the flow chart. (The rationale behind these alternatives is that the group's climate may be appropriate for dealing with some problems but not with others.) If you have decided that the group's climate is appropriate for the problem facing you, proceed to the first module in the next flow chart.

b. *Analyze the input module.* Information needed to analyze inputs is described in Figure 4-3 (and in Chapter 5). The first step in analyzing the inputs is to determine whether the problem is ill structured, because only ill-

Figure 4-2. Beginning the modular approach.

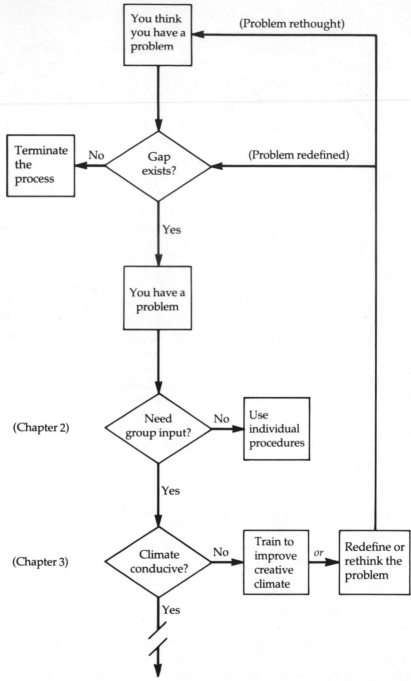

Figure 4-3. Analyzing the input module.

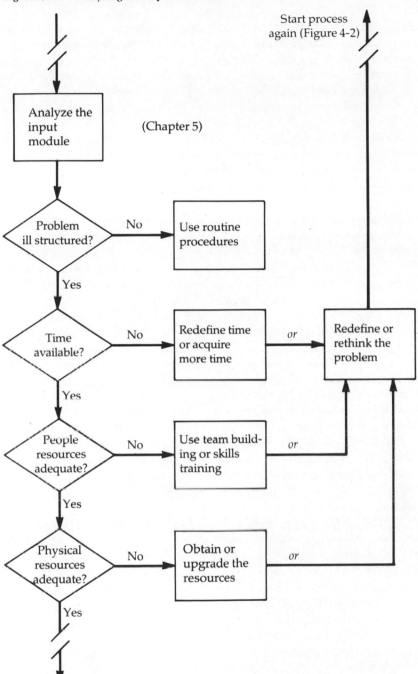

structured problems are appropriate for creative problem solving. You can use the problem structure rating form (Figure 5-1) to help you make this determination. If you decide that the problem is not ill structured, you can use routine procedures to solve it; if you decide that the problem is ill structured, proceed to the next decision point in the flow chart.

At this point, you must decide whether you have enough time to solve the problem using the modular approach. If the amount of time is inadequate, you will need to redefine your perceptions of time or acquire more time. If neither of these options is suitable or appropriate, your only recourse is to redefine or rethink the problem and recycle back to the flow chart in Figure 4-2. If you decide that you have adequate time, proceed to the next decision point.

The next decision point requires you to evaluate the adequacy of your people resources. If you judge these resources to be inadequate, you can use team building or skills training to upgrade them. Or you can consider redefining or rethinking the problem and returning to Figure 4-2. (Another alternative, not included in Figure 4-3, would be to use other people. This alternative was not included because it was assumed that most managers would have to work with the people available, that is, their subordinates.) If you decide the people resources are adequate, move to the next decision point.

The next decision point involves determining whether the available physical resources are adequate. If your physical resources are inadequate, you will have to obtain additional resources, upgrade your available resources, or redefine or rethink the problem and return to Figure 4-2. If the physical resources are adequate, you are ready to begin working on the next module.

However, note first that the decisions required for analyzing the input module can be facilitated if you use the Problem input analysis form (Figure 5-2). This form considers the adequacy, availability, applicability, and importance of problem information, time, people resources, and physical resources.

c. *Analyze the content module.* The four major decisions involved in analyzing the content module are shown in Figure 4-4. A discussion about the content variables used to develop these decisions, as well as pertinent questionnaires, can be found in Chapters 6 and 7. Groups that are experienced in working together on ill-structured problems may want to delete or devote the least amount of time to analyzing this module. A group that has worked together successfully may need very few adjustments in member composition, role clarity, task clarity, and environmental conduciveness. Most of these variables have probably already been dealt with and worked out to everyone's satisfaction. However, if there is the least bit of doubt about these variables, the group should analyze each one carefully for

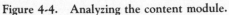

Figure 4-4. Analyzing the content module.

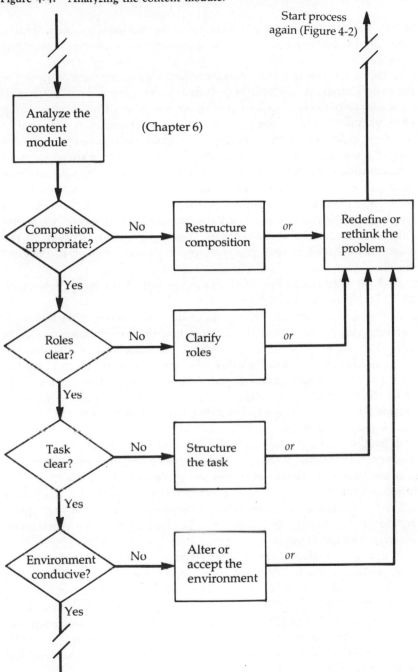

at least the first problem it works on using the modular approach. This is especially important for groups working in unstable or constantly changing environments.

In Figure 4-4, the first decision point inquires about the appropriateness of the group's composition (group composition is discussed in detail in Chapter 6). If the composition is not appropriate, you will need either to restructure it or to rethink or redefine the problem. In the latter case, you may need to recycle to Figure 4-2. If the composition is appropriate, your next decisions involve assessments of role clarity, task clarity, and physical environment conduciveness (Chapter 7). If your answers to any of these decision questions are negative, you will need to clarify roles, structure tasks, or alter or accept the group's physical environment. Of course, at any one of these decision points, you could redefine or rethink the problem, in which case, you would need to return to the first flow chart (Figure 4-2). If you answer all the questions in the affirmative, however, you are ready to move to the next module.

d. *Analyze the process module.* This module is depicted in the flow charts shown in Figures 4-5 and 4-6.

In Figure 4-5, your first decision is to determine whether all the group members clearly understand the process module. The process module is integral to the entire creative problem-solving process. It is vital that the group members understand the different stages within this module, so that they can work through the stages with little difficulty. If there is any doubt about the group members' ability to use the process module, you should provide training beyond the training that was provided before you began to use the modular approach.

When the process is well understood, proceed. The next two steps involve selecting redefinitional techniques and redefining the problem. Descriptions of a few sample redefinitional techniques are provided in Chapter 8. The techniques that you select will vary considerably with your skill in using them and with your preferences and those of the group members. In this regard, experience in using the techniques will be the best guide for determining which techniques to use.

After you have selected one or more techniques, use them to generate a list of potential problem redefinitions. Select one redefinition from this list, or use the original problem definition. The Problem redefinition culling and rating form (Figure 8-2) can help you decide which redefinition is adequate as a starting point for generating ideas. If the redefinition selected is not adequate, collect more information on the problem situation and develop a new redefinition. If the redefinition is adequate, proceed to the next flow chart, Figure 4-6.

In Figure 4-6, the first two activities involve selecting idea-generation

Figure 4-5. Analyzing the process module.

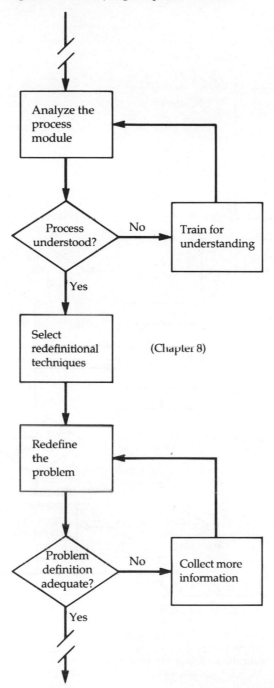

Figure 4-6. Analyzing the process module (continued).

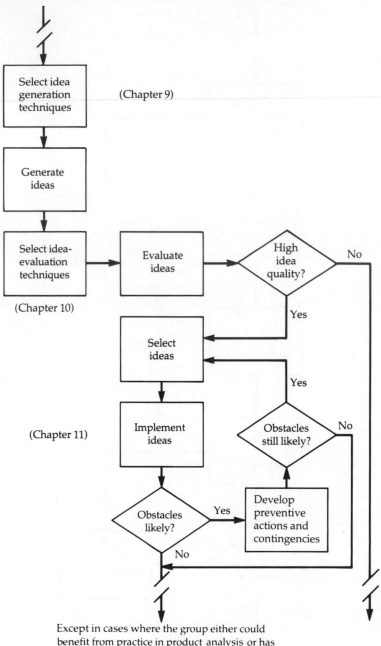

Except in cases where the group either could benefit from practice in product analysis or has difficulty achieving consensus, proceed from this point to Figure 4-8.

techniques and then generating ideas. Information and suggestions on how to perform these activities are presented in Chapter 8, along with a chart to use in selecting techniques. The questionnaire in Chapter 2 on choosing brainwriting and brainstorming techniques will also help you decide which techniques to use.

When the group has generated a list of ideas, move on. The next three activities are to select idea-evaluation techniques, evaluate the ideas, and select the idea or ideas to be used in developing a final solution. (Information relevant to these activities is discussed in Chapter 10. A rating scale for choosing from among the idea-selection methods is also presented in Chapter 10.)

Depending on the perceived quality of the ideas generated, you may need to move to the product module before selecting any ideas. If you and the group judge the ideas to be of low quality, you should use the product module at this point to ensure that the selected idea or ideas will be transformed into a workable solution likely to solve the problem. If you judge the quality of the ideas to be high, continue in the process module to the next step.

The final step in the process module is to implement the ideas selected. The specific actions and considerations involved in idea implementation are discussed in Chapter 11.

As shown in Figure 4-6, one aspect of idea implementation involves determining whether there are or are likely to be any obstacles that might hinder implementation activities. If such obstacles are likely, you need to develop preventive actions and contingency plans. If, after taking these actions, you feel that obstacles are still likely to block successful implementation, you might select a new idea or set of ideas to replace those selected originally. If no obstacles are likely after you select the first idea or after you develop preventive actions and contingency plans, you can proceed.

e. *Analyze the product module.* Normally, you will use this module, which deals with creative products, only if it is required after you have assessed idea quality within the process module. If the idea is of high quality and no obstacles are likely, you can skip the product module (unless you feel that group members could benefit from practice in product analysis or that the group had difficulty in reaching consensus).

A description of the product module can be found in Chapter 12, with relevant activities shown in Figure 4-7. Your first decision in analyzing this module is to determine whether the group members understand the different criteria. If they do not understand the criteria, you should provide training and evaluate the level of understanding again. When the product criteria are understood, use them to analyze the idea. When the idea has been analyzed, you will need to make a decision about revising the idea. If the idea needs revising, modifying, or combining with other ideas, discuss possible revisions

Figure 4-7. Analyzing the product module.

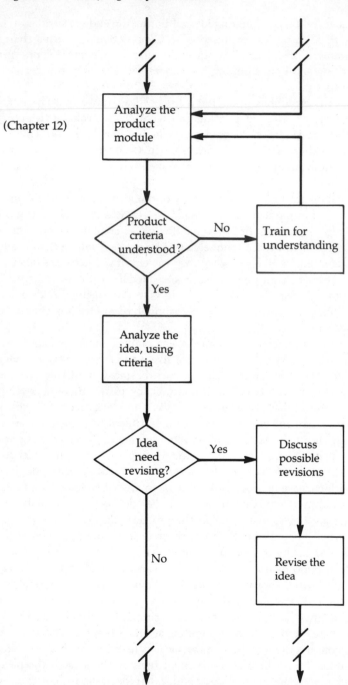

and transform the final revision into a workable solution. If the idea does not need revising, proceed to the last module.

f. *Analyze the outcome module.* The last module, which involves an assessment of group outcomes, is shown in Figure 4-8. (A more complete description of this module can be found in Chapter 13.) You first need to determine whether the group members are satisfied with the outcome and their growth and development. If they are dissatisfied, conduct a discussion to pinpoint the sources of dissatisfaction; if they are satisfied, go on to the next decision point.

The next decision involves determining whether the effect on the problem was positive or negative. If the effect was positive, terminate the process. If the effect was negative, the group should determine whether any adjustments are possible. If adjustments are not possible, the group should review and analyze the process to determine what might have produced a negative outcome. If there still is time and the problem still needs to be solved, the group might also consider beginning the approach again and returning to Figure 4-2. However, if adjustments are possible, the adjustments should be made.

Your last decision in the modular process is to determine whether any new problems were created as a result of your attempts to resolve the original problem. If new problems were created, the group should return to Figure 4-2 and, when appropriate, begin the modular process again. If no new problems were created, terminate the process.

Before we conclude the description of the modular approach one point needs to be repeated. As designed, the modular approach is not a fixed and rigid way to manage group creative problem solving. Rather, it is a loosely constructed set of variables that can be used in whatever way works best for a specific group in a particular setting. For example, some groups may find it appropriate to place less emphasis on the content and product modules. Furthermore, the sequence of activities within the different modules may be altered from time to time, depending on various constraining forces (e.g., available time, level of understanding, skill in doing particular tasks), the needs of the group leader and members, and the nature of the problem. In this regard, the results of a careful analysis of the inputs will be a major factor in determining how the modules are used.

Summary

Content Narrative

This chapter is a bridge between the introductory chapters and the chapters that describe the modular approach. This approach includes modules for inputs, the content, the process, the product, and group

Figure 4-8. Analyzing the outcome module.

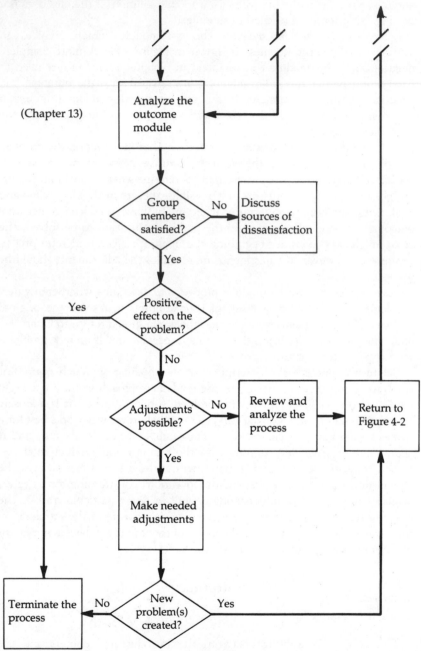

outcomes. Each of these modules has four components. The input module consists of problems, time, people resources, and physical resources; the content module consists of group composition, group roles, the task, and the external environment; the process module consists of redefining the problem, generating ideas, selecting ideas, and implementing ideas; the product module consists of types of products, understanding of the types, analysis of the types, and idea revisions; and the outcome module consists of effect on the problem, group member satisfactions, process adjustments, and new problems.

A major advantage of the modular approach to group creative problem solving is that it breaks down the variables involved into more manageable units so that the creative process becomes more efficient and effective. Another advantage is that the modular approach provides more flexibility in the control and direction of the creative process. Modules can be rearranged and joined in different ways to suit the needs of a particular group and set of circumstances.

The basic element underlying the use of the modular approach is diagnosis. Group creativity cannot be managed without some analysis of existing conditions and resources. Groups and their environments change over time, thereby requiring continual diagnosis whenever a group works on a problem. The group must thoroughly understand the problem and the context in which it exists before it attempts any solutions.

Determining problem-solving readiness through analysis of the context can be described as contextual problem solving. Actually working on a specific problem causing some "pain" to a group can be referred to as focal problem solving. Both of these types of problem solving are important to the overall process, but contextual problem solving is frequently overlooked or done only minimally, if at all. The modular approach provides a balanced emphasis on both types.

There are four major elements involved in using the modular approach: a group leader, group members, assessment questionnaires, and flow charts for guiding the process. The group leader and the group members should have a solid understanding of the approach before attempting to use it. The assessment questionnaires will help the group in making diagnostic decisions, and the flow charts will help in guiding and structuring all of the activities involved in using the modular approach.

The procedure used to implement the modular approach consists of six major stages: (1) Decide whether you want to use the modular approach. (2) Study the approach in depth. (3) Describe the approach to the group members. (4) Determine the amount of interest in using the approach. (5) Provide group training in using the approach. (6) Apply the approach to a real problem. The first two stages focus on the group manager, the next three stages focus on the group, and the last stage involves the manager's working with the group to apply the approach.

No matter how you use the stages, remember the modular approach is meant to be a flexible way to manage group creativity. You may not always need all the modules, and you may alter activities in the modules as needed. Still, you should make a careful diagnosis of the inputs to ensure effective outcomes.

Checklist of Activities

1. Decide whether you want to use the approach.
   a. Read about the approach.
   b. List advantages and disadvantages of using the approach.
   c. Decide whether the advantages outweigh the disadvantages.
2. Study the approach in depth.
   a. Skim this book.
   b. Read this book for understanding.
   c. Select a practice problem and work it through, using the approach.
   d. Check for understanding.
3. Describe the approach to the group members.
   a. Provide a brief overview of the approach.
   b. Describe the approach's advantages and disadvantages.
   c. Ask for questions and check for understanding.
4. Determine the amount of interest in using the approach.
   a. Consult with the group on an individual basis, if necessary.
   b. Meet with the entire group and clarify any possible misconceptions.
   c. Decide whether or not to try the approach.
5. Provide group training in using the approach.
   a. Have group members skim the book.
   b. Have group members read the book for understanding.
   c. Have individuals work on a real or a hypothetical practice problem.
   d. Meet as a group and ask for questions.
   e. Ask for evaluative comments and discuss them with the group.
   f. Work together on a practice problem, using the approach.
6. Apply the approach to a real problem.
   a. As a group, select a problem to work on.
   b. Work through the modular approach.
      (1) Determine whether a gap exists.
      (2) Determine whether to use individual or group procedures.
      (3) Assess the group's creative climate.
      (4) Analyze the input module.

(Checklist continues on page 84.)

Figure 4-9. Summary evaluation rating form.

1. Conduciveness of group climate?	Unconducive	1	2	3	4	5	6	Conducive
2. Degree to which the problem is structured?	Structured	1	2	3	4	5	6	Ill structured
3. Adequacy of available time?	Inadequate	1	2	3	4	5	6	Adequate
4. Adequacy of people resources?	Adequate	6	5	4	3	2	1	Inadequate
5. Adequacy of physical resources?	Adequate	6	5	4	3	2	1	Inadequate
6. Appropriateness of group composition?	Inappropriate	1	2	3	4	5	6	Appropriate
7. Clarity of group member roles?	Unclear	1	2	3	4	5	6	Clear
8. Clarity of group task?	Unclear	1	2	3	4	5	6	Clear
9. Conduciveness of physical environment?	Conducive	6	5	4	3	2	1	Unconducive
10. Degree to which the CPS process is understood?	Not at all	1	2	3	4	5	6	Completely
11. Adequacy of problem definition?	Adequate	6	5	4	3	2	1	Inadequate
12. Quality of ideas generated?	High	6	5	4	3	2	1	Low
13. Success in dealing with implementation obstacles?	Unsuccessful	1	2	3	4	5	6	Successful
14. Degree to which product types are understood?	Not at all	1	2	3	4	5	6	Completely
15. Adequacy of product type analysis?	Inadequate	1	2	3	4	5	6	Adequate
16. Degree to which idea revision was needed?	Not at all	1	2	3	4	5	6	Completely
17. Effect of outcomes on the problem?	Positive	6	5	4	3	2	1	Negative
18. Satisfaction of group members?	Satisfied	6	5	4	3	2	1	Dissatisfied
19. Degree to which process adjustments were possible?	Not at all	1	2	3	4	5	6	Completely
20. Degree to which new problems were created?	Not at all	1	2	3	4	5	6	Completely

(5) Analyze the content module.
(6) Analyze the process module.
(7) Analyze the product module (if needed).
(8) Analyze the outcomes module.

Summary Evaluation Rating Form

In order for you to pull together the major questions used in diagnosing various phases of the modular approach, the Summary evaluation rating form (Figure 4-9) has been developed. This form contains most of the questions represented by the major decision points throughout the flow charts. This form is not intended to yield a single summary score. Instead, it is simply a checklist of most of the decisions that will have to be made in using the approach.

This form's major value may be as a record of the decisions made by the group while working on a problem. After the group has worked on several problems using the modular approach, you and the members can evaluate progress in various areas by examining the responses to each item for every problem dealt with. In this way, the form could serve as an additional outcomes module for assessing the modular approach across several different problems.

5

Inputs

Inputs are the raw materials or the resources that a group has to work with. They are the fodder a group uses to transform and produce a creative product. Inputs are what go into a group's blender to be whipped around, changed, and combined until a creative outcome results. Inputs are people, material, energy, information—anything that is needed to get the job done.

Nature of the Inputs

There is nothing predictable about any given set of inputs. The outcome produced from identical sets of inputs may vary considerably, depending on the manner in which they are combined and the extent to which some inputs are relied on more than others. The link between inputs and outputs in groups is especially unpredictable because of the differences that exist among people as inputs. The creative product produced by one group of people with varying values, needs, skills, and experiences, for example, is likely to be very different from the product produced by another group. When different people are combined with other input variables, such as time or information, the transformation of these variables is apt to produce an outcome unlike that of any other group.

Inputs are indispensable to group creative problem solving. They provide the electricity needed to juice up a group as well as the resources needed for a group to achieve its goals. Plugging in the input module is, in fact, what begins the creative problem-solving process. A group's creativity cannot be managed unless the group recognizes, assesses, and then applies its input resources to solving problems. A group's inputs provide it with the drive needed to begin problem solving and with the sustaining action needed to complete implementation and follow-up of potential solutions. Inputs are not just the first module to be considered in managing group creativity, they are the energizers that give a group its creative life.

Inputs can be either tangible or intangible. Tangible inputs include such resources as equipment, material, supplies, facilities, money, and people. These inputs can be seen and touched and physically altered. Intangible inputs include resources that cannot be seen or touched. Intangible inputs can be altered mentally but not physically. Examples of primary intangible resources include perceived time, values, expectations, knowledge, skills, motivation, and information. Note that people inputs have qualities of both tangible and intangible resources. The physical presence of people constitutes a tangible input, while the mental functions of people are more intangible.

Organization and Description of the Inputs

The major inputs needed by groups to produce creative products can be organized into four categories. Because of the flexibility that people, as inputs, bring to groups, these categories are interdependent. That is, the categories are not discrete entities that exist in isolation from each other. Rather, the degree, quality, and quantity of any one input is likely to depend on the degree, quality, and quantity of other inputs. Thus, if a group member (an input) is knowledgeable about materials needed to solve a problem (another input), the extent of this person's knowledge may affect the quality and quantity of materials that the group obtains to use in solving a problem. Viewed in a slightly different light, the needed materials would not be used as an input if the group member did not have knowledge about them and their relation to the problem.

The four major categories of inputs are problem information, time, people resources, and physical resources. Because of their importance to managing group creativity, these inputs will be discussed in some detail.

Problem Information

Problem information is anything that can be considered to be even remotely related to the problem. Whether complete or incomplete, any facts that bear on the problem should be collected so that their potential bearing on the problem can be assessed.

When analyzing this input, a group should not discard a single bit of information—information should not be discarded until much later in the process, when the information's relevance can be more reliably ascertained. Premature rejection of problem information during the input module could seriously affect the quality of the final creative product. A good rule of thumb is to defer judgment on all information until a problem solution is actually implemented. Even though the input module represents a "front end" aspect of the creative process, the likelihood of obtaining additional information during subsequent modules is very high. Therefore, view the information collected at this point as tentative, subject to further refinements as the nature of the problem begins to take on a more visible form.

Problem Structure

Perhaps the most important type of problem information is information that a group can use to classify a problem according to its degree of structure. Most problems can be classified as being well structured, semistructured, or ill structured. Well-structured problems present clear and sufficient information about the current state of a problem, its desired state, and how to make the current state like the desired state. Baking a cake, for example, is a well-structured problem, since for most people it is clear what ingredients are needed, what the final product should be like, and how the ingredients need to be combined to produce the final product. Ill-structured problems, in contrast, typically present insufficient and often ambiguous information about the state of a problem. How to find a cure for lung cancer, for instance, is an ill-structured problem. Semistructured problems fall in between these two types and are characterized by moderate amounts of information in regard to the problem states.

Two aspects of problem structure merit special mention. First, the degree of problem structure is a subjective, perceptual matter. Any two people are likely to classify a problem's structure differently, depending on their past experiences with similar types of problems. Second, only semistructured and ill-structured problems are appropriate for creative problem solving. The routine procedures available for solving well-structured problems would make the development of a custom-made solution redundant and inefficient.

To assist you and your group in classifying the degree of a problem's structure, you can use the problem structure rating form presented in Figure 5-1. The group should complete this form together and should strive for agreement on all the ratings. Averaging should be used only when it is impossible to reach a consensus.

The three criteria used in this form to classify problem structure are availability, adequacy, and clarity. Availability refers to how ready to use the problem information is. Adequacy refers to the sufficiency of the information in contributing relevant data. Clarity refers to the degree to which the information is understandable and unambiguous.

Figure 5-1. Problem structure rating form.

Instructions: This instrument is designed to help you classify problems as well structured, semistructured, or ill structured. Based on what you now know about the problem situation, circle the one number following each question that best describes the adequacy, clarity, and availability of your information.

	Inadequate	Somewhat inadequate	Partly inadequate and partly adequate	Somewhat adequate	Adequate
Adequacy					
1. The information I have about the current state of this problem situation is:	1	2	3	4	5
2. The information I have about the desired state of this problem situation is:	1	2	3	4	5
3. The information I have about the procedures needed to make the current state like the desired state is:	1	2	3	4	5

	Unclear	Somewhat unclear	Partly unclear and partly clear	Somewhat clear	Clear
Clarity					
1. How clear (well defined) is the information you have about the current state of this problem situation?	1	2	3	4	5
2. How clear (well defined) is the information you have about the desired state of this problem situation?	1	2	3	4	5
3. How clear (well defined) is the information you have about the procedures needed to make the current state like the desired state?	1	2	3	4	5

	Strongly disagree	Disagree	Neither agree nor disagree	Agree	Strongly agree
Availability					
1. It is easy for me to obtain information about the current state of this problem situation.	1	2	3	4	5
2. It is easy for me to obtain information about the desired state of this problem situation.	1	2	3	4	5
3. It is easy for me to obtain information about how to make the current state like the desired state.	1	2	3	4	5

Scoring and Interpretation: Total your scores for adequacy, clarity, and availability. Record each of these scores on the graph below by circling the appropriate number.

Availability:	3	4	5	6		7	8	9	10	11		12	13	14	15
Adequacy:	3	4	5	6		7	8	9	10	11		12	13	14	15
Clarity:	3	4	5	6		7	8	9	10	11		12	13	14	15

Ill structured	Semistructured	Well structured

If all your scores fall within the same box, the problem can be classified according to the box in which the numbers were placed. However, if one score is in one box and the other scores are in one or more other boxes, the problem should be considered semistructured. Whenever a problem is classified as well structured, you should rethink using creative problem-solving procedures, since more routine methods probably are available to you.

Example: Suppose you have defined your problem as, "In what ways might we make our staff meetings more efficient?" Your total scores for adequacy, clarity, and availability are 9, 10, and 10, respectively. In this case, the problem would be classified as semistructured and suitable for creative problem-solving procedures. Suppose, however, that your total scores for the three criteria are 12, 13, and 12. With these scores, the problem would be classified as well structured and no creative solutions would be required.

In using this scoring form, remember that it is the perceptions of the individual raters and not the objective nature of a problem that will determine its classification.

Problem Dimensions

There are at least eight dimensions of problem information to consider when analyzing inputs. Before trying to solve any problem, the group should gather as much informtion as possible about these dimensions. This will permit you to develop a perspective on the problem that can be used to generate alternative redefinitions and can eventually lead you to a unique and workable solution. The eight dimensions are:

Magnitude. What is the scope of the problem? Compared to other problems the group has dealt with, how big is this problem? What are its boundaries? How widespread is this problem? Very large problems often command more attention and lead to more immediate action than smaller problems.

History. What events led to this problem? How long has it been a problem? Why is it a problem? When did it first come to your attention? Who else, if anyone, has been involved with this problem in the past? Where did the problem begin? The information gathered by taking a historical perspective can often be useful for estimating a problem's magnitude as well as for increasing clarity about the problem's key components.

Location. Where is the problem located? Is this problem linked with other problems? How widespread is this problem? Determining a problem's specific location can greatly increase the overall efficiency of the problem-solving process.

Multiple causes. How many different factors contributed to the creation of this problem? If more than one factor contributed to the problem, what was distinctive about the way the factors were combined? Many situations become problems only when certain factors cluster together in a unique way to produce a perception that a problem exists. For example, individuals may not view a situation as a problem until they interact with certain other people.

Threat. To what extent is the problem seen as a threat to some value or resource possessed by the group? How likely is it that this threat will increase or decrease in magnitude? Are individuals more threatened than the group? Has the group experienced similar threats? To some degree, all ill-structured problems convey some amount of threat to the affected persons. When the amount of perceived threat exceeds a group's threshold of tolerance, the group may find that its ability to deal effectively with the problem is severely curtailed.

Time horizon. Does it appear that the problem will have a short- or long-term effect on the group or other involved individuals? Does the group seem to have a short- or a long-range perception of this problem? How long will it take to solve this problem? The time horizon of a problem will be an important factor for a group to consider in planning its strategy. Problems that have long-term effects, for example, will necessitate long-term allocations of resources and will affect the ability of a group to deal with other problems.

People affected. How many people are affected by the problem? Who are they? Which people are affected more than others? How are the involved people affected by the problem? Why are they affected in this way? Although this dimension is related to other dimensions, it is important that it be considered alone because of its importance in defining the boundaries of a problem.

Complexity. How complex is the problem? How many different elements does it contain? To what extent are these elements interdependent? How do the problem elements interact? Which elements should be treated separately as subproblems? Collecting information about this dimension is crucial to effective problem solving, because changes in one aspect of a problem often will affect other aspects. Most problems can be viewed as systems in which several different components must be dealt with simultaneously.

Time

Time is the next most important input because of its potential constraining influence on problems. When it exists in abundance, time can operate as a valued ally to a group in permitting it to explore a greater number of alternatives and make needed solution revisions; when it is in short supply, time can become an enemy by restricting the quantity and quality of a group's problem-solving efforts.

Time can delimit a problem so severely that it can create psychological and physiological effects on the individuals involved. Anxiety, frustration, rage, anger, and increased pulse and respiration levels all can be produced by time pressures. Time is a stressor that, if not handled properly, can make the difference in whether or not a problem is solved.

Time is also an intangible construct that regulates biological functioning. But we have ascribed properties to time that go beyond mere control of our biological selves. We use time as a standard of control that governs the way most of us live. Some of us are more controlled by time than others, however, so that the extent to which time controls us varies considerably from individual to individual.

Time is also relative. No two persons view time in the same way, nor are they affected by it in the same way. Time can be experienced as slow or fast, pleasant or unpleasant, good or bad. Time can also be real or perceived, depending on how it is used.

Real Time

When you have two hours to solve a problem, that is real time. It can be measured quantitatively in discrete units such as seconds, minutes, hours, days, weeks, months, and years. Real time has a definite beginning and end. Its boundaries are circumscribed and prescribed. One minute contains 60 seconds and there are 3,600 seconds in an hour, 24 hours in a day, and 744 hours in a 31-day month. Real time is precise and absolute. Any deviation from a prescribed interval can be accurately measured using quantifiable standards.

As an input, real time tells a group how long a problem has existed, how long it has to solve it, and how long it has to evaluate the effectiveness of its solution. When a group begins work on a problem, real time is one of the constraints that it uses to guide its overall problem-solving strategy.

Perceived Time

In contrast to real time, perceived time is measured subjectively by the human mind. Its boundaries are ill defined, constantly changing in depth, breadth, and form. Beginnings and ends become blurred images. One minute contains 60 seconds, 6 seconds, or 600 seconds; hours blend into days, days into weeks, weeks into months, months into years. Infinity is never and forever. Deviations coalesce into obscurity, defying all attempts at measurement. Generalities become the standard: "a long time," "quickly," "soon," "slowly."

Like real time, perceived time tells a group how long a problem has existed, how long it has to solve it, and how long it has to evaluate a solution's effectiveness. Perceived time also imposes a very real constraint on a group's problem-solving capabilities. When a problem is ill defined, a group frequently has only as much time as it thinks it has or as much time as it imposes on itself.

Because real time and perceived time are interrelated, distinctions between the two can become blurred. In the course of creative problem solving, time frequently blends in with the problem. Time affects the problem and the problem affects time. Sorting out the boundaries of time and the problem is one way that the amount of problem-solving effort can be decreased. To do this, however, requires concentration on both the real and the perceived dimensions of time.

People

People represent the tangible tools that are used to produce creative problem solutions. Without people, there can be no creative problem solving. A machine has yet to be developed that can duplicate the creative powers of the human mind. In fact, it is the uniqueness of our minds that makes us capable of individually and collectively producing unique ideas.

In any given group, the individual members interacting together provide a mosaic of resources unique to just that group. When these resources are mobilized and combined, they can produce a pattern of interactions that can far outstrip an individual in creative potential. Even considering the possible dysfunctional consequences of group interaction (see chapter 2), groups exist as a wellspring of resources that can be brought to bear on a problem.

Of the many attributes that people bring to groups, six seem to be most applicable as inputs for managing group creativity. There is some overlap among these inputs, yet each one possesses a distinctive quality that can dramatically influence a group's creative problem-solving effectiveness. The six primary people inputs are skills, knowledge, experience, values, motivation, and expectations.

Skills

Skills are abilities to do something and to do it competently. In creative problem solving, numerous skills are required on the part of the group leader and the group members. Among these skills are the ability to: diagnose problem situations, develop remote problem perspectives, generate large numbers of ideas, withhold judgment when appropriate, image, relate effectively to others, control the pacing of a group's problem-solving activities, resolve conflicts, and accommodate the socioemotional needs of others.

Knowledge

Whatever information the group members have acquired and retained serves as a knowledge input. In relation to creative problem solving, this knowledge may be in regard to process, content, creative products, and outcomes. The effective utilization of such knowledge requires considerable skill on the part of the group leader and the other group members.

Experience

Past events that have shaped an individual's perceptions and behaviors contribute to the uniqueness of a group's creative climate. Generally speaking, the more diverse the experiences of a group's members, the more diverse and unique are the solutions they are capable of producing.

Values

Values are based on beliefs that evidence themselves as preferences for certain states of being or modes of behavior. A large portion of people's behavior is guided by their values.

Fortunately or unfortunately (depending on one's frame of reference), people do not all have the same set of values. When group members' values are similar, the group will probably take fewer risks and make less innovative decisions; when groups members' values differ, conflict is usually inevitable. However, such conflict, if properly managed, can increase the uniqueness and diversity of ideas that the group is capable of producing.

Motivation

The drive that impels people to achieve a goal is motivation. Motivation can result from awareness of a gap between what is and what should be, from contingent, positive reinforcement of behavior, from expectancies that certain behaviors will result in certain outcomes and rewards, or from an inherent need to achieve. People differ in their motivation levels and tend to be more motivated in some situations than in others. As a result, if the most valuable resource members in a group are not adequately motivated, a group's overall motivation to solve a problem will not always be sufficient to ensure successful resolution.

Expectations

Expectations are the particular anticipations that people have about the occurrence of some future event. Typically, expectations imply that there is a given probability of occurrence of an event. Furthermore, the expectations that people hold usually vary with the type of situation. For example, when a minister gives a highly inspirational sermon, most people do not expect to jump to their feet and give the minister a standing ovation while shouting, "Author, author!" It is just not expected in that situation.

In group creative problem solving, the situation is not much different. There are both individual and group expectations about how the group should behave, when it should do certain things, how it should carry out its activities, and so forth. Thus most group members probably expect a certain amount of task orientation, a certain amount of social interaction, adherence to a schedule, some participation in the discussion, and a final product that is satisfactory to most group members as well as being likely to solve the problem.

Some individuals in a group, however, may not share these expectations. In this situation, the group leader must be aware of these individuals and try to accommodate their needs. The trick is to do this without sacrificing achievement of the group's task or alienating other members in the group. Leader skills, knowledge, and experience will be most helpful in these situations.

It should be obvious that the nature and interrelatedness of these six inputs present a complex pattern of attributes for a group leader to consider for any one problem. It would be unrealistic to expect a leader to conduct an intensive analysis of people resources every time there is a problem to be solved. Yet, some form of analysis must be conducted at some time if the group members are to be utilized effectively.

Perhaps the most important thing that a group leader can do in regard to the people inputs is to become aware of the general types of resources that each group member possesses and the degree to which each one possesses these resources. Thus group leaders should be able to quickly identify the general skills, knowledge, experiences, and so forth, that each group member brings to the group. It is also important that the group leader be able to distinguish between stable or general inputs and those that are likely to vary with a particular problem. For example, one person may be exceptionally skilled at resolving conflicts among other group members (a general input) and at diagnosing mechanical problems (a more specific input). Another person may be exceptionally skilled at diagnosing problems pertaining to money matters. Obviously, the lesson is to maximize use of the people resources to ensure efficiency and effectiveness of operation in solving any type of problem.

Physical Resources

The least crucial (although not necessarily the least needed) input is all the physical resources involved in solving a particular problem. For most groups, the requirements for these resources and their availability will vary considerably. (Often, this discrepancy can be traced to a lack of foresight or to a lack of money.) Four physical resources will be considered: equipment, supplies and materials, facilities, and money.

Equipment

This category includes any technological apparatus that might aid a group in solving a problem. Computer hardware, photocopying machines, communication systems, and any equipment directly applicable to a problem are examples of equipment inputs. Sometimes the equipment is available but is not adequate and requires modifications or replacement. Certain computers, for example, may not have the processing capabilities required to help solve a particular problem.

Supplies and Materials

Paper, pens, paper clips, staplers, forms, tests, electrical wiring, lumber, and so forth, if they bear some relation to a problem, are examples of the supplies and materials input. Like the equipment input, this input may be available but not adequate and require modification or additions.

Facilities

The physical facilities that house a group can have some impact on a group's problem-solving abilities. Size of the facilities, color of the walls, temperature, humidity, number and arrangement of chairs and tables, and decorations can exert a minimal influence on a problem-solving group. There is some evidence, for example, that wall color can have a psychological impact on people, with cooler pastels probably being more conducive to creativity. And it is fairly well known that temperature extremes can dramatically affect human operating efficiency.

Money

Like lifeboat passengers floating in an ocean of undrinkable water, we often seem to be surrounded by money but we just don't have any. We know it's out there. It's just not always ours, or it's not accessible to us when we need it. Yet, money is the root of all the physical inputs. As such, it can determine the adequacy and availability of equipment, supplies and materials, and facilities. Money can't solve all our problems, but there are many situations in which it certainly could help.

Analyzing and Evaluating Inputs

Simply being aware of the different inputs that can affect a problem is not sufficient. Awareness must be translated into analysis, analysis into evaluation, and evaluation into action. Making these translations, however, can be difficult.

Individuals are complex, and groups are even more complex, because of the different combinations of interactions that can develop among individual group members. When the impact of such inputs as information, time, and physical resources is factored in, the complexity of the situation is magnified even more. Further complicating the picture are the tradeoffs implicit from the weightings of the different inputs. For example, it is easy to inventory and analyze physical resources, but they are less important than the other input resources. In contrast, people resources are extremely important, but they are much more difficult to inventory and analyze. Clearly, any procedure for dealing with inputs must be viewed as more art than science—at least until the technological capabilities for making precise and accurate predictions about people are developed.

Although input analysis and evaluation have an upper limit on their predictability, a group can take steps to make the process more systematic and thorough. A problem input analysis form is presented in Figure 5-2 to facilitate the group's search, analysis, evaluation, and interpretation of inputs through the use of probing questions, discrepancy analysis, and subjective ratings. This form is divided into three parts: input inventory, input evaluation, and input action.

In the input inventory, record all the inputs you currently have in the four major areas (information, time, people, and physical resources) and the inputs you need. Discrepancies can be easily identified in this way.

A second feature of the input inventory is the use of the probing questions, Who? What? Where? When? and Why? Use these questions to pull out all the information you can about each of the input areas. For example, ask such questions as: Who has the information? Who else has it? Who can get it? What information do you have? What information do you need? What do you know about the problem? What don't you know? What is the validity of your information? Where is the information? Where did the problem first occur? When did the problem first occur? When did other people recognize the situation as a problem? Why is it a problem? Why did the problem occur?

Three primary considerations in using these questions are to withhold all judgment when asking and answering them, to ask as many different questions as possible, and to involve the group members to the extent that they would like to be involved.

Other guidelines for using the input inventory are to (1) use a separate sheet of paper for each major input, (2) divide each sheet into two columns headed by the words "Have" and "Need," (3) be as specific as possible in answering the probing questions and in recording all other data, and (4) make special notations for all significant discrepancies between what you have and what you need.

After you have completed the input inventory, move to the input evaluation. On this form, rate each of the four inputs, using the criteria of adequacy, availability, and applicability. The importance criterion is a supplemental measure. Suggestions for scoring and interpretation follow. For purposes of this form, the criteria are defined as follows:

Adequacy: The extent to which the inputs can "get the job done" and are sufficient for use.

Availability: The extent to which the inputs are ready for use and are easily obtainable.

Applicability: The extent to which the inputs are usable and relevant.

Importance: The extent to which the inputs are required for resolution of the problem.

The final portion of the problem input analysis form is concerned with input action. In the input action section, guidelines are provided for additional interpretations and for specific steps you might take based on your input inventory and input evaluation.

Figure 5-2. Problem input analysis form.

Input Inventory

Instructions: Write down a tentative statement of your problem. Use a separate sheet of paper for each input category. In the Input column, list all the information you can think of about each input by using the probing questions. In the Have column, list all the specific inputs for each category that you currently possess and that you consider relevant to the problem. In the Need column, list the inputs that you currently don't have that you will need to solve the problem. Finally, review all your responses and determine which areas will require the most attention to begin work on the problem.

Input	Have	Need
1. Problem information (Who? What? Where? When? Why?)		
2. Time (Who? What? Where? When? Why?)		
3. People (Who? What? Where? When? Why?) a. Skills b. Knowledge c. Experience d. Values e. Motivation f. Expectations		
4. Physical resources (Who? What? Where? When? Why?) a. Equipment b. Supplies and materials c. Facilities d. Money		

Input Evaluation

Instructions: Review all the information described in the Have column of the input inventory. Then read over the definitions of the four criteria. Using the scales described for each criterion, rate each input variable by writing in the one number that best describes that variable.

Adequacy

1 = Inadequate
2 = Somewhat inadequate
3 = Neutral or undecided
4 = Somewhat adequate
5 = Adequate

Availability

1 = Unavailable
2 = Somewhat unavailable
3 = Neutral or undecided
4 = Somewhat available
5 = Available

Applicability

1 = Inapplicable
2 = Somewhat inapplicable
3 = Neutral or undecided
4 = Somewhat applicable
5 = Applicable

Importance

1 = Unimportant
2 = Somewhat unimportant
3 = Neutral or undecided
4 = Somewhat important
5 = Important

	Adequacy	Availability	Applicability	Total	Importance
Problem information	_____	_____	_____	____	_____
Time	_____	_____	_____	____	_____
People resources	_____	_____	_____	____	_____
Physical resources	_____	_____	_____	____	_____
Total	_____	_____	_____	____	_____

Scoring and Interpretation: The format of the Input Evaluation provides two different sets of scores. The first set describes your rating of each input variable across the three primary criteria of adequacy, availability, and applicability. The second set of scores presents your rating of each criterion across the four input variables of problem information, time, people resources, and physical resources. To score both sets, sum your ratings across the criteria and across the input variables. The row totals, obtained from adding across the criteria, indicate your ratings for each input variable. The column totals, obtained from adding down the input variables, indicate your ratings for each criterion. Add together all the row totals (or the column totals) for a rough indication of how all your input variables stack up against all the criteria.

The importance criterion is used as a supplemental measure and will be discussed in the input action section.

In general, a total score (obtained from adding either row or column totals) between 36 and 60 indicates that you can proceed in problem solving. That is, you have the resources you need, and they are, on the average, adequate, available, and applicable. A total score below 36, however, indicates that you might need to reconsider beginning work on the problem. Some of the specifics you should consider in proceeding or halting work on the problem are discussed in the input action section.

Input Action

The actions you take will be determined by how satisfied you are with the results of your analysis. The extent of your satisfaction, however, should be guided by more than a single quantitative score. Instead, you should closely examine the different facets of your evaluation.

Such an examination is especially critical if your quantitative score is relatively high, since you may be lulled into a false sense of security. Or you may overestimate the importance of some of your inputs. In this case, you may unnecessarily expend resources in attempting to accommodate these inputs.

As an illustration of how to analyze your score, suppose that your evaluation produced a relatively high total score. On close examination, you might note that you gave one of your variables a low or moderate score on one or more of your criteria. For example, you might have rated problem information high on all the criteria except availability. If you did, you might want to determine what aspect of availability is problematic for you. It could be that the information is not currently available but will become available at a later date. Or you may be able to make the information more available by seeking out other sources. If you ended up with a low total score, you might want to examine all the lowest-rated areas to determine what actions, if any, might lead to an improved score.

In both these cases, you can guide your analysis by noting the importance ratings that you gave to the lowest-rated input variables. If you rated one of these variables as low in importance, it may not be problematic for you and no further action will be required. For instance, if you rated the amount of time you have as low on two or three of the criteria and low in importance, little or no action may be required. Such ratings indicate that time is not problematic for this particular problem.

One way to make this process more systematic is to refer back to your input inventory form. On this form, you listed the input resources that you have and that you need. Using this form as a checklist, you can evaluate systematically the areas in which you have to acquire additional resources or modify or adapt existing resources to satisfy your input requirements.

If, after examining all your ratings and developing action plans for acquiring any needed resources, you still don't have the inputs you need, there is one final action you can take. Simply stated, this action is: If you can't change the situation, change the problem. If it doesn't appear likely that you will be able to solve the problem with your current resources, try redefining the problem. In doing this, you will create another situation, with its own unique requirements. Hopefully, this will be a situation in which the problem is more compatible with your existing inputs.

To summarize, the following actions should be taken after you have completed the input inventory and input evaluation forms:

1. Examine all the low-rated scores to determine which input conditions are likely to make the problem more difficult to solve.
2. Check the importance rating you gave to each low-rated input to see whether any further actions might be required with respect to the input.
3. If you consider a low-rated input to be important, determine how the input might be acquired or modified or how you might be able to adjust to the situation by adapting existing resources.
4. Review the input inventory and note where the largest discrepancies exist between the inputs you need and the inputs you have; develop action plans for acquiring, modifying, or adapting these inputs.
5. If all your analyses and actions indicate that you will not be able to proceed in solving the problem, consider redefining the problem to make it more compatible with your existing resources.

Before we leave the input module, one concluding note should be made. As complex as the process described may seem, any less systematic procedure can lead to much inefficiency and decrease the uniqueness of any solutions. However, it also must be recognized that not all problem situations will require the same depth and scope of analysis. This undoubtedly would lead to even greater inefficiency. What is needed is a balance in the amount of effort and time devoted to the many problems faced by groups. Use the intensive process only when the importance of a problem and the risk associated with not solving it (or with solving it incorrectly) justify its use. Beyond this consideration, the systematic aspects of the process should become easier to use over time, as the essential ingredients become integrated into the group's normal way of approaching problems.

Summary

Content Narrative

Inputs are whatever goes into a group to be transformed into a creative product. Because of the vast differences that exist within groups, no two groups have exactly the same inputs and no two groups will produce the same product.

The major inputs used in managing group creativity are problem information, time, people, and physical resources. Considerable overlap may exist among these inputs in that the degree, quality, and quantity of any one input may vary with the degree, quality and quantity of other inputs. Put another way, inputs are interdependent.

Problem information can be classified according to the perceived degree of structure that a problem possesses and the nature of the various dimensions that characterize the information. Problems can be categorized as well structured, semistructured, or ill structured. Only semistructured and ill-structured problems are suitable for creative problem solving. The structure of any given problem can be determined by rating problem information using the criteria of adequacy, clarity, and availability. Eight major dimensions of problem information are magnitude, history, location, multiple causes, threat, time horizon, persons affected, and complexity. Collect information on these dimensions to provide alternative perspectives to use in redefining a problem.

Time, the second major input variable, can function as a major constraint on problem solving. It can produce both physical and psychological effects that can alter a group's effectiveness. The effects of time, however, will vary from person to person.

Two major aspects of time are real time and perceived time. Real time is based on objective standards, and perceived time is measured using subjective perceptions. Both types of time are interrelated and frequently blend with a problem, making it difficult to isolate the problem's boundaries.

People inputs are the primary tools used to produce creative products. As sources of unique ideas, groups have no equal when they are operating effectively. The number of problem perspectives that can be provided by combining the divergent resources that people bring to groups is almost infinite. The six primary inputs that people bring to groups are skills, knowledge, experience, values, motivation, and expectations. To effectively manage group creativity, group leaders should become aware of these inputs in regard to each group member. In addition, the group leader should be able to quickly identify the members who possess the inputs that may be most relevant to a particular problem.

Physical resources are the tangible inputs needed to solve a problem. Four inputs are included in this category: equipment, supplies and materials, facilities, and money.

After considering the nature of the inputs that pertain to group creative problem solving, make an inventory of the inputs possessed by the group. Using the probing questions, Who? What? Where? When? and Why? collect information on each major input category. Next, list the inputs that are needed, and note any discrepancies between the current and the needed inputs. After collecting input information, evaluate each input area, using the criteria of adequacy, availability, and applicability. An importance criterion can also be used, as a supplemental variable. Finally, conduct an input analysis to determine what adjustments might need to be made in the inputs or the definition of the problem.

Checklist of Activities

1. Evaluate the problem structure.
2. Classify the problem as well structured, semistructured, or ill structured.
3. If you classify the problem as semistructured or ill structured, collect information on the problem dimensions.
4. Complete the input inventory, using the probing questions, and classify the inputs according to those that you have and those that you need.
5. Evaluate the inputs you have, using the criteria of adequacy, availability, and applicability. Use importance as a supplemental criterion to help you identify areas of major concern.
6. Conduct a final analysis of all the inputs to determine what, if any, adjustments might need to be made.

6

Composition

Introduction

The next two modular components deal with the content and the process and form the core of the modular approach. Both these modules are essential for managing group creativity successfully. If they are not analyzed and considered seriously, the group product and outcomes are likely to be of low quality. More important, however, failure to give due consideration to the content and process may decrease significantly the odds of solving a problem.

Examining either one of these modules without simultaneously examining the other will do little to solve a problem. Both must be considered at the same time, since each will be only as good as the other. Neither the content nor the process alone can solve a problem. The content is needed to provide the foundation on which the inputs can be transformed using the process. Without this foundation, the inputs cannot be processed and no problem solutions will be produced.

The particular focus of this chapter and the next one is on the content variables involved in using the modular approach. These variables include the composition of the group, group roles, the task, and the physical environment. Each of these variables plays a central role in moderating the input variables so that they may be used efficiently and effectively within the process module. However, each of the content variables must be considered separately, in view of their importance in determining the products and outcomes resulting from the process module.

Group composition is important because of its direct relation to a group's synergistic creative potential. That is, the combination of certain individual personality variables plus various group characteristics determines how effectively a group can mobilize its resources to develop creative products exceeding those obtainable by simply adding together individual contributions. Group roles are important primarily in their effect on the overall creative problem-solving process. The roles in a group must be clearly differentiated in order for the group to successfully complete a creative problem-solving task. The task itself is important because its clarity, structure, and complexity determine the procedures that the group needs to use to produce a workable problem solution. Finally, the role played by the physical environment of a group is important because of its potential to affect group behavior in the successful performance of problem-solving tasks. Furthermore, the physical environment plays a critical role in its effect on the interpersonal relationships of the group members.

Because of the overriding importance of group composition, this entire chapter is devoted to it. Group roles, tasks, and the environment will be discussed in Chapter 7.

As mentioned in Chapter 4, groups that have worked well together in solving ill-structured problems may want to skip a thorough examination of the content module or give it only a cursory review. As the old saying goes, "If it's not broken, don't fix it." Groups that are successful in creative problem solving and are satisfied with their success probably already have an appropriate composition and clear roles and tasks and are able to deal effectively with their physical environment. However, if you have any question about overlooking this chapter, complete the questionnaires presented in conjunction with each of the content variables to assist you in making this decision. If the results of these questionnaires indicate even marginal outcomes on each of the variables, analysis of this module should be seriously considered.

In the remainder of this chapter and in the next chapter, the nature of the content variables and the issues involved in assessing them will be discussed. When reading over this material, remember that a considerable amount of subjectivity is involved. Research on group creativity is still in its infancy. As a result, many of the specific features used to characterize each content variable may not reflect accurately what is actually involved in managing group creativity. In many cases, it is only hypothesized that certain variables and their components are correlated with creative group products. Most of the variables included reflect research outcomes gained from investigating group processes not directly concerned with creative problem solving. In some cases, the results from this related research are directly applicable to group creativity; in other cases, the results are not so directly applicable. Unfortunately, little comparative research exists. Thus the discussion that follows must be interpreted with some caution.

Group Composition

The composition of a group refers to the particular manner in which a collection of two or more individuals is put together for the purpose of accomplishing specific tasks. Composition can be achieved either formally or informally. Groups that are composed formally exist as the result of some need within a formal authority structure to achieve cultural, social, economic, political, and/or technological objectives. Informally composed groups usually exist to achieve similar objectives, but they arise without the direction or input of a formal authority structure. For example, a department in an organization that develops computer programs is a formally composed group designed to achieve formally prescribed objectives. A group of community members who band together to protest a zoning change is an informal group with no prescribed roles or formally circumscribed higher authority structure.

The composition of both types of groups is an important factor in determining how successful they will be in achieving their objectives. However, the composition of most formal groups can be controlled, while the composition of most informal groups cannot. Because of the authority vested in a formal private or public organization, the membership of its groups can be controlled with respect to the size of the groups and who will be in them. And once a formal group is formed, control of its composition usually rests with higher management—at least in highly centralized, hierarchical organizations. Managers appointed to supervise the general operation of individual groups may have some say about who is in their group, but the final authority to make such decisions typically rests with higher management. Because the major focus of this book is on formal groups, the discussion in this chapter and the next is directed primarily to such groups.

That the presence of one or more other people can affect group behaviors is fairly well documented in the research literature. Numerous studies have demonstrated that being around others can increase motivation to perform (e.g., Zajonc, 1965; Zajonc and Sales, 1966; Kelly and Thibaut, 1969) and that social facilitation can be enhanced by the expectation of positive evaluations by others (Good, 1973; Martens and Landers, 1972).

Perhaps the most significant variable related to group composition, however, is what is known as the assembly effect (Shaw, 1976). Behavior in any given group is determined by the specific combination of people in the group, independent of their individual characteristics. Thus, when the same people are arranged differently into groups and behaviors are compared, any differences likely beyond chance should be attributable directly to group composition. It is this assembly effect, that is, whom people interact with, that determines group behavior and not just the sum of the individual characteristics of the group members. Support for this notion has been found in at least one research study, in which individuals made different contributions on a problem-solving task depending on the particular people placed with them in a group (Rosenberg, Erlick, and Berkowitz, 1955).

Although knowing that different combinations of people can produce different outcomes is useful, it is not sufficient for analyzing the content module. The specific characteristics that people bring to groups also need to be considered if the effects of their combination are to be understood. As mentioned previously, since not much research is available, we don't know definitively which characteristics will be most predictive of group characteristics. Even less is known about what combinations of these characteristics will be best for different situations. Nonetheless, the literature does suggest a cluster of factors that seem to be related to creativity and creative problem solving to varying degrees. These factors can be grouped into individual characteristics and group characteristics.

Individual Characteristics

The study of personality traits in general has consumed considerable time among psychologists for many years. Many studies have attempted to identify individual characteristics that are common among creative people. Unfortunately, the outcomes of these research efforts have failed to produce any definitive conclusions about common creativity factors. There is, however, at least intuitive agreement on a group of factors that seem to appear in most people society would consider creative. This is not to say that everyone needs to possess all these characteristics, especially when they are considered in the context of group creativity. The absence of a characteristic in one individual frequently can be compensated for by its presence in another. Fifteen of these characteristics are discussed next.

Intelligence. Creative people typically are above average in intelligence—at least as measured by standard measures of intelligence. However, being intelligent does not guarantee that a person will be creative. In fact, little correlation has been found between creativity and general intelligence (MacKinnon, 1978). Only a certain amount of intelligence is required for creativity. Beyond that amount, intelligence becomes a nonsignificant variable in relation to creativity.

If creativity and general intelligence are not correlated, what value, then, is there to having intelligent group members? The answer is that intelligent people can make a contribution to group creativity if they use their intelligence appropriately. By appropriately, I mean that they can apply the types of intelligence that will help to develop unique problem solutions. For example, many types of verbal intelligence (which essentially involve sequential, analytical thinking) may be relatively useless for dealing with some aspects of ill-structured problems. On the other hand, spatial intelligence (which involves dealing with spatial arrangements and is more intuitive) may be appropriate for viewing problems as wholes and thus result in a better understanding of a problem situation.

Absence of repression and suppression. Repression and suppression are psychological mechanisms that involve either forcing ideas, impulses, and experiences into the unconscious (repression) or concealing psychological material from consciousness (suppression). In both cases, the net effect is that a person is predisposed to behave in certain ways without knowing why and is less open to experiences.

People who repress or suppress their experiences quite naturally do not have these experiences available to them as aids to creative problem solving. By repressing or suppressing experiences, these people cannot use impulse and imagery to solve problems that require intuitive and symbolic information processing. Creative people are more prone to express their psychological experiences and to use them on a conscious and unconscious level to solve problems. By being open to experiences, creative people have a vast experiential reservoir on which they can draw to aid them in developing creative problem solutions.

Feminine and aesthetic interests. On tests of masculinity/femininity, more creative males typically score higher on femininity than do less creative males (MacKinnon, 1978). Like an absence of repression and suppression, a degree of femininity indicates an openness to expression and particularly to feelings and emotions, an essential attribute for creative thinking. Males who score higher on masculinity generally are less open to their feelings and thus less prone to creative expression.

Creative people tend to be concerned with form and beauty that exist outside themselves. As one criterion of a creative product, elegance of solutions is commonly achieved by people with an aesthetic sense. Simply solving a problem very often is not enough for such people. They have a high concern for the final form of the product—a concern that often results in a higher-quality solution.

Self-esteem and self-confidence. The beliefs that people have about their worth and competence might be expected to be positively correlated with creativity. That is, people who think highly of themselves and believe in their own competence should be more creative than people who think less of themselves. Solving ill-structured problems requires a certain amount of self-esteem and self-confidence for dealing with what basically are ambiguous situations. To be able to deal with uncertainty, you must believe that you can succeed.

Although no studies directly linking these variables with creativity could be found, the research that does exist suggests some degree of relationship. For example, Carlston (1977) and Hochbaum (1954) found that self-confident members tend to dominate group discussions. In some cases, dominance can arouse others and cause them to be less likely to accept ideas passively (Pepinsky, Hemphill, and Shevitz, 1958)—and a lack of passivity is desirable in creative problem-solving groups. However, it is possible that self-confident group members who tend to dominate discussions may prevent the ideas of others from receiving equal consideration.

The relationship between self-esteem and problem solving has generally been found to vary with the nature of the task. Gergen and Bauer (1967), for example, produced results suggesting a curvilinear relationship between conformity and self-esteem when the task is low or medium in difficulty but no relationship when the task is high in difficulty. We might infer from this that tasks that are too difficult will not affect self-esteem, because it would not be reasonable to expect that the problem could be solved. Thus high task difficulty might wash out any effects that self-esteem might have on conformity during problem solving.

In another, more related study, Weiss and Knight (1980) found that individuals with low self-esteem searched for more information while solving a problem and were significantly more efficient at problem solving than were high self-esteem individuals. In addition, the low self-esteem individuals were more likely to offer correct problem solutions. However, interpretation of these results must be tempered by the fact that the task was one in which one correct solution was possible. In creative problem solving, many different solutions are possible and it is difficult to identify any one solution as being correct or incorrect. Consequently, high self-esteem individuals may be better solvers of ill-structured problems, where the costs of information searching may outweigh the benefits. Low self-esteem individuals, in contrast, may perceive ill-structured problems as requiring too much information searching in proportion to the likelihood of developing an appropriate solution. As the costs of information searching quickly begin to outweigh the perceived benefits, low self-esteem individuals may give up in despair, while high self-esteem individuals may persist because they are confident that they can succeed.

In general, it might be concluded that high self-esteem and confidence will be assets during information searching involving ill-structured problems that are low or medium in difficulty. During the idea-generation phase, however, highly confident group members might decrease group creativity if they tend to dominate the discussion. During idea generation, it would seem that individuals with a moderate level of self-confidence would work best.

Tolerance for ambiguity. Because ill-structured problems represent ambiguous situations, an ability to deal with ambiguity should be indispensible to creative problem solving. People who are intolerant of ambiguity tend to stereotype situations as being either one thing or another. Confronted with an ill-structured problem, such people will tend to classify it as being one type of problem or another and look for a quick solution. As a result, they risk correctly solving the wrong problem. In contrast, people who are more tolerant of ambiguity will be less likely to see a problem situation in this way and will focus more of their attention on understanding the situation before they attempt to solve it. Consequently, people who can tolerate ambiguity should be more effective problem solvers than people who can't.

The value to problem solving of being able to tolerate ambiguity has been demonstrated by Brightman and Urban (1978), who investigated the relationship among intolerance of ambiguity, dogmatism (being narrow-minded), and problem-solving effectiveness (as measured by performance ratings). The data were collected from management supervisors who completed a psychological instrument. The results indicated that supervisors who were flexible and tolerant of moderate ambiguity were also effective problem solvers and managers.

Willingness to take risks. Closely related to tolerance of ambiguity, willingness to take risks also should be a desirable attribute of creative problem solvers. Dealing with ambiguity involves taking certain risks, the most prominent of which is failing to solve the problem. If an individual is unwilling to risk failure, the individual is not likely to solve an ill-structured problem—or at least not with a high-quality solution.

However, being willing to assume risks does not mean that problem solvers should rush headlong into every problem situation and let the chips fall where they may. Risk taking in creative problem solving involves taking calculated risks. That is, the amount of perceived risk should be such that the expected benefits are likely to outweigh any possible costs. Making such an assessment is usually a matter of examining all possible consequences of different courses of action and selecting the course with the highest probable payoff. In other words, look at the worst possible thing that could happen if the problem is not solved and select the course of action with the most realistic, most harmless outcome.

Ability to use convergent and divergent thinking. The creative problem-solving process involves two basic, alternating styles of thinking. The first, convergent thinking, occurs when the scope of the search for problem information is reduced or whenever the bits of information or ideas must be narrowed down to a more manageable number. For example, the act of selecting from among a pool of ideas is a convergent activity. The second type of thinking, divergent thinking, is just the opposite: The search for problem information and the generation of ideas (just two instances of divergent thinking) are expanded as more information and ideas are sought. Ideational fluency, to be discussed later, is an example of divergent thinking, since it involves the rapid generation of many ideas.

Both convergent and divergent thinking are essential to creative problem solving, because without them none of the different stages could be completed and the problem could not be solved. Unfortunately, many people are better at one type of thinking than the other. Although there is nothing wrong with this, the ability of a group to solve a problem is diminished if most of the members excel in one type of thinking. Obviously, what is needed in most creative problem-solving groups is a balance between both types of thinking or a group composed entirely of people proficient at both types of thinking.

Originality. Originality is often equated with creative behavior. However, it is only one of several primary creativity variables. Being creative involves more than being original. Although originality is an important variable, it must be considered in conjunction with other creativity measures.

According to Guilford (1950), originality refers to "statistical infrequency." This means that an idea is original to the extent that it is unlikely to occur among the universe of ideas possible for a particular problem. For example, someone in the publishing business might consider a book proposal original if it is one that would not normally be expected to occur.

However, originality must also be viewed as a relative concept. What one person considers original may not be considered original by another person. Many ideas are original only to their creator or within a specific group, organization, or professional area. In addition, originality can vary in relation to specific characteristics. For instance, an idea for a radio may involve using only original colors, knob sizes, or means of selecting different situations. In this case, it would not be the product that is original but specific aspects of it.

In any event, originality is a prerequisite for members of a creative problem-solving group. The more original ideas a group is capable of producing, the more likely it is that the group will be capable of solving a problem satisfactorily. However, unless several members of a group are high in originality, the group climate may not be sufficiently conducive to sustaining group originality over a period of time.

To help stimulate originality, Torrance (1959) suggests doing the following:

1. *Provide adequate time for idea generation.* The originality of ideas seems to increase with time, up to a certain limit.
2. *Allow group members to play with ambiguities and uncertainties.* Encourage people to experiment with their ideas and examine different idea combinations.
3. *Heighten concern about the seriousness or importance of the problem.* If a problem is viewed as trivial or inconsequential, the motivation level may be too low to result in original ideas.
4. *Make original thinking legitimate.* Provide rewards (if only recognition of originality) to help create a norm that reinforces and encourages production of original ideas.

Ideational fluency. Closely related to originality is ideational fluency—the ability to generate a large number of ideas in response to a particular problem situation. The more ideas a group can produce, the higher will be the quality of the ideas and the greater will be the probability that it will successfully solve the problem (Osborn, 1963; Parnes, 1967). Thus, if a group is composed of individuals who are highly fluent and they use this fluency to produce a large number of ideas, many original ideas are likely to result. Furthermore, the likelihood that at least one of these ideas will lead to a successful problem solution is increased substantially.

Two ways in which ideational fluency in groups can be increased are by using brainstorming rules and checklists of idea stimulators. Osborn's (1963) four brainstorming rules for groups can also be applied to individuals. The four rules are:

1. Criticism is ruled out; defer all judgment.
2. Freewheeling is welcome; the wilder the ideas, the better.
3. Quantity is wanted; the more wild ideas, the better.
4. Hitchhiking and combination are sought; whenever possible, build on previous ideas to produce new ones.

Torrance (1959) recommends training pairs of group members in using each of these rules. Increasing ideational fluency through the use of stimulator checklists might involve asking group members to focus on how problems might be solved using one or more of these methods.

Substitution:	One idea or product used in place of another.
Combination:	Putting together either ideas or products.
Adaptation:	Use of a similar idea or product.
Modification:	A change in one or more elements of an idea or product.
Magnification:	An increase in the size or scope of some aspect of an idea or product.
"Minification":	A decrease in the size or scope of some aspect of an idea or product.
Rearrangement:	An alteration in the order of one or more elements of an idea or product.

Flexibility. This component of creative behavior has two aspects. The first is the ability to view a problem from many different perspectives. Because understanding of a problem situation is critical for solving the problem, a person who is flexible should be able to gain a better understanding of the focal problem and then smooth the way for solving it. The second aspect of flexibility involves the different types of ideas that are generated for a given problem. For example, a problem of how to recruit more students for a university might involve ideas for recruiting students of specific races, ages, geographical locations, income groups, and so forth. Both types of flexibility are important to creative problem solving, because both are needed for different stages in the creative problem-solving process.

Note that flexibility and ideational fluency do not go hand in hand. Being able to generate ideas rapidly (ideational fluency) does not necessarily mean that a person will be able to break a mental set and generate different kinds of ideas for the same problem (flexibility). Thus flexibility is not a prerequisite for ideational fluency. However, a person needs some degree of fluency in order to be flexible.

This difference between ideational fluency and flexibility suggests that, ideally, creative problem-solving groups should be composed of individuals who are high in both behaviors. If this is not possible, the majority of group members should be high in ideational fluency, with fewer members high in flexibility. In this case, the high-flexibility members could increase the diversity of ideas produced by expanding or building on ideas of the other members. Because they are high in flexibility, these individuals should be able to increase the range of possible ideas by using their ability to generate ideas within different categories.

Elaboration. This aspect of creative behavior involves adding detail to ideas already generated. A simple example is that of a novelist who develops a basic story outline and then builds a story by the addition of details to the outline. The final story thus represents an elaboration of the original story ideas as described in outline form.

In general, there seems to be an inverse relationship between elaboration and fluency, flexibility, and originality (Henrickson, 1963). Elaboration of ideas requires time that usually results in decreases in other components of creative behavior. People who are high in all four components frequently must choose which component to emphasize. In groups, however, creative output probably will not suffer as long as there are enough members proficient in each.

The importance of elaboration to creativity should be evident. For one thing, an idea is much more likely to be implemented and to successfully solve a problem if it has been elaborated so that if required, the acceptance by others can be obtained. Second, most ideas emerge from our subconscious as only partially completed images. Elaboration helps us to add definition and value to such ideas. Finally, elaboration is a skill that is essential to any form of planning involving the coordination of many details. Nevertheless, too much elaboration can cause problems by confusing the developers or users of a creative product.

Independence of judgment. In a society that often reinforces conforming behavior, it is difficult for some people to develop independence of thought. Yet, the ability to be relatively free from convention and the constraints imposed on most people is a primary determinant of creative behavior. For example, in a study in which creative architects were rated on 22 traits, independence of thought had a positive correlation of .44 (correlations can range from −1.00 to +1.00) with creativity ratings (MacKinnon, 1978).

However, being an independent thinker can be dysfunctional if it is carried to extremes. People who are independent thinkers often develop a rigidity of thought or tunnel vision that makes it hard for them to develop broader problem perspectives. When such extreme thinking develops in groups, a phenomenon known as groupthink (Janis, 1972) often occurs. The group begins thinking it is always in the right, insulates itself from outside opinion, begins to feel invulnerable, and censures any group members who deviate from the group's way of thinking. To avoid this pitfall, creative problem-solving groups should be composed of individuals who are independent thinkers who can also remain open to new ideas and viewpoints.

Although not essential to the creative process, independence of thought helps to predispose people to creative thinking. We can do without it and still be creative. But our ideas are more likely to be unique when we have a moderate sense of independent judgment.

Dual-brain hemispheric dominance. All of us have left and right brain hemispheres that enable us to perform different motor activities and mental functions. In relation to mental activities and creativity, the left brain seems to be primarily involved in verbal behavior, logical and sequential thinking, and analytical and judgmental approaches to problem solving. The right brain is more concerned with spatial relationships, intuitive and nonsequential thinking (or parallel information processing), and the use of symbols and images.

The functions residing within both hemispheres are equally important to creative problem solving. Unfortunately, the left hemisphere has been dominant in most of us. The reasons for this dominance are unclear, but it is likely that our cultural and social conditioning play a major role. At a young age, most of us were instructed to think logically and not jump to conclusions. We were trained to develop our left brains while our right brains were left to their own devices.

We use both brain hemispheres whenever we attempt to solve a problem. But because the left hemisphere has received more attention, we frequently use inappropriate problem-solving strategies. For instance, we might try to solve a problem primarily with logic when mental imagery might be more effective.

If a group is composed of primarily left- or right-brain thinkers, it may be limited in its ability to produce creative solutions. Ideally, creative problem-solving groups should have a more or less equal number of left- and right-brain thinkers. Although it is difficult to determine who such people are, it often is possible to make subjective determinations simply by observing people work on developing creative solutions or asking them to describe the approach they use. In addition, such instruments as Raudsepp's (1981) Left/Right Brain Orientation questionnaire and Hermann's (1980) Learning Profile Survey Form can also be used to assess brain hemispheric dominance.

Perseverance. People who develop highly original problem solutions usually do so after immersing themselves in solving their problems. They are driven by a "stick-to-itiveness" that may not be characteristic of less creative people. When working on a problem-solving task, creative people have a need to complete the task that motivates them to see it through to a solution. Just identifying a problem usually is not sufficient for most creative people. They want to solve it and frequently will drive themselves until they do.

A group composed of members with a fairly high level of perseverance is much more likely to solve ill-structured problems successfully than is a less persevering group. However, if several group members lack the motivation to persevere, the performance of the entire group may suffer unless the more persevering members are willing to shoulder a disproportionate share of the effort. Unfortunately, this is how many groups (and organizations) survive—with a few doing most of the work.

Locus of control. One personality variable that has received considerable attention in the research literature over the last decade and a half is locus of control. As conceptualized by Rotter (1966), locus of control refers to the extent people believe that things that happen to them are in their control or are due more to luck or powerful others. People with an internal locus of control generally view themselves as being in control, while those with an external locus of control see luck or others dictating what happens to them.

Research based on the locus of control measure indicates that internals actively seek out information that can be used to help them achieve their goals. Externals are much less likely to seek out such information.

Because information searching is a vital element of the creative problem-solving process, it seems plausible to predict that internals would be more effective problem solvers than externals. Because of their greater alertness to environmental factors likely to affect their problem-solving effectiveness, internals should be able to clarify and redefine problem situations with greater ease than externals. As a result, ill-structured problems should be less ambiguous and uncertain for internals.

Some support for this hypothesis has been found by Organ and Greene (1974), who report a significant positive correlation between locus of control and role ambiguity among senior research scientists and engineers. Specifically, people with an internal locus of control tend to perceive less ambiguity about their roles than do people with an external locus of control. Although these results are not related directly to creative problem-solving effectiveness, they suggest a plausible relationship—at least until more conclusive research is conducted.

Group Characteristics

As discussed earlier in this chapter, an assembly effect in groups often determines group behavior. That is, group behavior is partially determined by specific combinations of individuals interacting together and not just the sum of all the individual characteristics. In this regard, the individual characteristics that go into defining a group's composition must be considered in relation to specific group characteristics. The composition of a group cannot be considered properly unless the interaction of both sets of characteristics is taken into account. In the remainder of this section, six group characteristics will be discussed, all of which determine the contributions possible from using the individual characteristics.

Group-member sex. In general, mixed-sex groups produce higher-quality problem solutions than same-sex groups (Hoffman and Maier, 1961). Because of the different social perspectives that men and women bring to groups, mixed-sex groups are likely to consider a broader range of problem viewpoints and solution alternatives than same-sex groups. Consequently, mixed-sex groups are likely to produce more creative solutions than same-sex groups.

However, the research results supporting this conclusion are somewhat mixed. For example, in a signal detection task, Clement and Schiereck (1973) found that same-sex groups performed more efficiently than mixed-sex groups. In another study, Kent and McGrath (1969) reported that same-sex groups produced more original products than mixed-sex groups. And Reitan and Shaw (1964) observed that more interpersonal disagreement and conformity occurred in mixed-sex groups than in same-sex groups.

It appears that mixed-sex groups may be more concerned with social-emotional problems and less concerned with the task than same-sex groups, in which the focus may be more on getting the job done (Shaw, 1976). When social-emotional issues exist in mixed-sex groups, the group members may conform more to what they perceive to be the expectations of others. As a result, social-emotional problems may be smoothed or resolved, but at the expense of group creativity. If a group is concerned with conformity, the synergistic creative potential of its members is not likely to be released and solutions are likely to be mundane and conventional.

Nonetheless, mixed-sex groups probably do not need to be avoided entirely. There undoubtedly are many mixed-sex groups in which social-emotional problems have been resolved and a productive task orientation has been developed. Much of the research in this area has been conducted using artificial groups in laboratory settings, where there is usually not enough time to resolve social-emotional problems. Thus, in deciding on the sex composition of a creative problem-solving group, consider the extent to which a group has worked through its social-emotional problems.

Group homogeneity-heterogeneity. Although diversity of group membership with respect to sex may or may not facilitate group creativity, diversity with respect to personality profiles does seem to promote group creativity. Hoffman (1959), for example, administered a personality assessment instrument to a group of individuals and divided the individuals into groups consisting of those with similar profiles and those with dissimilar profiles. The groups then worked on two problems involving realistic work settings. The results indicated that the heterogeneous groups performed better overall and produced more inventive solutions than the homogeneous groups. Similar results were obtained on different tasks in a study conducted by Hoffman and Maier (1961)—the heterogeneous groups produced higher-quality solutions.

A three-part study more relevant to creativity was conducted by Triandis, Hall, and Ewen (1965). Participants were formed into dyads based on their high, medium, or low cognitive similarity in regard to opinions toward various social issues (e.g., war and socialized medicine). The dyads were then instructed to work on resolving various social problems. The heterogeneous dyads with previous experience on such tasks outperformed those without previous experience. In the other experiments, dyads were composed of people with varying attitudes and creative ability (e.g., homogeneous attitudes and creative ability or heterogeneous attitudes and homogeneous ability). The results suggested that the most original, most practical, and highest quality solutions were produced by the dyads that were dissimilar in attitudes but similar in creative ability.

It appears that creative problem-solving groups should be composed of members who differ in their personalities but are relatively homogeneous with respect to their creative abilities. However, differences in personalities can create dysfunctional conflict that must be controlled by a skilled group leader or by using group techniques (such as various brainwriting methods) that minimize or eliminate interpersonal conflict. It is desirable for creative groups to possess personality heterogeneity, but only if the group members are not too dissimilar or if they have learned how to work together smoothly.

Group cohesion. This characteristic of groups refers to the extent that individuals want to remain members of the group. The members of highly cohesive groups generally are more motivated to participate in their group's activities and identify more with their group's successes and failures than do the members of less cohesive groups. Unless a group has a minimal level of cohesiveness, it will not be able to function effectively as a group.

Research on group cohesiveness has revealed that members of high-cohesive groups, in contrast to members of low-cohesive groups, tend to communicate more with one another (Back, 1951; French, 1941), exhibit more positive and friendly interactions (Shaw and Shaw, 1962), exert greater influence over one another (Berkowitz, 1954), are better at achieving group goals (Goodacre, 1951), and are generally more satisifed with their group and its products (Gross, 1954; Exline, 1957).

Cohesiveness also seems to be related to a group's ability to produce unique ideas, if the group members have received some training in creative thinking. Cohen, Whitmyre, and Funk (1960) investigated the effects of problem type and training on the creative behavior of nominal and real dyads. The participants in the study each ranked the other participants according to their preference to work with another person as a brainstorming partner and in terms of the others' perceived brainstorming skills. Dyads then were formed consisting of cohesive and noncohesive pairs who were either trained or untrained in creative thinking (as defined by their participation in a ten-hour course). The findings indicated that dyads who were both cohesive and trained produced more unique ideas than the other pairs.

Although group cohesiveness can contribute toward a group's creative output, too much cohesiveness may be dysfunctional. As noted earlier, groups that are very cohesive may insulate themselves from outside opinions and develop a norm of conformity that places cognitive restrictions on the group members. In other words, too much cohesiveness may decrease a group's ability to produce divergent problem viewpoints and ideas.

Group compatibility. Group members who get along together are compatible. Hypothetically, compatible groups should be characterized by less interpersonal conflict, a more congenial atmosphere, and more efficient task functioning than incompatible groups. In addition, when group members are compatible, they should be more effective in achieving group goals— especially goals that require cooperative efforts. Group members who can mutually satisfy their needs and who possess personality characteristics that mesh are likely to spend less time dealing with social-emotional problems, thus leaving more time for working on group tasks.

Although somewhat inconclusive, the research literature does offer some support for these hypotheses. For example, Haythorn, Couch, Haefner, Langham, and Carter (1956) found less interpersonal conflict and more goal-directed behavior in compatible groups than in incompatible groups. Schutz (1955), testing his tridimensional theory of interpersonal behavior, found compatible groups to be more productive than incompatible groups. Of particular significance to creative problem solving was Schutz's finding that productivity in compatible groups tends to increase in direct proportion to task complexity. With respect to complementary personality characteristics and compatibility, research by Smelser (1961) and Fry (1965) has demonstrated that groups are more effective when the group members are different on the personality variables of dominance and ascendance.

Clearly, then, groups are much more likely to be creative if the group members are compatible with one another. Compatibility undoubtedly affects a group's creative climate but is not a primary determinant of climate. That is, groups should be compatible in order to develop and sustain a creative climate. However, compatibility is not a sufficient condition, the variables discussed in earlier chapters must also be present in sufficient quantity. Nevertheless, compatibility probably is one of the most important group composition variables.

Group aging. This is an interesting, although often neglected, variable in group research. Most studies on groups use a static methodology that assumes that groups exist at only one point in time. This "slice of group life" approach, while necessary, fails to consider the dynamic, developmental aspects of groups. The group aging concept involves looking at the effects produced on group members by their interacting together over time.

In general, research in this area suggests that newer groups tend to be more creative than older groups. For example, Shepard (1956) had research directors rank work units on their creativity and found that the highest-ranked groups were under 16 months in group age. Simliar results were found when team members ranked the groups, although a slight increase in creativity was observed for groups between 2 and 5 years of age. In a related study, Pelz and Andrews (1966) assessed the rated usefulness of contributions of 83 scientific research teams. Their results were similar to those of Shepard, with scientific usefulness of contributions being curvilinearly related to group age. Usefulness gradually increased with age until it peaked at about 4 or 5 years of age and then gradually declined, although slight increases were noted at older ages, gradually diminishing during the 10- to 12-year period.

Although young groups seem to be less rigid in their thinking than older groups, it is obviously not realistic to expect all groups to be young. What, then, can be done? The secret involves making an old group think young. Thus the chronological age of a group may not be as significant as the group's psychological age.

There are at least four ways in which an older group can counteract the effects of rigid thinking that occur over time. First, new group members can be assigned to the team or rotated in on a temporary basis. The infusion of "new blood" can often stimulate new perspectives. Second, the group might consider participating in creative-thinking training, which might result in the group's developing new ways of looking at problems. Third, the appropriate application of various group creative problem-solving techniques can also spark a group's creativity. The group should alternate the use of several different techniques to avoid becoming locked in on one particular approach. Finally, the group leader can help an old group think like a young group. The Pelz and Andrews (1966) study found that the group leader can help the group members by actively playing the role of a sounding board for new ideas. In addition, the group leader can encourage members to challenge one another and to acknowledge individual contributions.

Group size. The resources available to a group for creativity and problem solving will increase in direct proportion to the number of group members. The more people in a group, the more abilities, knowledge, and skills that they can draw on to work on a problem. Unfortunately, increases in problem-solving effectiveness cannot be expected by simply adding more group members. As the size of a group increases, the number of coordinating problems involved also increases. Furthermore, larger groups reduce opportunities for participation, make shy members feel less inclined to volunteer ideas, and increase the possibility that interpersonal conflicts will develop. (As a rough rule of thumb, large groups consist of six or more people).

The research conducted on group size has several clear implications for managing group creativity. In particular, studies dealing with the effects of group size on participation, group climate, uniformity, and performance suggest possible applications for group creativity.

Bales, Strodtbeck, Mills, and Roseborough (1951) demonstrated that with increasing group size, a few group members tend to dominate the discussion. When participation is unequal, all solution possibilities are not likely to be considered and the final solution may be of lower quality than when participation is more or less equal. In such situations, the group leader can alleviate the effects of size on participation by controlling the discussion and soliciting comments from all group members. In addition, brainwriting procedures (see Chapters 2 and 9), which ensure equality of participation, could be used.

In the general area of group climate, Katz (1949) found larger groups to be less cohesive than smaller groups; Slater (1958) found that members of smaller groups tend to view their group experience more positively; and O'Dell (1968) observed that intermember tension, disagreement, and antagonism tend to increase with increases in group size. These results suggest that development of a creative climate will be accomplished more easily in smaller groups. Consequently, group leaders might consider using only three to five group members at any one time for creative problem solving.

Research on uniformity suggests a tentative positive relationship with group size. That is, larger groups may tend to be characterized by more conformity to majority judgments (Gerard, Wilhelmy, and Conolley, 1968).

However, the research in this area is not conclusive. Asch (1951) also found a positive relationship, but only with increases in group size by a maximum of three people. Nevertheless, group leaders might be best advised to limit group size with respect to this variable also. Conformity of thought is obviously counterproductive for group creativity and should be avoided if at all possible.

A final variable affected by group size is performance. The literature in this area indicates that large groups perform less well than small groups when the task is conjunctive (Frank and Anderson, 1971). That is, when group performance depends on the performance of the least competent member, small groups will outperform large groups. The reason for this is that large groups simply are more likely to have at least one incompetent member than are small groups. The literature also indicates that the most competent member will determine group performance when the task is disjunctive (Ziller, 1957). With disjunctive tasks, the outcome of the group's efforts will depend on at least one person's being able to complete a task successfully. When disjunctive tasks have been studied in relation to group size, larger groups have been found to perform better, although not in direct proportion to the number of group members (Frank and Anderson, 1971). Because creative problem-solving groups deal with ill-structured problems that essentially are disjunctive tasks, relatively small groups (up to about five persons) should be used. Caution must be exercised to avoid the potential negative effects that might be produced by large groups.

Assessing Group Composition

In order to determine the appropriateness of a group's composition for creative problem solving, the group members could read over the preceding material and make a subjective determination. A more objective and quantitative assessment requires the use of a rating scale. The group composition questionnaire (Figure 6-1) is a quantitative rating scale that a group can use. In most cases, an entire group should discuss each of the items in the questionnaire and attempt to reach consensus on the ratings. In doing this, there will be greater ownership of the outcome.

Figure 6-1. Group composition questionnaire.

Instructions: The purpose of this questionnaire is to help you assess the extent to which the composition of your group is appropriate for group creative problem solving. For each of the following items, indicate the extent to which you believe the group as a whole possesses the characteristic or ability described by circling the one number that best describes your assessment. Do not spend too much time on any one item; your first reaction is likely to be the most accurate one.

1 = Not at all
2 = A little
3 = Somewhat
4 = Quite a bit
5 = Completely

Individual Characteristics
To what extent are the members of this group:

1. Able to tolerate ambiguity?	1	2	3	4	5
2. Above average in intelligence?	1	2	3	4	5
3. Able to view a problem from many different perspectives?	1	2	3	4	5
4. Able to generate many different kinds of ideas?	1	2	3	4	5
5. More expressive than repressive or suppressive?	1	2	3	4	5
6. Able to use both convergent and divergent thinking?	1	2	3	4	5
7. Able to use both analytical and intuitive thinking with ease?	1	2	3	4	5
8. Able to produce original ideas?	1	2	3	4	5
9. Characterized by a belief that they are in control of their lives and what happens to them?	1	2	3	4	5
10. Characterized by perseverance when working on a problem?	1	2	3	4	5
11. Moderately high in self-esteem and self-confidence?	1	2	3	4	5
12. Willing to take calculated risks?	1	2	3	4	5
13. Able to generate large numbers of ideas rapidly?	1	2	3	4	5
14. Able to add detail to ideas?	1	2	3	4	5
15. Moderately high in femininity and aesthetic interests?	1	2	3	4	5
16. Able to think independently?	1	2	3	4	5

Group Characteristics
To what extent is this group:

1. Composed of members of the same sex?	1	2	3	4	5
2. Composed of members with diverse personalities?	1	2	3	4	5
3. Composed of members who are nearly equal in creative abilities?	1	2	3	4	5
4. Moderately cohesive (in terms of being able to work together well)?	1	2	3	4	5
5. Compatible (i.e., mutual needs are satisfied and personality characteristics mesh)?	1	2	3	4	5
6. Composed of members with less than two years of experience in working as a unit?	1	2	3	4	5
7. Composed of three to five members?	1	2	3	4	5

Scoring and Interpretation: Add up each number circled to obtain your group composition score (GCS). Possible total scores range from 23 to 115.

If your GCS was between 23 and 53, the composition of your group is probably inappropriate for group creative problem solving. That is, your group most likely would not be as successful at solving ill-structured problems as would groups with higher scores. Groups with scores in this range probably will produce creative products that are lower in value when measured against whatever criteria might be used. If your GCS is within this inappropriate range, you should analyze each item that received a low score and take any actions possible that might raise your score.

If your GCS is between 54 and 83, your group is moderately appropriate for group creative problem solving. On the basis of group composition alone, the odds of your group's being successful at solving ill-structured problems are about even. You should examine all the low-scoring items and make any adjustments possible to increase your score.

If your GCS is between 84 and 115, the composition is very appropriate and probably needs few adjustments. If you can take any actions that are low in cost (in terms of time, money, etc.) to increase the composition appropriateness, go ahead and take them. However, a score within this range indicates that efforts might be better directed at other aspects of the modular approach (e.g., giving more attention to honing problem redefinition skills).

Summary

Group composition is one of the most important content variables in the modular approach. A particular group's combination of individual and group characteristics can significantly influence group creativity.

The composition of any group is determined by formal or informal factors (in some cases, by a combination of both). Groups with a formal composition (i.e., the composition has been prescribed by a formal authority structure) can have their membership controlled to a much greater extent than informal groups. In other words, members of informal groups generally will have more say over who is in the group and the group's size.

It is fairly well established that the presence of others can have an arousing effect on the motivation to perform in groups. In this regard, what is known as the assembly effect plays a major role in determining group effectiveness. The behavior observed in a group is determined more by the particular combination of individuals in the group than by the sum total of the individual characteristics. However, knowledge of specific individual and group characteristics is also important for assessing the appropriateness of a group's composition.

Major individual characteristics related to creativity include intelligence, absence of repression and suppression, feminine and aesthetic interests, self-esteem and self-confidence, tolerance of ambiguity, willingness to take risks, ability to use convergent and divergent thinking, originality, ideational fluency, flexibility, elaboration, independence of judgment, dual-brain hemispheric dominance, perseverance, and an internal locus of control. Some major group characteristics related to creativity are group-member sex, group homogeneity-heterogeneity, group cohesion, group compatibility, group aging, and group size.

When some control over group composition is possible, consider including group members who are able to tolerate ambiguity, above average in intelligence, able to develop different problem perspectives, able to generate many different kinds of ideas, more expressive than repressive or suppressive, able to use both convergent and divergent thinking, equally adept at intuitive and analytical thinking, able to produce original ideas, believers in their own abilities as a major factor in determining what happens to them, able to persevere when solving problems, moderately high in self-esteem and self-confidence, willing to take calculated risks, able to generate large numbers of ideas rapidly, able to add detail to ideas, moderately high in femininity and aesthetic interests, and able to think independently.

In addition, creative problem-solving groups should be composed of members of the same sex (unless a skilled facilitator is available or social-emotional difficulties have been resolved), members with diverse personalities, members who can work together well, members whose mutual needs are satisfied and whose personality characteristics mesh, members with under two years of experience working as a unit, and three to five members (larger groups should be subdivided).

7

Roles, Tasks, and the Environment

The three remaining components of the content module are discussed in this chapter. The first component, group roles, is discussed by examining the nature of roles, different role types, and the concept of role clarity. Group tasks are discussed next, with the emphasis on task characteristics and task clarity. Finally, a group's physical environment is looked at from the perspective of its conduciveness to group creativity.

Group Roles

All the people who determine a group's composition play various roles. The literature on group dynamics is replete with examples of the different roles played within groups. The focus in this section, however, is on those roles that pertain most directly to creative problem solving. The general nature of the concept of a role will be discussed first, followed by a description of role types, and finally we take a look at the concept of role clarity.

The Nature of Roles

A role consists of the set of expectations that are held about a person who occupies a particular position. A group leader, for example, is expected to provide the group members with information that may affect the way they do their jobs, with information about how they should do their jobs, and with feedback about how well they have performed. Each group member performs roles expected of him or her by the leader as well as other group members and even people outside the group.

When a person is expected to behave in a certain recurring manner, the set of expectations constitutes an expected role. However, there are at least two other components that make up the concept of a role. One of these is the perceived role, which consists of the set of recurring behaviors that role occupants believe they should perform. A perceived role differs from an expected role in that role perceptions are based on the perceptions of role occupants and not the perceptions of others. The third component of the role concept is known as the actual or enacted role. This role involves the actual behaviors used by an individual in carrying out his or her role. Obviously, the behaviors of an actual role may be quite different from those of an expected role and even a perceived role.

According to Katz and Kahn (1966), the motivation to perform a role derives primarily from three sources. The first source pertains to the information sent to individuals about how they are expected to perform. This information is received by individuals in terms of what they must and must not do in performing their jobs. The second source of motivation is more situational and derives from the task being performed or from previous experience individuals might have had with similar tasks. Thus a computer operator responds to data that appear as continual reminders of what needs to be done. The third source of motivation stems from the internal forces that drive individuals to perform, regardless of external expectations. For instance, an insurance claims adjuster might take special care in completing the required forms—not because of any external standards, but because of pride in her work and the intrinsic satisfaction of doing a job well.

In addition to the general components of the role concept and the sources of role motivation, note that all roles exist on two interrelated planes—the formal and the informal. Formal roles are those prescribed by the organization or others in the authority structure. These are prescribed roles that usually emanate from legitimate authority in the form of job descriptions and would be classified as formal, expected roles.

However, informal, expected roles also exist in all organizations and often determine actual role behavior more than formal, expected roles do. Informal roles typically are based on the prevailing norms that characterize a particular group or organization. For example, members of a work group may informally dictate the pace at which work is done, how it is done, and when it is done.

As long as these informal standards do not interfere with the achievement of formally prescribed standards, they are likely to be tolerated by the formal authority structure. However, if the organization perceives the formal and informal roles to be incongruent, it usually will institute changes to correct the situation. (Unfortunately, many such changes are made using formal sanctions that often do not take into account the strong psychological influences exerted by informal roles.)

Types of Roles

In the literature on small group behavior, the actual roles played by group members usually are described in terms of task and maintenance behaviors. Task-oriented role behavior refers to actions directed toward achieving the group's tasks. Setting and defining goals, processing task-relevant information, and pushing for task completion are examples of this type of role behavior. Maintenance-oriented role behavior involves maintaining harmonious relationships and group cohesiveness. For this type of role behavior, the focus is more on the people who are attempting to accomplish a task. It generally is agreed that both types of role behavior are necessary for effective group problem solving.

In addition to these two broad categories of role behavior, more specific roles have been differentiated. Benne and Sheats (1948) described such task roles as Initiator, Information Processor, Summarizer, and Evaluator and such maintenance roles as Encourager, Harmonizer, Compromiser, and Gatekeeper-Expeditor. Although not all these roles will be in evidence to the same degree during every small group discussion, some degree of several of the roles will be evident in most groups. The extent to which the different roles can be observed will depend on the characteristics of the task being worked on and the needs of individual members to fulfill one or more of the roles.

Similar roles can be observed in creative problem-solving groups. However, the roles specific to creative problem-solving groups can be better discussed using slightly different terminology. Furthermore, roles not specifically included in the roles described by Benne and Sheats also need to be discussed. These roles are both descriptive and prescriptive; the roles just discussed are primarily descriptive. Thus, in the discussion that follows, the emphasis is on roles usually played by members of creative problem-solving groups as well as roles not frequently observed but often required for effective performance.

The task roles specific to creative problem-solving groups are those of Fact Finder, Problem Finder, Idea Finder, Solution Finder, Acceptance Finder, Evaluator, and Creativity Monitor. The first five of these roles correspond to basic stages of the creative problem-solving process, and the remaining two are specific roles needed to supplement the other five. The maintenance roles observed or needed in creative problem-solving groups are Mediator, Comic, Scapegoat, and Maintenance Facilitator.

Task Roles

Fact Finder. People who fulfill this role are concerned primarily with supplying information to help the group better understand a problem situation. Whenever a group member contributes any information—relevant or irrelevant—he or she is performing a fact-finding role. For most groups, the people who assume this role will vary considerably across different problems. Each group member brings to a group different levels of knowledge and experience that might apply to some problems but not to others. People who behave as Fact Finders play a central role in determining how an initial problem situation will be perceived and possibly be redefined.

Problem Finder. People who play this role help the group determine the specific problem that it will work on. The key to being an effective Problem Finder is the ability to distill, synthesize, and clarify information generated by the Fact Finders. From a mass of relevant and irrelevant problem facts, these role players are able to help a group crystallize its thinking about a general problem situation and help it decide how the facts can be sorted out and pulled together to produce an acceptable problem redefinition. Most effective Problem Finders are able to delineate the core issues of a problem (a problem's "essence") and communicate these issues in a manner understandable to all group members.

Idea Finder. Once a group has agreed on a problem redefinition, it can begin the task of generating ideas—the raw material of problem solutions. Good Idea Finders usually score high on measures of fluency, flexibility, originality, and elaboration. Somewhat less analytical than Problem Finders, people fulfilling an idea-finding role are relatively unconstrained in their thinking and rely heavily on intuitive thinking. In addition, they are willing to take risks, jump to conclusions, and put forth any idea that pops into their minds without evaluating it or fearing that it will be received negatively by others. Idea Finders also stimulate other group members by providing ideas that might prompt new ideas or by suggesting possible combinations of previously generated ideas.

Solution Finder. Solution Finders have the ability to toy around with ideas and transform them into solutions capable of solving a problem. In contrast to Idea Finders, who are proficient mostly at divergent thinking, Solution Finders excel at convergent thinking. They are able to narrow down a large number of ideas and produce one or two potential solutions. However, Solution Finders must also be capable of some divergent thinking, because they must generate a list of criteria against which ideas can be judged. Then, using a combination of analytical and intuitive skills, they must be able to formulate a solution likely to solve the problem.

Acceptance Finder. People in this role are the PR people of creative problem solving. One of their jobs is to "sell" the problem solution selected to dissenting group members. However, their primary responsibility is to convince those who are at higher levels or external to the group or organization to accept the solution selected by the group. In addition, Acceptance Finders frequently are responsible for seeing that solutions, once accepted, are implemented and that outcomes are then evaluated against the process that led to the development of the solution.

Evaluator. The evaluator role is usually played by at least one group member throughout the creative problem-solving process. This role is especially noticeable in unstructured groups, where little control is exerted over the process and a group leader is either absent or unskilled at process facilitation. Evaluators tend to be highly critical and analytical. As a result, they can be detrimental to group creativity, especially during the fact-finding, problem-finding, and idea-finding stages. However, Evaluators can be helpful during the solution-finding stage. Furthermore, Evaluators can provide a valuable service to groups by functioning as "devil's advocates" and ensuring that a group does not become a victim of groupthink. Nonetheless, some control must be used with Evaluators so that they do not impede a group's creativity.

Creativity Monitor. This role can often make the difference between success and failure in problem-solving groups. The major responsibility of Creativity Monitors is to oversee the group's progress through the creative problem-solving stages and to promote and encourage creative thinking. Although these functions are typically performed by a group's formal leader, individual group members can also act as the Creativity Monitor when they possess the necessary skills. Group leaders may even want to encourage the other members to perform this role for their professional or individual development. Creativity Monitors are essential for groups inexperienced in using creative problem solving; they will perform a much less active role in more experienced groups.

Maintenance Roles

Mediator. People who perform this role attempt to settle interpersonal conflicts and differences of opinion. Although highly cohesive groups whose members have similar personalities may not require a Mediator, there usually are some instances when such a role is indispensable. However, Mediators are most useful in groups in which interpersonal conflict is likely. In particular, highly creative groups frequently require a Mediator to resolve disputes. The independence of judgment, risk taking, and differences in personality profiles that characterize most creative groups usually involve interpersonal clashes that are unavoidable.

Although conflict is not always an undesirable group attribute (in moderate amounts, it often can enhance creativity), too much conflict can cause group members to become dysfunctional problem solvers. If a group devotes too much energy to resolving interpersonal disputes, it may not have enough energy for task concerns. A competent Mediator can reduce the amount of effort spent on settling disputes and thus free up more of a group's time and efforts for creative problem solving.

Comic. Many groups have at least one Comic. In some cases, this individual serves as a generalized outlet for the release of tension that might exist in and among some of the group members. Furthermore, a Comic can enhance group creativity by helping to loosen up a group and thus unleash the members' creative potential. There is a close association between creativity and humor, and when humor is incorporated as a group norm, it can result in the generation of unique problem perspectives and ideas.

A Comic in a group also can be destructive if he or she is performing the role primarily for self-serving ends. For example, overly insecure individuals might crack jokes frequently, solely to attract attention to themselves. These frequent interruptions may distract the group from its task, and it may not perform very effectively. The Comic's role needs to be monitored to ensure that the group is not overly distracted.

Scapegoat. This role probably can be best described as that of a "dumpee"— the person "dumped on" by other group members acting out the role of "dumpers." More precisely, a Scapegoat is someone who bears the blame for the mistakes of others. Like the Comic, the Scapegoat frequently can serve as an object for others to project their frustrations on, with a resulting reduction in interpersonal tension. In this respect, group creativity might be enhanced if one or more members act as the group Scapegoat. By allowing blame to be placed on themselves, Scapegoats can free up the other group members to devote more of their psychic energies to the problem. However, Scapegoats must be willing to assume their role. Otherwise, their dissatisfaction could create more conflict than their role is capable of dissipating.

Maintenance Facilitator. As the counterpart to the Creativity Monitor, the Maintenance Facilitator promotes involvement of the group members in the problem-solving process, is accepting of the other group members and their ideas, encourages harmonious relationships, and generally seeks to develop and maintain a group climate conducive to creative thinking. Although the role of Maintenance Facilitator is typically assumed by the group leader, it can be fulfilled by other group members who have the required human relations skills. Regardless of who acts as Maintenance Facilitator, the major outcome of performing this role should be increased group compatibility. Unless the group members can work well together, they are unlikely to produce many unique creative products.

Not all the distinct task and maintenance roles will be observed in every group. In groups with an experienced leader, the majority of the roles will be assumed by the leader. In inexperienced groups, it will be especially necessary for the group leader to assume many of these roles. However, most groups probably will be more effective in the long run if the roles are more evenly distributed and assumed by all the group members at varying times and to varying degrees.

Perhaps the most important consideration of role types is the need for group members to develop role awareness. That is, group members should determine which roles they play most of the time. This determination can be made by using introspection and by receiving feedback from other members. Once group members have described their roles realistically, they can work at determining whether they are effective at the role (or roles) and whether the contribution their role makes toward group efforts is justified.

Role Clarity

The preceding sections dealt with descriptions of the general nature of roles and specific types. This section is concerned more with the quality of roles. In particular, the focus is on role clarity. Because of the relationship between role clarity and problem-solving effectiveness, role clarity is one of the most important aspects of group creativity. Groups whose members are clear about their roles are more likely to be effective problem solvers than groups whose members have low role clarity.

The extent to which group members are clear about their roles is determined by the amount of role conflict and role ambiguity they perceive to exist when working on ill-structured problems. Role conflict occurs when people receive two or more sets of expectations that make it difficult for them to do all that is expected of them. Put more technically, role conflict is "the simultaneous occurrence of two (or more) role sendings such that compliance with one would make more difficult compliance with the other" (Katz and Kahn, 1966, p. 184). For example, a group leader may expect a member to assume the role of Idea Finder, and the other group members may expect the same individual to play the role of Maintenance Facilitator. Role ambiguity occurs when people do not understand what is expected of them. For example, a group member might be uncertain as to how the role of Problem Finder should be performed.

Of these two determiners of role clarity, role ambiguity is the more important and the one more likely to be associated with perceptions of job-related stress (House and Rizzo, 1972). Perceptions of extreme stress when working on a task can restrict cognitive functioning and decrease problem-solving ability. Consequently, it is important for leaders of creative problem-solving groups to determine how much, if any, role ambiguity exists among the group members. Little or no ambiguity indicates that the group members are clear about their roles.

When group members appear to have low role clarity, the group can carry out a relatively simple team development effort. Begin the exercise by having all group members individually write down a description of what they perceive their primary role to be during group creative problem-solving efforts. (Although all group members will participate to some extent in the five task roles, one or more members may excel at each one of these roles. Thus group members should be instructed to describe what they consider to be their major role or roles.) Next, ask each member to describe his or her roles for the other group members. It is often helpful to list key descriptors on a chalkboard or flip chart. After this information has been provided, the group members should discuss how each role occupant's perceptions mesh with their own perceptions of that individual's roles. Repeat this process until all group members have had their roles discussed. All group members should write down what they heard and develop a revised role description to be discussed at a later meeting.

Assessing Role Clarity

To help group members assess their degree of role clarity, a role clarity questionnaire (Figure 7-1) is presented. This questionnaire is designed to be completed by the group members individually. The results can then be pooled to determine the overall role clarity of the group members. This questionnaire can also be used as a pre- and post-test measure of role clarity when the group carries out the team development effort just described.

Figure 7-1. Role clarity questionnaire.

Instructions: For each of the following statements, indicate how true the statement is for you when you are participating with the other group members on a group creative problem-solving task. Circle the one number following each statement that reflects your belief about the statement. Do not spend too much time on any one statement; your first reaction is likely to be the most accurate one.

1 = Not at all true
2 = A little true
3 = Somewhat true
4 = Very true

1. I am able to predict what others will expect of me the next time we work together.   1 2 3 4
2. I have enough facts and information about my role to perform it well.   1 2 3 4
3. There is very little conflict among the roles played by members of this group.   1 2 3 4

4. The expectations I have about my role are nearly identical to
   those held by other group members about my role.   1   2   3   4
5. I understand clearly what others expect of me.   1   2   3   4
6. I understand clearly the roles played by the other group
   members.   1   2   3   4

Scoring and Interpretation: Possible scores on the Role Clarity Questionnaire range from a low of 6 to a high of 24. To score this instrument, group members should add up the numbers they have circled for their individual questionnaires. The total scores for each member then should be summed and divided by the number of members completing the questionnaire. This operation will produce an average role clarity score for the group. If the average score is between 18 and 24, the group members are, on the average, clear about their roles. A score between 12 and 17 indicates moderate role clarity. And a score between 6 and 11 indicates low role clarity.

If your group's average role clarity score is low or moderately low (between 6 and 14), the group should examine the individual questionnaire responses to determine the specific sources of low role clarity. Training or coaching could then be used to increase the clarity in the areas identified. If your group's average score is moderately high (between 15 and 17) or high, very little will need to be done to make improvements. However, regardless of the score obtained, all groups should make periodic checks of role clarity.

Group Tasks

Tasks and Task Selection

Groups exist because they have goals to achieve. Collections of individuals are organized for the purpose of achieving something—a decision, a tangible product, a policy, or simply satisfaction of mutual needs.

If groups have goals, they also must have tasks. Therefore, a group task can be viewed as whatever is done in an attempt to achieve a group goal or subgoals. Without group tasks, group goals cannot be achieved. If group goals are not achieved, the very existence of a group will be in question. Group tasks and goals go hand in hand.

Most group tasks serve as a stimulus and as a moderator (Hackman and Morris, 1975). The stimulus role occurs when the tasks themselves directly affect group member behavior through the instructions involved in performing the tasks and through the specific cues emitted by the tasks. For example, a supervisor instructing workers on how to assemble an electrical component serves as a stimulus to the workers. And the information presented by the task itself serves as a stimulus if it provides cues on how to proceed. The moderator role of tasks is slightly more complex. It can be said that the relationship existing between a group's process variables and its process outcomes is usually contingent on specific task characteristics. Thus the relationship between group effort and satisfaction may be moderated by the degree of task difficulty.

When a group uses creativity as a primary process, the group's primary task is to solve an ill-structured problem—to close a gap between what is and what should be. In particular, the task is to add structure to an ambiguous situation to reveal solution possibilities. In other words, the task of creative problem solving is to make the ill-structured structured. When this has been accomplished, a group goal will be realized.

The general tasks facing groups may be either assigned or unassigned. If a task is unassigned, a group must choose from among several potential tasks that it might perform to achieve one or more goals. In some cases, it is even necessary to select tasks on the basis of the order in which they must be performed to achieve a goal; in other cases, task order is much less important, and goal attainment requires only that all the required tasks be performed. Assigned tasks may permit little latitude in how they are to be performed. However, numerous exceptions are possible.

Although the problems worked on by creative problem-solving groups in formal organizations typically are assigned, the specific subtasks involved in achieving the goal of problem resolution may be unassigned. Thus a group may be assigned the task of developing a new market for personal computers but be given considerable discretion in how to attain this goal. In this instance, a group may have complete freedom in its choice of both the process and the creative problem-solving techniques to be used. Thus each stage of a process used by a group represents a separate task with its own goal (which actually would be a subgoal of the primary problem).

Although the research on task selection is rather sparse, what does exist suggests that task selection is based on prior success with similar tasks, the existence of social pressures outside the focal group, and various group-oriented motives (Shaw, 1976). Research on task selection, suggests the following tentative conclusions:

1. Groups that have been successful in solving earlier tasks are more likely to select a more difficult task than groups with a history of failure at tasks.
2. Potential external sources of pressure on task selection are: (a) the performance history of a group in comparison to that of other groups, (b) outsiders' predictions about a group's future performance, and (c) the needs and objectives of the larger organization of which a group is a part.

3. Highly cohesive groups with a strong achievement motivation will select tasks intermediate in difficulty; groups with little or no achievement motivation will select tasks that are very low or very high in difficulty (Zander, 1971).

One major implication of this research for creative problem solving is that prior problem-solving success may be a key variable in creative problem-solving performance. If a group has a history of task success and seeks out difficult tasks, it may be more successful in solving ill-structured problems than a group with a history of task failure. A group with a history of failure may avoid ill-structured problems altogether or, if such problems cannot be avoided, it may perform inadequately. In contrast, a group with a history of task success may have greater motivation that can provide it with the persistence needed to resolve ill-structured problems.

Tasks and Creativity

It is fairly well established that tasks can influence group behavior. The relationship between tasks and creativity is less well established. However, from the preceding discussion, it can be seen that ill-structured problems may be stimulating and may actually enhance creativity within some groups. Because of their often nonroutine nature, ill-structured problems also may increase motivation in group members who desire variety in their work and, consequently, lead to the production of highly creative solutions. On the other hand, individuals with little need for variety may react negatively to ill-structured problems, have reduced motivation to solve them, and produce low-quality creative solutions.

Although there is little empirical research available that directly supports these predictions, there is some research that addresses the relationship between tasks and creativity. For example, in a laboratory study using 24 three-person groups, Kabanoff and O'Brien (1979) found that the type of task (production, discussion, and problem solving) has a significant, although small, influence on creativity. Production and problem-solving tasks were rated as more creative than discussion tasks, where more emphasis was placed on idea evaluation.

Another study, however, has clearer implications for managing group creativity. In studying the effects of group strategy formulation on task performance, Hackman and Morris (1975) reported that the frequency of strategy comments is positively (and significantly) related to group creativity. That is, groups who defer task performance in favor of planning how to proceed tend to be rated high in their creative products. Although it cannot be said that strategy formulation "caused" creativity, subsequent analyses by

Hackman and Morris suggested a plausible explanation for the relationship found. Examination of the transcripts of group discussions suggested that strategy formulations might help many groups to loosen up and veer away from more traditional task approaches. Simply taking the time to explore various task alternatives apparently opened up the groups enough to allow them to seek the most effective approach.

Although not mentioned by Hackman and Morris, it is also possible that strategy discussion helped to produce a climate more conducive to creative functioning. In addition to the task focus of a strategy discussion, there is an aspect of social interaction that can "thaw" group members' inhibitions and increase their receptivity to new ideas. As a result, it may be that any type of loosening-up discussion could be beneficial to creative problem solving. Nevertheless, it seems much more reasonable for creative problem-solving groups to use some form of strategy discussion. Such a discussion could make their task performance more efficient and result in higher-quality creative solutions as well.

Task Dimensions

A major focus of the task module is task clarity; that is, the extent to which the group members are clear about how to proceed in producing creative problem solutions. Your analysis of task clarity can be aided by an understanding of the basic components or dimensions that differentiate group tasks. In this section, seven such dimensions will be discussed: solution multiplicity, intrinsic interest, cooperation requirements, intellectual-manipulative requirements, task difficulty, population familiarity, and task complexity (Shaw, 1976).

Solution multiplicity. This dimension refers to the extent that more than one solution is possible. Tasks rated high on this dimension also will provide different means for achieving a solution and provide few clues as to whether a solution is "correct." In general, most ill-structured problems will be rated high on solution multiplicity.

Intrinsic interest. On the basis of their subjective perceptions, individual group members can rate most tasks from dull to interesting. Group members will see tasks with a high intrinsic interest value as attractive and usually motivating. Group members with a high tolerance for ambiguity and a desire for task variety, will probably view ill-structured problems as intrinsically interesting.

Cooperation requirements. A task that requires an integrated group effort to coordinate the behaviors of all group members would be rated high on this dimension. A task with low cooperation requirements could be completed more effectively by independent actions of each group member and involve no integrative efforts. Research on this dimension has found that when working on a task with high cooperation requirements, compatible groups perform better than do incompatible groups (Schutz, 1955). Most creative problem-solving tasks will probably require either high or low cooperation, depending on the compatibility of the group members and their preferences for techniques that require different amounts of cooperation (e.g., brainstorming versus brainwriting groups).

Intellectual-manipulative requirements. Some tasks require a great deal of intellectual effort and very little physical manipulation; other tasks require a great deal of physical manipulation and little intellectual effort; and still others require almost equal amounts of each. When the ratio of intellectual to manipulative requirements is high, the task can be performed best by using basic mental functions such as thinking, reasoning, and deducing. Thus most ill-structured problems would be rated high on this dimension.

Task difficulty. Task difficulty is the amount of effort that must be expended to finish a task. Some tasks are high in their requirements for skill, knowledge, and procedures, while others are low in these requirements. Up to a point, increases in the level of task difficulty may result in corresponding increases in motivation. When difficulty is perceived as too great, group members' motivation will decline and task performance will be inhibited. For most ill-structured problems, task difficulty probably will range from moderate to high, depending on the information, skills, and experience of the group members in using creative problem solving and in dealing with similar types of problems.

Population familiarity. If members of the larger society have had experience with a task, the task would be rated high on this dimension. When a task is totally unfamiliar to the larger society, it would be rated low on population familiarity. However, for purposes of group creativity, familiarity with a task should be viewed in regard to the members of a specific group. If group members are not aware of others' experience with a task, this experience will be of little value to the group. In general, population familiarity probably operates as a moderator of task difficulty. If group members have had experience with a task, they will be less likely to perceive the task as difficult. However, caution must be used—especially in creative problem-solving groups—to ensure that the previous experience is relevant to the task at hand. Otherwise, the group risks correctly applying incorrect or inappropriate solutions to a problem.

Task complexity. The complexity of task is determined by the number of different operations that group members must perform to complete it. For example, securing clock hands to clocks would be a relatively simple task; assembling an entire clock would be a much more complex job. Because dealing with ill-structured problems involves different stages, most creative problem-solving tasks can be classified as high in task complexity. And the often nonroutine nature of such problems make them all the more complex. As with task difficulty, this dimension may be moderated somewhat by task familiarity—although to a lesser extent.

Task Clarity

Most of the seven task dimensions just discussed are related—at least minimally—to the general concept of task clarity. For example, a clear task might be one that is low on solution multiplicity, high on intrinsic interest, high or low on cooperation requirements, low on task difficulty, high on familiarity, and low on task complexity. There is, however, an additional dimension that is more directly related to task clarity: goal-path clarity.

Task clarity can be defined as the extent to which group members have clearly identified an assigned or unassigned task. That is, when members of a group know what it is they are to do to achieve a specific goal, the task can be rated high in task clarity. But in addition to knowing what task they need to perform, group members must understand *how* to perform the task. Understanding how to perform a task is known as goal-path clarity.

It should be obvious that group goals are more likely to be achieved when the group members are high on both task clarity and goal-path clarity. However, knowing how to complete a task to achieve a goal, but not clearly understanding what the task is, is a highly insufficient condition for goal attainment. It is much better to know what a task is and be uncertain of how to perform it than it is to be certain about how to perform an unclear task. In the case of the former, the right task will be correctly or incorrectly performed; in the case of the latter, the incorrect task will be correctly performed.

There are several major implications for creative problem solving from this brief discussion on task clarity. First, an ill-structured problem can be viewed as a task that a group must perform to achieve some larger goal or outcome. If this problem is not correctly defined (task clarity), the group will be in danger of correctly solving the wrong problem. On the other hand, if the problem is understood, but inappropriate processes are used to solve it (goal-path clarity), the group may incorrectly solve the right problem. Finally, there is an important relationship between task clarity and role clarity. In order to perform a task effectively, group members need to understand more than what the task is and how to perform it. They also need to know what roles they play and whether or not these roles are appropriate for a particular task. For example, a task with high cooperation requirements usually requires some degree of maintenance facilitation to ensure that the desired level of cooperation is achieved.

Assessing Task Clarity

To help you assess the overall task clarity of your group, the task clarity questionnaire that appears in Figure 7-2 can be used as a rough guide. In general, it is best to have the group members complete this questionnaire individually and then compute an average score for the group.

Figure 7-2. Task clarity questionnaire.

Instructions: For each of the following statements, circle the one number that best indicates the extent of your agreement with the statement. Do not spend too much time on any one statement; your first reaction is likely to be the most accurate one.

> 5 = Strongly agree
> 4 = Agree
> 3 = Neither agree nor disagree
> 2 = Disagree
> 1 = Strongly disagree

Most of the ill-structured problems worked on by this group:

1. Have only one "correct" solution.	1	2	3	4	5
2. Are extremely interesting.	1	2	3	4	5
3. Require a moderate amount of effort on the part of group members.	1	2	3	4	5
4. Are similar to those worked on by the group in the past.	1	2	3	4	5
5. Involve very few procedures and operations to achieve a solution.	1	2	3	4	5
6. Are clearly understood by all the group members.	1	2	3	4	5
7. Provide enough information on how to proceed in solving them.	1	2	3	4	5

In general, most people in this group:

8. Clearly understand how to use the creative problem-solving process.	1	2	3	4	5
9. Clearly understand how to use most major creative problem-solving techniques.	1	2	3	4	5
10. Understand the appropriate roles to use in performing group tasks.	1	2	3	4	5

Scoring and Interpretation: Possible scores on this instrument range from a low of 10 to a high of 50, with low scores indicating low task clarity and high scores indicating high task clarity. If the group's average score is between 10 and 23, the group members—on the average—do not have a very clear understanding of the tasks facing them when they deal with ill-structured problems. Groups scoring within this range, might discuss the individual items in the questionnaire during a group meeting to pinpoint areas of special concern and areas needing immediate attention. If the group average is between 24 and 36, the group has moderate task clarity. Again, the group should examine the individual items to search out areas of particular concern. Special attention should be paid to items that are rated low by a majority of the group members. If the group's average score is between 37 and 50, most of the group members are clear about their problem-solving tasks. However, a brief discussion of the items frequently can reveal specific difficulties that should be dealt with. If these difficulties are not dealt with, the group's overall task efficiency may be seriously impeded.

The Physical Environment

The three content variables described earlier—composition, roles, and tasks—deal with factors that influence the creative behavior of group members. The physical environment of groups also influences creative behavior, although its effects may be less potent than the effects of the other factors. Nonetheless, the physical environment is of sufficient importance to justify its inclusion in the content module.

All groups have different physical environments that can influence the performance of their members to varying degrees. Group activity occurs in different types of rooms, under different temperature conditions, and with different seating positions and interaction distances among the members. And the relation of the objects and people may be quite different from one setting to the next. These factors can help determine how creative a group will be.

This discussion of a group's physical environment centers on four aspects: concrete aspects, territoriality, personal space, and spatial arrangements. Although each aspect is discussed separately, there will be some overlap among these aspects in regard to their ability to influence group behavior. That is, it may not be the presence of any one aspect that makes a difference; rather, potential effects on group behavior may be determined by the combined action of two or more of the aspects.

Concrete Aspects

The concrete aspects of the physical environment include such things as rooms, color, lighting, temperature, and noise.

When groups use creative problem solving, the members often cast about the room consciously or unconsciously, looking for external sources of idea stimulation. If the room is a familiar one, the group members are not likely to receive much stimulation. The use of different rooms may help to spark ideas because of the creative stimuli they can provide. In addition, the aesthetic qualities of a room can affect attitudes and perhaps behavior. Mintz (1956), for example, found that experimental subjects in a "beautiful" room had more energy and experienced less fatigue than subjects in an "ugly" room.

The colors of a room can also have a psychological effect on group members. Vivid shades on the red end of the spectrum, for instance, can be disconcerting to group members, make them irritable, and cause them to avoid the room. Rooms painted in warm yellow or pastel green can have a more soothing effect.

Evenly distributed lighting in a work area can help make workers more efficient (Tinker, 1939). However, the effects of lighting may be due more to individual perceptions than anything else. For example, the famous Hawthorne studies suggested that increasing light intensity was correlated with productivity increases. Additional analysis indicated that the productivity changes were due more to the attention being paid the workers than any changes in lighting. Nevertheless, lighting must be at a certain minimal level to permit task accomplishment. And lighting can have an emotional impact on workers when used for aesthetic purposes.

From a strictly physiological viewpoint, the temperature in a room must be maintained within an acceptable range for groups to be productive. If group members perceived a room to be too hot or too cold, their concentration and efficiency will suffer along with their morale. Furthermore, an interaction effect between the temperature and the color of a room can occur. Seghers (1948) noted that rooms painted a "cool blue" resulted in worker complaints about the cold when the temperature was set at either 70 or 75 degrees. When the color was changed to more "restful" shades of yellow and green and the temperature was set at 75 degrees, the workers complained about being too hot. You just cannot please everyone, especially where temperature is concerned.

Numerous studies have been conducted on the effects of noise on worker attitudes and performance. As with lighting, however, the actual effects of noise may be more imagined than real. Glass, Singer, and Friedman (1969) found that unanticipated noise can bring about reduced performance, but only if people believe that they have no control over termination of the noise. Noise exceeding a certain decibel level can be physically harmful as well as distracting. Groups will need to decide whether the external noise in their environments is detrimental to their task performance.

Territoriality

Many research studies have demonstrated that individuals tend to assume territorial rights over physical space (e.g., Whyte, 1949; Altman and Haythorn, 1967). Individuals also will defend their territory against invaders (e.g., Lipman, 1968; Sommer, 1969). And individuals will communicate their ownership of their territory through various types and combinations of signals.

If you have been a member of an ongoing group that always met in the same room, you may have observed territoriality firsthand. Some people become visibly disturbed and will even jokingly comment about how someone has taken over "their" chair. New group members are frequently the recipients of such comments.

When territoriality becomes an issue in a creative problem-solving group (or in any group, for that matter), the group may need to deal with it openly. Often the assertion of territorial rights can be a symptom of an underlying interpersonal conflict. If some group members feel that their territory has been invaded, they may not be able to participate in group tasks effectively until their concerns have been dealt with. Usually this means using conflict resolution strategies, rather than simply trading seat locations.

Personal Space

Closely related to territoriality is the concept of personal space. Both involve perceptions of invasion of one type or another. The difference between the two, however, is based on the relation of one person to another. Territoriality refers to a specific geographical area; personal space refers to the area around an individual in which interactions occur with others. Personal space is flexible; everyone has different space requirements. Territoriality is inflexible because it involves a specific area.

Although personal space in general is flexible, the area around any one person may be perceived as relatively rigid. And although this "private" space may remain unchanged, the reactions people have to invasion of their space may be flexible. Depending on who the invader is and the behavior this person uses, the reactions of the person whose space is being invaded may vary considerably. For example, a person working next to another person on the same task may not feel there is much space invasion if the other person is perceived as having similar values and facilitates the group's task accomplishment. In contrast, another person seen as having dissimilar values and working at cross-purposes to the group may be viewed as invading a significant amount of space.

A major variable related to the concept of personal space is interaction distance. Most group members have individual preferences for the amount of distance between themselves and others when they are interacting. Research has shown that these preferences usually vary with the degree of intimacy in the relationship between two people. For instance, Willis (1966) found that women require more interaction distance with "close friends" than with "friends." Although not related directly to intimacy, Willis also found that people who approach women to start a conversation use less interaction distance than people approaching men.

Other research on personal space, although not conclusive due to problems in controlling the many variables involved, suggests that the sex and status of group members may be important variables. Cheyne and Efran (1972) reported that invasion of personal space varies with the sex of the group members. There was a tendency for less invasion to occur in mixed-sex groups than in same-sex groups. In regard to status, research indicates that interaction distance will be greater between people seen as high and low in status than between people relatively equal in status (Lott and Sommer, 1967).

Spatial Arrangements

The physical positioning of one person in relation to another in a group can have important influences on group behavior. Two areas that illustrate how spatial arrangements can affect behavior are seating preferences and seating arrangements. Both have fairly strong implications for managing group creativity.

In general, most people prefer to sit side by side when cooperating with someone else and to sit face to face when competing with someone else (Sommer, 1969). Although the motives underlying these and other preferences are not clear, it is possible that emotional reactions associated with seating preferences may affect arousal levels to cooperate or compete. Furthermore, people may see certain seating positions as more rewarding than others (e.g., sitting at the end of a rectangular table).

Perhaps more important than seating preferences are the effects of seating arrangements on group member interactions and behaviors. In the research on where people sit around a table, it has been observed that people at a round table tend to communicate most with persons seated across from them (Steinzor, 1950); that people sitting at ends of rectangular tables have more influence on a group and participate more in group discussions (Strodtbeck and Hook, 1961); and that the greater the distance between people sitting at tables, the less friendly and talkative the people will be (Russo, 1967). However, it must be noted that all of these findings can be moderated by the personal qualities of the group members. For instance, Mehrabian and Diamond (1971) found that quantity of conversations among group members and its relationship with seating position vary with the sensitivity of the members to rejection.

Implications for Group Creativity

The information on factors in the physical environment that can affect group behavior and performance has several implications for managing group creativity. Since some of these implications are more research-based than others, caution must be used in interpreting them and in using them as guidelines to structure behavior. The variances in personality variables across groups make it difficult to prescribe absolutely what will work in all groups all the time. Group leaders will have to decide what works best for them.

The implications that follow are presented in the form of decision rules or, perhaps more accurately, heuristics. That is, they are rules of thumb and should be regarded as nothing more.

1. Use a variety of rooms for group problem solving.
2. Use rooms that are pleasant aesthetically.
3. Use rooms painted in warm pastel colors of yellow, green, blue, or tan.
4. Provide adequate, evenly distributed room lighting. Avoid glaring lights, and occasionally vary lighting intensity.
5. Maintain a comfortable room temperature.
6. Experiment with different noise levels in a room. Try using "white noise" or soft background music from time to time.
7. Allow group members to develop their own territorial areas. If necessary, deal openly with territorial issues and establish guidelines.
8. If interpersonal conflict develops, try to assess group members' satisfaction with the amount of personal space that they perceive to exist. Be especially attentive to the individual requirements of the group members for a specified interaction distance with other group members.
9. If invasion of personal space seems to be a major problem, consider using mixed-sex groups with members who are relatively equal in status.
10. Whenever possible, use square or round tables for group discussions and verbal problem solving. Limit the number of people at any table to four to seven.

Assessing the Physical Environment

The abstract level of two of the physical environment factors—personal space and territoriality—makes it difficult to assess reliably the conduciveness of the physical environment to group creativity. The more tangible nature of concrete aspects and spatial arrangements makes it quite easy to assess these factors. As a result, the questionnaire in Figure 7-3 must be used with considerable caution.

Figure 7-3. Physical environment questionnaire.

Instructions: This questionnaire is designed to assess your perception of how conducive your physical environment is to creativity. For each of the following statements, indicate the extent of your agreement by circling the appropriate number after the statement. Do not spend too much time on any one statement; your first reaction is likely to be the most accurate one. In recording your responses, use the following scale:

1 = Strongly disagree
2 = Disagree
3 = Neutral or undecided
4 = Agree
5 = Strongly agree

1. The room (rooms) used for group creative problem solving is (are) of adequate size.   1 2 3 4 5
2. Different rooms often are used by the group.   1 2 3 4 5
3. The room (rooms) used is (are) pleasing aesthetically.   1 2 3 4 5
4. The room (rooms) used has (have) adequate lighting and comfortable temperatures.   1 2 3 4 5
5. The room (rooms) used is (are) free of distracting noises.   1 2 3 4 5
6. There is very little assumption of territorial rights among the group members.   1 2 3 4 5
7. Group members rarely feel that their personal space is invaded when working together.   1 2 3 4 5
8. Group members are comfortable with the physical distance between themselves and other group members.   1 2 3 4 5
9. The group has a mixture of males and females.   1 2 3 4 5
10. Except for the group leader, there are very few status differences among the group members.   1 2 3 4 5
11. There is very little competitive behavior between group members who sit opposite one another.   1 2 3 4 5
12. The group usually works together while seated around a circular or square table.   1 2 3 4 5

Scoring and Interpretation: Possible scores on this questionnaire range from 12 to 60. A low score would be between 12 and 28; a moderate score would be between 29 and 43; a high score would be between 44 and 60. Groups whose members' scores average out in the high range probably have a physical environment conducive to creativity. An average score in the moderate range suggests the need to examine specific factors that might be altered to produce a more conducive environment. An average score in the low range clearly indicates problems with the physical environment. Nevertheless, do not view a low score on this factor with too much alarm. Although important, the long-range influence of the physical environment may be less critical than the other content variables. Consequently, groups scoring in the low range should make any adjustments possible but not be overly concerned if they cannot completely overcome the physical limitations of their environment.

Summary

Three of the remaining group content factors were examined in this chapter: group roles, group tasks, and the physical environment. All these factors play a role in determining a group's creativity level.

A role is a set of expectations held about a person who occupies a particular position. A perceived role refers to the expectations that role players have about how they should behave. An actual or enacted role consists of the behaviors actually used in carrying out a role. The motivation to perform a role stems from information sent to a role player, from the specific task being performed, and from internal sources that drive individuals to perform.

Most roles in general problem-solving groups can be classified as dealing with either task or maintenance behaviors. Within these categories, more specific roles also have been identified, such as Initiator, Information Processor (task roles) and Harmonizer and Compromiser (maintenance roles). Task roles specific to creative problem-solving groups include Fact Finder, Problem Finder, Idea Finder, Solution Finder, Acceptance Finder, Evaluator, and Creativity Monitor. Maintenance roles specific to creative problem-solving groups include Mediator, Comic, Scapegoat, and Maintenance Facilitator.

In some groups, these roles may be distributed evenly; in others, most or all of them may be assumed by the group leader. However, the distribution of the roles is less important than group members' awareness of the roles they play.

The degree to which group members are aware of their roles is known as role clarity. When group members are not clear about their roles, stress can result that restricts cognitive functioning. As a result, creative ability may be diminished. When group members are unclear about their roles, the group leader can conduct a team development exercise to clarify roles. The focus of this exercise is on receiving feedback from other group members as to their role expectations for every other group member.

The task component of the content module is important because all groups exist to achieve goals. And the primary way that goals are achieved is through task completion. In general, most group tasks serve as stimuli to energize group behavior and as moderators of process variables and group outcomes.

The primary task of creative problem-solving groups is to resolve ill-structured problems. These problems are either assigned or unassigned. When tasks are unassigned, a group's selection of a particular task will be guided by its prior success with similar tasks, the existence of social pressures outside the group, and various group-oriented motives. In general, successful problem-solving groups are more likely to select difficult tasks than are less successful groups. Because groups often view ill-structured problems as difficult tasks, a group's problem-solving history will be a major variable in determining its success. Prior success may increase group motivation and provide a group with the persistence it needs to cope with ill-structured problems.

Although somewhat sparse, research on tasks and creativity reveals some interesting findings. For example, a group that devotes a portion of problem-solving time to deciding how it will proceed in dealing with a problem usually can increase its level of creativity by the loosening up that is a by-product of such discussions.

The clarity of tasks plays an important role in the content module. Members' understanding of task clarity can be enhanced by examining such task dimensions as solution multiplicity, intrinsic interest, cooperation requirements, intellectual-manipulative requirements, task difficulty, population familiarity, and task complexity. The degree of task clarity will depend on the extent to which each of these dimensions is perceived to be a part of a particular task.

A major aspect of task clarity is goal-path clarity. To the extent that group members understand how to perform a task, it can be said that the task is high on goal-path clarity. The successful resolution of ill-structured problems requires that group members understand both the task and how to perform it to achieve a goal.

Although somewhat less important than the other content factors, the physical environment nonetheless plays a role in determining group problem-solving behavior and performance. Four major components of a group's physical environment are concrete aspects, territoriality, personal space, and spatial arrangements. All these components overlap to some extent in influencing group behavior.

Concrete aspects of a group's physical environment include such things as rooms, color, lighting, temperature, and noise. Territoriality in groups occurs when one or more individuals assume "rights" over a particular physical space and perceive that their space has been invaded. Personal space refers to the space perceived to exist around an individual in relation to other individuals. The extent to which invasion of personal space occurs will depend on subjective reactions. People define space invasion differently. Also related to the concept of personal space is the notion of interaction distance. Depending on the degree of intimacy among individuals, physical interaction distance can vary considerably. Spatial arrangements refer to the seating preferences and seating arrangements within a group. Group members who sit side by side are more likely to use cooperative behaviors than are group members sitting across from one another.

The research on the physical environment of groups has several implications for managing group creativity. Among these implications are such things as using a variety of rooms painted in warm pastel colors, evenly distributed lighting, and a comfortable temperature level. Furthermore, territorial and personal space issues should be dealt with openly to avoid severe interpersonal conflicts, mixed-sex groups whose members are equal in status should be used whenever role invasion is a problem, and square or round tables should be used to help promote cooperative behaviors.

8

Redefining the Problem

Problems are abstract representations of what we perceive reality to be. They help to provide meaning for the many different situations we encounter. Without problems, we would be unable to distinguish between what is real and what is unreal.

Just as an artist uses canvas and paint to portray some feature of life, so do we use problems to paint pictures of our existence. Like the artist, we sketch a rough outline of a problem in our minds, fill in details, use shading and perspective, and produce a finished product. The result is how we depict reality.

What we consider to be real and unreal is entirely subjective. There are no absolute standards. We each create our own reality to use in interpreting our existence. Depending on our experiences and psychological makeup, what is real for one person will not necessarily be real for another. What you consider to be a problem may be of little concern to me, and vice versa. In one respect, your problems help you deal with your world and my problems help me deal with mine. Occasionally, such as in group situations, our worlds may collide or overlap. When this occurs, our individual perceptions of reality may blend, enabling us to work together to deal with our problem situations.

Defining Redefining

Problems contribute to our individual perceptions of reality by setting limits. Because we interpret a situation as a problem, we automatically assign boundaries to it. Without such boundaries, we would be unable to cognitively or experientially grasp the significance of our lives. Yet such boundaries can also constrain our view of reality. We can construct walls that make it difficult for us to see the larger fabric of a problem that exists outside the walls.

When we establish limits or boundaries for a situation, we are defining a problem; when we attempt to break away from these boundaries and see what lies on the other side, we are redefining a problem. Both these actions are highly interrelated and without a beginning or an end. Where one problem ends another may begin.

To define is to understand. When we say that we are defining a problem, we are actually clarifying our understanding of a situation by the use of a concept we call a problem. Problems are not situations. Problems are ways of understanding situations. Thus, when we redefine a problem, we are providing ourselves with a circumscribed way of viewing reality.

To redefine is to change our understanding of a situation. We may achieve such change by pushing out situational boundaries or by drawing them in, by altering the shape of the boundaries or by substituting other elements into the mix that makes up our problem situation. The situation always stays the same—only our understanding changes, because we have reconstructed the boundaries or changed the elements of the situation. The result is a new definition of the problem.

At this point, you might ask why anyone would want to redefine a problem. Why not just leave things the way they are and proceed from there? The answer stems from the preceding discussion: We need to redefine problems in order to increase our understanding of situations.

Because creative problem solving deals primarily with ill-structured and semistructured problems, anything that can increase our understanding of situations will put us that much further along in developing solutions.

Redefining a problem increases the amount of information and structure we can use to guide us in generating solutions. In addition, when we have extensively redefined a situation, the odds are greatly increased that we will be able to avoid correctly solving the "wrong" problem. (Note that a "wrong" problem in this instance refers to a situation that is not clearly understood.) This is perhaps the most important reason for redefining a problem situation.

In actual practice, an extensively redefined problem usually is a solved problem. As our understanding of a delimited situation gradually increases, the emerging clarity about the situation will reveal various solution possibilities. From another perspective, it can be said that for every solution we generate, there is a corresponding problem situation. Furthermore, these solutions may be interrelated, just as problem situations may be interrelated.

Closely allied with this view of redefining problems is the matter of problem scope. Most problem definitions can be categorized as narrow, moderate, or broad in scope. What usually distinguishes these types is the level of abstraction. For example, a problem of how to ensure world peace is highly abstract. A problem of how to design a new type of writing pen is not very abstract at all. The former is a broad-scope problem, and the latter is a narrow-scope problem. The difference between the two, however, is purely subjective, since both problems may be representations of the same situation that vary only in their degree of abstraction.

As an illustration of this way of viewing problems, consider the following question: IWWMW (In what ways might we) make our meetings more efficient? Depending on the amount and quality of information you have about this problem, you could classify it as narrow, moderate, or broad in scope. If levels of abstraction can be conceptualized as existing on a continuum ranging from low to high abstraction, it should be possible for you to classify this problem on the basis of such criteria as information clarity, adequacy, and availability.

Using these criteria, you might judge the problem of how to make meetings more efficient to be moderately low in abstraction along a continuum of ten different problem situations. As shown in Figure 8-1, the problem could rank fourth from the bottom in abstraction level. (Remember, however, that a problem's rank on such a continuum is a subjective, perceptual matter that will vary across individuals.) The limits of the continuum define the lower and upper ranges of the general situation. The problem, as initially defined, is one person's attempt to understand the situation; the other problem statements represent redefinitions that result in either broadening or narrowing the problem's scope.

Note also that in this case the definitions can be grouped according to different levels of impact—group, organizational, and societal. These levels are, of course, relative categories, since another individual might have limited the range of the situation to just individual and group levels, for example, while someone else might have broadened the range. What is significant about these particular categories, however, is that they can contribute to our understanding of the total situation—the primary purpose of redefining an initial problem statement.

Guidelines for Redefining Problems

For all the reasons discussed, redefining the problem is probably the most important stage of the creative problem-solving process. It makes very little sense to try to solve a problem if you don't really know whether it is the problem you want to solve (or need to solve) and if you have very little information about the overall context of the problem situation. The goal of redefinitional activities is to overcome these obstacles so that you can develop a better grasp of the problem area to be worked on.

The actions involved in attaining such an understanding can be greatly facilitated if you follow certain basic guidelines. The underlying objective of

Figure 8-1. Hypothetical relation of an initial problem definition to situational abstraction level.

Abstraction Level		Problem Statements	Impact Level
High	10	IWWMW* make the world a better place in which to live?	Societal
	9	IWWMW help stimulate the national economy?	
	8	IWWMW help the organization earn more money?	Organizational
	7	IWWMW contribute more to organizational productivity?	
	6	IWWMW accomplish more as a group?	Group
	5	IWWMW use our time more wisely during group activities?	
Medium	4	IWWMW make our meetings more efficient?	
Low	3	IWWMW work together better as a group?	
	2	IWWMW help group members to better understand how to do their jobs?	
	1	IWWMW help group members receive more job-related information?	

*In what ways might we . . . ?

these guidelines is to view an initial problem statement from another perspective, to see a problem situation with new eyes. Awareness, understanding, and use of the following guidelines will ensure that the group will be able to develop workable creative products.

1. *Develop as many different redefinitions as possible.* The more redefinitions a group is able to come up with, the easier it will be for it to develop solutions, and the higher will be the quality of the solutions. In addition, developing multiple redefinitions can contribute to a group's efficiency by reducing the potential number of solution and problem definition revisions that frequently are required in groups that don't redefine their initial problem statement.

2. *Include only one problem area in a redefinition.* Many inexperienced groups use the double-barreled shotgun approach to redefinitions by combining two redefinitions into one. An example of such a redefinition would be: In what ways might we better use our personnel resources and our time? There are two possible redefinitions in this statement, and they should be stated separately. Otherwise, the focus of any solution-generating activities is likely to be disjointed and diffuse, and frustration may result.

3. *Withhold all judgment when listing redefinitions.* This is perhaps the most important guideline. The possibility of producing many unique problem perspectives will be greatly curtailed if suggested redefinitions are met with some form of negative criticism. Evaluation of the redefinitions comes later in the process. All the group members should clearly understand this. If some group members seem incapable of restraining themselves from making unfavorable comments, the leader can suggest that each group member submit redefinitions in writing, to be collected and then evaluated at a later time.

4. *Avoid searching for "correct" redefinitions.* Because of the way we were brought up, we often find ourselves categorizing things as either correct or incorrect. Such actions are useful in some situations but not during redefinitional activities. The purpose of the redefinitions is not to find the "correct" definition of a problem. Instead, the primary objective of redefining a problem is to create new perspectives, so that a situation can be better understood. Any attempt to search for "correct" redefinitions, therefore, is self-defeating. When this principle is fully understood, the tendency of some individuals to criticize redefinitions will be greatly diminished.

5. *Develop redefinitions that are as remote as possible from the initial problem statement.* The more distant a redefinition is from the initial problem statement, the more diverse will be the perspectives generated about the overall problem situation. Diverse perspectives make it easier for the group to gain more understanding about the general problem situation. Redefinitions that provide only small incremental changes in how a problem is viewed are unlikely to increase the group's understanding by any appreciable amount.

For instance, if the initial problem statement is: In what ways might we decrease worker absenteeism? and it is redefined as, In what ways might we decrease worker absenteeism on Mondays? very little additional information has been added. A more substantial redefinition might be: In what ways might we increase participation during staff meetings? As long as the group sees such a redefinition as being part of the general problem situation, the increment in understanding will be much greater than had the former redefinition been selected.

6. *Make sure all group members clearly understand all the redefinitions.* Some redefinitions have implied meanings that are not always evident from the way they are stated. If any group members do not understand a redefinition, their perceptions of the problem situation will also be inaccurate. Eventually, such individuals will be looking for solutions to a problem entirely different from the one the others are solving. In effect, a misunderstood redefinition represents another redefinition of the problem.

To avoid this situation, the group leader should check for understanding of each redefinition and specifically ask members about the clarity and meaning of the redefinition. One way to do this is to ask the group members how they interpret each of the key words in a redefinition. For example, in the problem dealing with ways to increase participation during staff meetings, the leader might ask for interpretations of the words "increase" and "participation." The more specific the redefinitions are, the less likely it is that they will be misunderstood.

7. *Consider all redefinitions to be tentative.* Because most problem situations are extremely complex and have interrelated parts, it would be presumptuous on the part of anyone to assume that his or her redefinitional efforts have provided a complete understanding of a situation. Information is not always available or adequate and events (both internal and external to the group) over time can drastically alter the nature of a problem situation. Thus, even when a group has selected a final redefinition for use in generating ideas, it should consider the redefinition tentative until the potential solutions must be implemented. Premature acceptance of any redefinition can only decrease a group's problem-solving efficiency.

Redefinitional Techniques

When a group has developed an integrated understanding of the basic redefinitional guidelines, it can turn its attention to aids for generating redefinitions. To use these aids before gaining an understanding of the guidelines would be like trying to scuba dive without receiving any instruction. When the group has learned and understood the instructional material, it can begin the task of actually using the aids.

The redefinitional techniques described in this section are the "equipment" that a group can use to develop alternative problem perspectives. Although there may be a few similarities among the techniques, each one provides a unique framework for developing redefinitions. It is strongly recommended that you always try to use at least two techniques—depending on the amount of time available, motivation to solve the problem, importance of the problem, and the group's ability to use the techniques. To use just one of these methods would severely limit the total number of potential redefinitions.

When the group has practiced with the techniques, it probably will develop preferences for certain methods. Although such attachments can stimulate participation and increase motivation, there is always the danger that a group's uniqueness of perspectives will decrease over time if it relies on the same methods continuously. To avoid this situation, the group leader should periodically suggest that the group alternate use of some of the techniques to provide more variety and help maintain production of remote redefinitions.

There are six redefinitional techniques that I have found to be useful in most group situations: analogies, boundary examinations, five Ws, reversals, two words, and the why method. There are other techniques, but too many approaches from which to choose can overload a group.

Analogies

An analogy is a statement of comparison in which the similarity of a situation is compared with another situation. For example, in introducing this section, I compared learning to use redefinitional techniques with learning how to scuba dive. Both require mastery of basic principles and guidelines before any attempt can be made to use the "equipment" (in this case, techniques). Another example would be to say that motivating people is like taking pills. Everyone reacts differently, and it is important to know what kind of pill, dosage, and frequency of use will be best for each person. Similarly, it is important to know what kind of motivation people need, how much, and how often. Like pills, some people can receive too much motivation and overreact, while attempts to motivate other people will produce no effect at all. In addition, some people need to be internally motivated.

Developing the pill analogy with the problem of motivating people could be continued at some length in this manner. The more the analogy is developed, the more information is revealed about the problem. With each new bit of information that emerges, a stimulus is provided for suggesting a possible redefinition. For example, with the pill analogy, two redefinitions would be: (1) IWWM (In what ways might) group leaders determine the motivational needs of group members? and (2) IWWM group members motivate themselves? Note that in both these cases different problem perspectives have resulted.

In using analogies to aid in generating redefinitions, a group should follow these guidelines: (1) Avoid criticism of any analogies suggested. (2) Try to develop analogies that are unrelated to the problem. (3) Begin each analogy with the phrase "This problem is like . . . " (4) Develop at least five different analogies. (5) Select one analogy that looks interesting and seems to hold promise for generating a variety of perspectives. (6) Develop the selected analogy by continuing to make comparisons between it and the problem. (7) Look over all the comparisons and select information that can be restated in the form of a redefinition. (8) Write down all the redefinitions suggested.

Boundary Examinations

Certain assumptions underlie every problem statement. Some of these assumptions are tested in the course of formulating a problem, while others go untested, to be revealed only during a later stage in the problem-solving process.

By using boundary examinations, a group can more systematically bring out the major assumptions underlying a problem early in the overall process. Perhaps more important, however, is the value these assumptions have for providing the group with new problem perspectives.

The procedure for using boundary examinations to suggest redefinitions involves (1) writing down the initial statement of the problem, (2) underlining key words and phrases in this statement, (3) examining the key words and phrases for assumptions that were not previously considered, and (4) using the hidden assumptions, developing as many redefinitions as possible.

As an illustration of this method, consider again the problem of how to motivate workers. If the problem were stated as: IWWM workers be motivated to use less sick leave? the words, "workers," "motivated," "less" and "sick leave" might be underlined to check assumptions. Then questions could be posed, such as: Why just workers? Why do they have to be motivated? Why less sick leave? and Why sick leave? Finally, the answers to these questions could be used to suggest redefinitions. For example, new redefinitions might include: IWWM managers and workers motivate themselves to use less sick leave? IWWM managers and workers be rewarded for using less sick leave? IWWM managers and workers use more sick leave during slack times? IWWM managers and workers be paid to be well?

Five Ws

The five Ws technique is one of the most basic yet comprehensive redefinitional methods. It is virtually identical to the probing questions used in the input inventory described in Chapter 5. In this case, however, the probing questions are applied directly to the initial problem definition.

The technique is used by asking who, what, where, when, and why questions about the problem definition. The key to success in using this method is for group members to ask as many different questions as they can think of for each of the Ws. The more questions the group asks, the more information it will have for generating possible redefinitions. To increase the amount of information that can be pulled out, the group members should focus on key words in the problem statement to direct their questions. Then, after the group has posed all the questions and supplied all the answers, it is just a matter of examining all the answers or implied redefinitions.

Using the problem of motivating workers again, this method can be illustrated in the following manner.

Problem: IWWM workers be motivated to use less sick leave?

Questions	*Answers*
1. Who are the workers?	Blue-collar employees. Workers in unpleasant work environments.
2. Who needs to be motivated?	Workers who use sick leave. Workers who are absent from work a lot.
3. Who uses sick leave?	Workers who are sick. Workers who want to complete personal business. Bored workers.
4. What needs to be motivated?	Personal health. The will to work.
5. What is motivation?	Something that prompts. Inducement. Drive. Need to achieve a goal.
6. What is sick leave?	A legitimate excuse to miss work. Being paid while you are sick.
7. Where are workers motivated?	Award ceremonies. Managers' offices. While doing their jobs.
8. When are workers motivated?	When they perform well. When they are recognized. When they participate in decision making. When they are rewarded. When they feel good about themselves.

9. When do workers use sick leave?	Mondays. Fridays. When sick. When bored.
10. Why do workers need motivating?	To use less sick leave. To produce more. To be absent less.
11. Why do workers use sick leave?	To get well. To complete personal business during the workday.

From the answers to these questions, the following are representative of the types of redefinitions that might be developed:

IWWM working conditions be improved?
IWWM the workers' personal health be improved?
IWWM workers complete personal business without missing work?
IWWM jobs be made more motivating to workers?
IWWM group goals be achieved better?
IWWM workers be rewarded for using less sick leave?
IWWM workers be paid for being well?
IWWM workers be rewarded for working on Mondays and Fridays?

There are several points that should be made about this technique. First, just as there is no such thing as a "correct" redefinition, there is no such thing as a "correct" question or a "correct" answer. Asking and answering questions are the important actions. Second, there may be considerable overlap among the answers. If this occurs, do not be overly concerned, since any question that brings out an answer is all that is needed. Duplicate answers can simply be ignored. It is, however, possible that two different questions will produce answers that are almost but not quite the same. Asking the question using a different perspective increases the odds of bringing out additional information. So go ahead and use duplicate answers, but try to look for different twists to your answers whenever possible. Finally, some of the redefinitions themselves may require additional redefining before they can be used to generate ideas. Depending on how questions are answered, some redefinitions may be more or less abstract than others.

Reversals

Reversing a problem statement is another way to achieve new problem perspectives. The key to this method lies in group members' changing their perspectives in as many ways as possible, even though the reversal may not appear to be logical. The reversal is then used to suggest more workable definitions or solutions. As with other redefinitional techniques, there is no such thing as a "correct" reversal.

Reversing problem statements involves making changes in key words or phrases, that is, using words or phrases that are opposite or different from those found in the original statement. The direction or appropriateness of the reversal is not as important as is introducing change into the meaning of the problem.

With the problem of how to motivate workers to use less sick leave, the following reversals might be generated:

IWWM workers be motivated to use more sick leave?
IWWM workers be rewarded for staying at home?
IWWM workers be punished for using less sick leave?
IWWM customers be motivated to use less sick leave?
IWWM workers be encouraged to remain healthy?
IWWM workers lose their motivation to use less sick leave?

It should be apparent that most of these redefinitions require further redefining, although some may be workable in their current state. It all depends on how capable a group is of drawing additional information from the redefinitions. For example, the redefinition involving rewarding workers for staying at home suggests the use of flexible working hours or the use of interactive computer systems for people who could do the same work at home. On the other hand, the redefinition that includes punishment of workers for using less sick leave suggests, to me, nothing more original than reducing their paycheck. Nevertheless, with the people resources available in a group, each of these redefinitions should have the potential for sparking at least one practical redefinition or solution.

Two Words

The two words technique is based on the semantics involved in redefining a problem. Words frequently vary in their meaning when interpreted by different people. Thus the wording used in a problem statement can, by itself, serve as a redefinitional stimulus within many groups. In addition, the deliberate use of alternate words of related meaning can help provoke redefinitions. The use of such alternate words forms the basis of the two words method.

To use this technique, a group selects two key words or phrases from the initial problem statement. Then it generates words that are associated in meaning or that are similar to these words for each of the key words or phrases. Finally, it forces together different combinations of the alternate words to provide redefinitions. Any solutions suggested by this focusing are written down and put aside for later evaluation.

As an illustration of redefining a problem with this method, consider again the problem about the use of sick leave: IWWM workers be motivated to use less sick leave? In this case, the words "motivated" and "to use less" are selected for examination. Using free association, a book of synonyms, or a thesaurus, alternate meanings for the word and phrase are generated. Some examples of alternate meanings are:

Motivated	*To use less*
Induced	To preserve
Stimulated	To conserve
Influenced	To save
Rewarded	To store
Enticed	To retain
Persuaded	To decrease
Prompted	To hoard

The redefinitions are generated by forcing together all the possible combinations. Thus the problem can be redefined in such ways as, IWWM workers be induced to preserve sick leave? Stimulated to conserve? Rewarded to decrease? Persuaded to save? Enticed to retain? and so forth. These redefinitions then would be used as stimulus sources for possible solutions.

Why Method

The major operational principle underlying the why method is the gradual increase in the abstraction level of the initial problem statement until no further redefinitions are practical or feasible. Problems that are initially defined with a narrow scope will benefit most from this technique.

Applying the why method is very simple. A group successively asks why it wants to solve a problem, answers the question, and uses the answer to redefine the problem. It then uses the redefinition to repeat the cycle of asking, answering, and redefining until it has achieved the desired level of abstraction. As with the other redefinitional aids, there is no one "correct" way to ask or answer any of the questions.

With the worker motivation problem, the why method could be used as follows:

Problem: IWWM workers be motivated to use less sick leave?

Question: Why do you want workers to use less sick leave?
Answer: To decrease the absenteeism level.
Redefine: IWWM worker absenteeism be decreased?

Question:	Why do you want to decrease worker absenteeism?
Answer:	To increase productivity.
Redefine:	IWWM worker productivity be increased?

Question:	Why do you want to increase worker productivity?
Answer:	To increase company profits.
Redefine:	IWWM company profits be increased?

Question:	Why do you want to increase company profits?
Answer:	To provide a better life for company employees and stockholders.
Redefine:	IWWM the lives of company employees and stockholders be improved?

The last redefinition in the example represents a fairly high level of problem abstraction. At this point, no further redefinitions are likely to be needed, because the purpose of achieving different viewpoints has been achieved. In addition, any further redefinitions are likely to lead to problems of broad philosophical issues, whose scope would need to be narrowed in order to work on them. The group could repeat the process, however, using different answers to the questions. By doing this, it could provide additional perspectives.

Evaluating and Selecting Redefinitions

After a group has generated a list of possible redefinitions, it must choose one tentative redefinition. This selection process can be a frustrating and tedious experience—depending on the time available, the number of redefinitions listed, and the group's commitment to solving the problem.

This process can be made considerably easier, however, if the group adopts a systematic procedure. The procedure should be one that is easy to understand, easy to implement, and agreeable to all group members. The procedure described next seems to satisfy these requirements. However, most groups find it expedient to modify or adapt features of any process they choose to use.

This procedure assumes that a relatively large number of redefinitions have been developed (e.g., 20 or more) and that no one redefinition stood out during the development process. Five different stages are involved in using this procedure: discussing for clarification, revising the redefinitions, combining and eliminating duplicates, culling and rating the redefinitions, and stating the "final" redefinition and checking for understanding.

1. *Discussing for clarification.* In beginning the procedure, the leader should

remind the group members that no criticism is to take place until the actual selection decisions are made. The redefinitions should be written on a flip chart or chalkboard visible to all. The leader then points to each redefinition and asks the group members if they have any clarifying questions or comments.

2. *Revising the redefinitions.* Based on the clarification discussion, the leader should change any words, phrases, or complete redefinitions that were not clear to the group. In doing this, the leader should primarily rely on the suggestions of the group members. However, the intended meanings of the redefinitions should be preserved. As in the first stage, no criticism should be permitted.

3. *Combining and eliminating duplicates.* The leader and group members should review all the redefinitions and combine any that would increase clarity and understanding and eliminate those that clearly are identical to others in content. Exercise caution during this stage so that combinations don't significantly alter a redefinition's intended meaning and so that two problems are not presented in one redefinition. Also, control elimination of duplicates so that a problem that differs only slightly in content from another is not eliminated. Like the two previous stages, there should be no criticism used during this stage.

4. *Culling and rating the redefinitions.* The primary purpose of this stage is to reduce the remaining redefinitions to a more workable number. The basic procedure involves using preliminary culling criteria to sort out redefinitions that clearly are not suitable for the group to work on at this point. The three criteria are urgency, threat, and appropriateness. In order to pass through this stage, a redefinition should receive a positive response on at least two of the three criteria. (For an exceptionally large number of redefinitions, passing could be based on satisfying all three criteria.) The redefinitions that survive the culling criteria are then subjected to rating criteria. Each rating criterion is evaluated on a 5-point scale, with a total score of 11 required for passing on to the next stage. There also are three rating criteria: importance, applicability, and commitment. The final selection is made using group consensus and/ or voting or ranking procedures.

The six criteria used in this process can be defined as follows:

Culling criteria

Urgency: The extent to which the problem redefinition commands the attention of the group members and requires immediate action.

Threat: The extent to which the group sees the consequences of *not* solving the problem redefinition as leading to the loss of some value or resource.

Appropriateness: The extent to which the problem redefinition is within the group's sphere of influence (i.e., does not require external authorization to solve).

Rating Criteria
   Importance: The extent to which the problem redefinition is viewed as likely to have a significant impact on the group and its activities.
   Applicability: The extent to which the problem redefinition is relevant to the concerns and needs of the group members.
   Commitment: The extent to which the group members are likely to persist in developing a solution to the problem redefinition.

A sample format for using the culling and rating criteria is shown in the problem redefinition culling and rating form (Figure 8-2). This form illustrates how a group might use the criteria. Because individual preferences may vary, you may use a slightly modified format.

Figure 8-2.   Problem redefinition culling and rating form.

Culling Criteria
   Instructions: For each problem redefinition, respond to each question by circling the appropriate response. Add up the number of positive responses circled and compare the total with the required passing score of 2. If two or more positive responses have been circled, go on to the rating criteria; if only one positive response has been circled, eliminate the redefinition from further consideration.

1. Does the problem require that immediate action be taken by the group to solve it?	Yes	No
2. If the problem is not solved, are the consequences likely to be serious?	Yes	No
3. Is the problem within the group's sphere of influence (i.e., does not require external authorization to solve)?	Yes	No

Rating Criteria
   Instructions: For each problem redefinition, respond to each question by circling the most appropriate number. Add up the numbers for all three items. If the total is equal to or greater than 11, retain the redefinition for additional evaluation by the group; if the total is less than 11, eliminate the redefinition from further consideration.

   (Note: If for any reason the group seems to be uncomfortable in eliminating a redefinition, set it aside for later evaluation. If a large number of redefinitions cause such a reaction, reevaluate the ratings, the criteria, or how the criteria are interpreted.)

1. How important is this redefinition to the group and its activities?

1 = Unimportant
2 = Somewhat unimportant
3 = Neutral or undecided
4 = Somewhat important
5 = Important

2. How applicable is this redefinition to the needs and concerns of the group?

1 = Inapplicable
2 = Somewhat inapplicable
3 = Neutral or undecided
4 = Somewhat applicable
5 = Applicable

3. How committed is the group to developing a solution to this redefinition?

1 = Uncommitted
2 = Somewhat uncommitted
3 = Neutral or undecided
4 = Somewhat committed
5 = Committed

If culling and rating the redefinitions result in just one redefinition that the group is satisfied with, the group can move on to the next stage in the selection procedure. However, if the group is left with two or more redefinitions, additional work will be required. (Should the number of remaining redefinitions exceed ten, the group may want to go through the culling and rating criteria again.)

If time permits, the group should discuss the remaining redefinitions and attempt to achieve consensus on just one. If time is in short supply or the consensus-seeking activity seems to be unproductive, the group can use ranking or voting procedures. In using rankings, each member should rank the redefinitions individually by assigning a 1 to the most preferred redefinition, a 2 to the second most preferred, and so forth, until all the redefinitions have been ranked. Then the rankings of all the group members should be added up and the one with the lowest score selected.

5. *Stating the "final" redefinition and checking for understanding.* After selecting a "final," tentative redefinition, the group should examine it to determine whether it is suitable for generating potential solutions. That is, the redefinition should be stated clearly and unambiguously, and it should have the potential to lead to divergent thinking. In other words, the redefinition should be one all the group members are comfortable with as a tentative statement of their problem and should appear amenable to creative thinking. Such a determination will be pretty much a subjective, intuitive decision that will vary with the preferences of different groups. However, if

the group is at all uncomfortable with the redefinition, it should start the process again using whatever techniques it deems appropriate. Once a tentative redefinition is agreed upon, the group is ready to move on to the module for generating ideas.

Summary

Content Narrative

Problems help us to interpret reality by establishing limits on situations. Establishment of such limits also can constrain our perceptions of reality. However, whatever we define to be a problem situation is highly subjective and based on individual interpretations.

To place limits on a situation is to define a problem; to attempt to change the limits is to redefine the problem. Because problems are simply ways of understanding broader situations, redefining problems involves changes in our understanding of these same situations. To redefine is to change understanding of a situation, not the situation itself.

We need to redefine problems in order to increase our understanding of the broader situation and to help add structure and information that can guide us in generating solutions.

Most problems that are appropriate for creative problem solving can be categorized as being narrow, medium, or broad in scope, depending on the abstraction level of the problem. Abstraction level defines the lower and upper limits of a general problem situation, with varying degrees of abstraction ranging across a continuum between the lower and upper limits. In redefining an initial problem statement, we will usually increase or decrease the degree of abstraction. With changes in the problem's abstraction level, there should be changes in our understanding about the situation.

There are seven guidelines that groups should follow when redefining a problem: (1) Develop as many different redefinitions as possible. (2) Include only one problem area in a redefinition. (3) Withhold all judgment when listing redefinitions. (4) Avoid searching for "correct" redefinitions. (5) Develop redefinitions that are as remote as possible from the initial problem statement. (6) Make sure all group members clearly understand all redefinitions. (7) Consider all redefinitions tentative.

Among the many techniques available to groups as redefinitional aids are analogies, boundary examinations, five Ws, reversals, two words, and the why method.

To evaluate and select the redefinitions produced from using the redefinitional aids, use this five-stage process: Discuss for clarification. Revise the redefinitions. Combine and eliminate duplicates. Cull and rate the redefinitions. And state the "final" redefinition and check for understanding. In the culling and rating stage, the group can use a culling and rating form that will help reduce the number of redefinitions. This form uses the criteria of urgency, threat, appropriateness, importance, applicability, and commitment. Redefinitions that survive culling and rating are narrowed down to only one through the use of group consensus, voting, or ranking procedures.

Checklist of Activities

1. Write down the initial problem statement.
2. Review the redefinitional guidelines with the group.
3. Select at least two redefinitional techniques.
4. Use the techniques to generate as many redefinitions as possible.
5. Discuss the redefinitions to seek clarity of understanding.
6. Make any revisions in wording suggested by the group.
7. Combine and eliminate duplicate redefinitions.
8. Reduce the remaining redefinitions using culling and rating criteria.
9. If necessary, use group consensus, voting, or ranking procedures to narrow down the number of redefinitions to just one.
10. State the "final" tentative redefinition, and check for understanding among the group members.

9

Generating Ideas

Ideas Versus Solutions

Although the primary focus of this chapter is on selecting and using group idea-generation techniques, a brief distinction first needs to be made between ideas and solutions. These two terms are often used interchangeably with little consequence, especially when they are interchanged in casual conversation. However, the difference between ideas and solutions assumes greater importance during the idea-generation process.

Ideas generated by a group will not always be solutions. An idea should be thought of as an approximate thought, conception, or image about how a problem *might* be solved. A solution is more refined than an idea and specifies behaviors, methods, or processes for how a problem *can* be solved. An idea, as initially proposed during idea generation, is a stimulus; a solution is a response.

It must be noted that a fine line exists between the concepts of ideas and solutions. An idea may be proposed in a form that closely approximates or equals a solution. That is, an initial conception of how to deal with a problem (an idea) may contain enough information to suggest clearly what needs to be done to produce a workable solution. When this is the case, the idea may actually be more of a solution. On the other hand, some solutions may not specify clearly what needs to be done and, as a result, may be considered more as ideas than as solutions.

Another way to view the difference between ideas and solutions is to compare them along various dimensions. Six possible dimensions are degree of definition, spontaneity of occurrence, outcome, static versus dynamic, complexity, and generality. Based on these dimensions, ideas and solutions might be compared as follows:

Ideas	*Solutions*
Are relatively amorphous concepts.	Are more well defined.
Often occur spontaneously.	Often evolve gradually over a period of time.
Help produce solutions.	Help stimulate new ideas.
Are more static, singular mental concepts.	Are more dynamic and exist as processes.
Are relatively simple concepts.	Are more complex concepts.
Are usually general and passive.	Are more specific and action-oriented.

Perhaps the best way to view ideas is as diamonds in the rough with the potential to be refined and combined to produce workable problem solutions. Every idea doesn't have to be a polished gem when it is first proposed. Just proposing an idea is a significant contribution to group problem solving, because all ideas have the potential to spark solutions.

This unpolished aspect of ideas is why it is so important for group members to defer all judgment of ideas. They can evaluate and judge them later. If ideas are not given the opportunity to be transformed into workable solutions, the solutions that result are likely to be of lower quality. Ideas are raw material; solutions are the final product.

In using the techniques described in this chapter, remember that they are intended to produce ideas, not solutions—although the ideas may lead to solutions. Idea-generation techniques are tools that people can use to tap the hidden resources of their minds for the material needed to construct problem solutions. When first excavated, this material usually will be in the form of ideas. In this regard, groups should view ideas as tentative hypotheses about what could be.

Classifying and Selecting Techniques

The two basic types of group idea-generation techniques—brainstorming and brainwriting—were discussed in Chapter 2 and will not be described in much detail here.

In general, brainstorming groups use oral idea-generation procedures and can be classified as either structured or unstructured. Structured brainstorming involves the use of an agreed-upon procedure to guide idea generation; unstructured brainstorming does not use an agreed-upon procedure and generally proceeds in a more or less haphazard fashion.

Brainwriting groups use written idea-generation procedures and can be classified as either nominal or interacting. In nominal brainwriting groups, individuals working alone write down their ideas and then pool them without any discussion and without seeing the ideas generated by the others; interacting brainwriting groups, in contrast, share the individually generated ideas and use them to help prompt more ideas.

In addition to these techniques, which might be described as "pure" brainstorming and brainwriting, there are techniques that combine elements of both. With these hybrid techniques, brainstorming either precedes or follows brainwriting.

Chapter 2 presented eight criteria to help you select brainstorming or brainwriting methods: idea quantity, idea quality, time/money costs, interpersonal conflict potential, accommodation of social interaction needs, contribution to group cohesiveness, pressure to conform, and task orientation. The brainstorming and brainwriting procedures were then rated low, medium, or high on each criterion (see Figure 2-1). When quantitative ratings were applied to these criteria, structured brainstorming and interacting brainwriting tied for highest rated, nominal brainwriting was a close second, and unstructured brainstorming was a distant third.

Your selection of a particular class of technique, however, should be guided more by the tradeoffs inherent in each technique class than by any global, quantitative ratings. That is, base your decision to use either brainstorming or brainwriting on what a group is willing to give up (in terms of the criteria) in order to gain something else. For example, if social interaction needs must be accommodated, brainstorming would be selected at the possible expense of interpersonal conflict developing. Conversely, the use of brainwriting to avoid interpersonal conflict eliminates any accommodation of social interaction needs. One way to minimize this tradeoff dilemma is to use techniques that incorporate both brainstorming and brainwriting. Although these hybrid techniques will not eliminate tradeoffs completely, they will allow their users to benefit—to a limited degree—from the strengths of both brainstorming and brainwriting.

In the next four sections, techniques are described in the categories of structured brainstorming, nominal brainwriting, interacting brainwriting, and combination brainstorming-brainwriting (unstructured brainstorming is excluded because only formal techniques are being considered). To help you to select from among these techniques and to better understand the tradeoffs involved in using each technique, use the rating chart presented in Table 9-1. As shown in Table 9-1, each technique has been rated high, medium, or low against each of the criteria discussed in Chapter 2.

In addition to these eight criteria, one other criterion has been used in Table 9-1: skill/experience requirements. Since some techniques require

Table 9-1. Criteria ratings for selected brainstorming and brainwriting techniques.

Technique	Idea Quantity	Idea Quality	Time/ Money	Conflict Potential	Social Needs	Group Cohesiveness	Conformity Pressure	Task Orientation	Skill/ Experience	Numerical Rating Total
Structured Brainstorming										
1. Classical brainstorming	M	M	L	M	H	H	M	H	H	21
2. Force-fit game	M	M	L	M	H	H	M	H	M	22
3. Gordon/Little	H	H	L	M	H	M	M	H	H	22
4. Phillips 66	M	M	L	H	H	M	H	M	L	19
5. PIPS	M	M	H	L	H	M	M	H	M	20
6. Semantic intuition	M	H	L	M	H	M	M	H	M	22
7. Stimulus analysis	H	H	L	M	H	H	M	H	H	21
8. Synectics	H	H	H	M	H	H	M	H	H	21
9. Visual synectics	H	H	L	M	H	H	M	M	H	20
Nominal Brainwriting										
10. NGT	M	M	L	L	L	L	L	H	M	20
11. Crawford slip writing	M	M	L	L	L	L	L	M	L	20
Interacting Brainwriting										
12. Gallery method	M	M	L	L	L	L	L	L	L	19
13. Pin cards	M	M	L	L	L	L	L	L	L	19
Brainstorming-Brainwriting										
14. BBB	H	H	M	M	H	H	M	H	M	23
15. SIL method	M	M	L	L	H	M	M	H	L	23

L = low; M = medium; H = high.

more skill and experience to use than do others, this criterion is important when selecting from among specific techniques. For purposes of technique selection, the skill/experience criterion refers to the extent that effective technique use depends on the existence of a group leader and group members who are both skilled and experienced in using a particular technique. To illustrate the basis for the ratings in Table 9-1, consider the ratings for classical brainstorming. According to these ratings, this technique is capable of producing a medium quantity of ideas with medium quality, is low in time/ money costs, has a medium potential to result in interpersonal conflicts, a high ability to accommodate social interaction needs and promote group cohesiveness, a medium tendency to promote uniformity of behavior, a high emphasis on getting the job done, and a high need for skilled and experienced group leaders and group members.

The quantitative rating totals in the last column of Table 9-1 were derived by assigning a score of 2 to each medium rating and either a 1 or 3 to each high or low rating, depending on whether or not a criterion is considered to be positive. In this regard, the criteria of time/money costs, conflict potential, conformity pressure, and skill/experience were scored a 1 when rated high and a 3 when rated low; the remaining criteria were scored a 3 when rated high and a 1 when rated low. For example, the low rating used for classical brainstorming on the criterion of time/money costs was scored a 3, since it is desirable to have low time and money costs. The high rating for group cohesiveness was also scored a 3, because it too is a generally desirable feature associated with a technique.

Two other aspects of Table 9-1 should also be noted. First, the numerical totals are based on the assumption that all the criteria are equal in weight or value. Determination of criteria weightings generally will vary with the requirements of a particular group. For instance, some groups may value low conflict potential and high cohesiveness more than time and money costs. As a result, the numerical rating totals reflect only a generalized assessment of each technique, with the technique advantages and disadvantages often offsetting each other. Second, the criteria used in Table 9-1 are not exhaustive. Several additional criteria could have been used, and individual groups may decide to add their own criteria. For instance, a group may decide to consider how comfortable it is in using a technique, the complexity of a technique, or the physical requirements for using a technique (e.g., room size, group size, and special materials). In any event, each group should use Table 9-1 as the basis for making technique selections and not as the final decision guide.

Making technique selections will be a much easier task for groups that have experimented with many different types of techniques. These groups may not need to resort to quantitative ratings as long as they are satisfied with the technique outcomes. However, groups with little experience in using formal idea-generation methods might be wise to use the ratings to help them make their initial selections. For such groups, the following procedure might be helpful:

1. Study the technique descriptions in the following sections to become familiar with the techniques.
2. Review and discuss the general technique ratings in Table 9-1. Pay particular attention to criteria that are important to your group.
3. Think of any additional criteria your group would like to add and any criteria it might like to delete or modify.
4. Develop a new list of criteria, if needed.
5. Develop weights for each criterion, using a scale of 1 to 5. Assign a value of 1 to a criterion that is least important, 2 to a criterion that is only somewhat important, and so forth, up to 5 for a criterion that is most important.
6. Multiply criterion weights by the numerical rating equivalents in Table 9-1 (e.g., if idea quantity is weighted with a 5 and a technique is rated medium on this criterion, you would multiply 5 times 2).
7. Calculate the new numerical rating totals for each technique by adding up the products obtained for each criterion across each technique.
8. Examine all the numerical rating totals and select the highest-rated technique (or techniques) to use in generating ideas.

The technique descriptions that follow are relatively brief and present only basic information on how to use them. This will not present an obstacle with some techniques, because of the simplicity of their procedures. For other techniques, however, the information presented may not be sufficient, depending on your degree of familiarity with these methods. If you believe that the descriptive information provided is insufficient, you should consult the appropriate references provided for each technique.

Structured Brainstorming Techniques

Classical Brainstorming

As developed by Osborn (1963), classical brainstorming uses four basic rules to guide a brainstorming session: (1) No criticism of ideas is allowed—idea evaluation comes later. (2) Freewheeling is welcomed—the wilder the ideas the better. (3) Quantity is wanted—the more ideas generated, the greater will be the quality of the solution. And (4) combining and improving on ideas are desirable—better ideas can be obtained by building on previous ideas. Using these four rules, a typical brainstorming meeting proceeds as follows:

1. Develop a problem statement.
2. Send the problem statement to a group of 6 to 12 participants. Include with the problem statement a description of the background of the problem, the four brainstorming rules, sample solutions, and the place and time of the meeting.
3. Before beginning the meeting, explain the procedures that will be used, review the rules, conduct a warm-up exercise (e.g., think of different uses for a brick), and, if needed, redefine the problem.
4. Write the problem statement on a chalkboard or flip chart and request ideas by asking for raised hands. Allow only one idea at a time to be suggested.
5. Have a recording secretary copy down all ideas.
6. Conclude the session after a period of 30 to 45 minutes.
7. Present the ideas to an evaluation group (which may or may not be the same as the brainstorming group) and have the group select the best ideas.

In brainstorming sessions, the role of the leader can be critical. You should be somewhat knowledgeable about the problem, experienced in conducting brainstorming sessions, and capable of promoting a relaxed and friendly atmosphere. You can also facilitate the process by encouraging equal participation, having group members snap their fingers when they want to build on a previous idea, suggesting ideas when the group slows down, asking the group to think of ways to modify different ideas, and setting goals for a certain number of ideas to be generated (as long as the goals are realistic).

When a few group members tend to dominate the process or some of the group members appear to be inhibited, try the brainstorming procedure known as sequencing. Sequencing makes the brainstorming activity a little more systematic by introducing some structure. To use sequencing, go around to each group member and give him or her a chance to suggest an idea. A group member who does not have an idea to offer simply says "Pass," and the next member is given a turn.

An additional resource on classical brainstorming is Rawlinson's *Creative Thinking and Brainstorming* (1981).

Force-Fit Game

The force-fit game, one of many techniques developed at the Battelle Institute in Frankfurt, Germany, was designed by Schlicksupp (Warfield, Geschka, and Hamilton, 1975) and uses forced relationships to prompt ideas.

The steps involved are:

1. Two small groups are formed.
2. Someone who is not in either of these groups assumes the role of referee/recorder.
3. The problem statement is written down for all participants to see and is read aloud by the referee/recorder.
4. The game begins by having a member from one of the groups suggest an idea that is unrelated to the problem. For example, if the problem is developing ways to avoid laying off personnel during difficult economic times, a member might suggest that the organization needs to buy more light bulbs.
5. The second group is told that it has two minutes to turn the unrelated idea into a practical solution to the original problem.
6. The second group is awarded one point if its solution is judged successful by the referee/recorder; if its solution is judged unsuccessful, the first group gets the point.
7. The referee/recorder writes down all solutions as they are proposed.
8. The groups reverse roles, and the second group proposes an unrelated idea that the first group develops into a practical solution. The solution is then judged as described in Step 6. The groups continue to reverse roles until the game ends (this step represents an addition proposed by VanGundy, 1981).
9. After a 30- to 45-minute period, the game is terminated and the group with the most points is declared the winner. All solutions are collected and evaluated at a later time.

Gordon/Little

The Gordon/Little technique was developed by William Gordon (see Taylor, 1961, or VanGundy, 1981) to offset the tendency of many people to propose obvious solutions. This technique also circumvents the problem of reduced originality that often occurs when people are knowledgeable about a problem (the "can't-see-the-forest-for-the-trees" syndrome, if you will). However, the success of the Gordon/Little method depends largely on the leader's ability to apply it correctly. The major steps are:

1. Introduce to the group a general subject area, somewhat abstract in content, saying, "Think of ways to . . ." (Don't reveal the problem at this point.) For example, if the original problem is to develop ways to reduce the number of drunk drivers on the highways, you might say, "Think of ways to prevent something from happening."
2. The group members then generate ideas for this general problem.

3. Ask the group to think of ways of doing something that is less general and abstract than the first instruction. In doing this, you gradually introduce key bits of problem information. For instance, you might now say, "Think of ways to keep people from doing something."
4. The group members generate ideas in response to the second instruction.
5. The process continues until you finally introduce the original problem.
6. When you reveal the original problem, the group members look over their ideas for solving the more abstract problems and use these ideas to help them suggest solutions to the original problem.

Phillips 66

A former college president, Donald Phillips (Phillips, 1948) is credited with developing the Phillips 66 method for gathering ideas from a large group of individuals. With this technique, many different ideas can be generated in a relatively short time. Another major strength is its ability to allow audience participation through small group discussions. Implementing the Phillips 66 technique involves the following steps:

1. Divide a large group into small groups containing six people each. The groups should be physically separated from one another, so that they cannot overhear each other's conversations.
2. Have the groups elect a discussion leader and a recorder/reporter.
3. Provide each group with a written statement of a problem and inform each group that it has six minutes to discuss the problem and generate ideas. The recorder/reporter writes down all ideas.
4. At the end of the six-minute period, have the group members evaluate their proposed solutions and select the most promising ones for presentation to the larger group.
5. Ask the individual groups to return to their original location, where the conference leader then records the ideas selected by each group (as reported by each group's recorder/reporter).
6. When the conference leader has recorded all the ideas, terminate the process and present the ideas to an individual or a committee for further evaluation. (If desired, the ideas could first be discussed by the larger group for purposes of clarification.)

Phases of Integrated Problem Solving

Most group idea-generation methods focus exclusively on the task of generating ideas and ignore the group process issues that often arise. The phases of integrated problem solving (PIPS) technique was designed to overcome this deficiency by incorporating both task and people concerns in its format. The result is a highly structured, six-step procedure that deals with task and process activities simultaneously. Although PIPS can be burdensome to use—especially for experienced and highly cohesive groups—it can be helpful for relatively inexperienced or new problem-solving groups. As described by its developers (Morris and Sashkin, 1976), PIPS should be used by following these six steps:

1. Problem definition
   a. Task activities: Search for relevant problem information. Develop a detailed understanding of the problem. And seek consensus on group goals relevant to the problem.
   b. Process activities: Ensure that all group members participate in the search for information. Encourage group members to feel open about sharing their information. Work toward consensus on a common goal. And select a problem statement that is satisfactory to all members.
2. Problem-solution generation
   a. Task activities: Generate ideas using classical brainstorming. Elaborate on the ideas generated. And develop a list of tentative problem solutions.
   b. Process activities: Encourage equal participation during the brainstorming activity. Discourage any criticism of ideas. And check to make sure everyone is aware of the solutions generated.
3. Ideas to action
   a. Task activities: Evaluate each idea's strengths and weaknesses. Examine ways of combining two or more solutions with high potential. And select a tentative solution.
   b. Process activities: Make sure criticism of ideas is avoided. Attempt to mediate disputes on how to combine ideas. Work toward consensus on the best idea to implement. And make sure that all members agree on the selected solution.
4. Solution-action planning
   a. Task activities: List activities needed to implement the solution. Identify resources needed to carry out each activity. And decide who will be responsible for seeing that each activity is carried through to completion.
   b. Process activities: Make sure all group members participate in developing the implementation activities. Make sure that potential resources are evaluated adequately in reference to each action step. And develop member commitment for carrying out the responsibilities involved in performing each implementation activity.

5. Solution-evaluation planning
   a. Task activities: Decide how to assess the success of each action step. Develop a timetable to monitor the results of each action step. And develop contingency plans in case any action steps require modification.
   b. Process activities: Make sure all group members participate in developing success measures. Determine whether all group members are comfortable with the action timetable. And develop commitment for putting contingency plans into operation.
6. Evaluation of the product and the process
   a. Task activities: Compare solution outcomes with original objectives. Determine whether any new problems have arisen. Decide whether any future actions will be needed. And discuss the adequacy of the group's procedures.
   b. Process activities: Evaluate the overall degree of group member participation. Evaluate the extent to which group members felt free to express themselves and to be supportive of others. And examine what the group has learned about itself and its ability to use the PIPS procedure.

Although these six steps describe the basic elements of the PIPS technique, they do not fully capture other considerations involved in using the technique. In their description of the PIPS process, Morris and Sashkin also provide a list of specific task and process questions to help guide the group in working through each of the steps. They also provide a rating scale that the group can use to evaluate its success in accomplishing each step. Without this material, it may not be possible to achieve very satisfactory results. Therefore, readers interested in trying the PIPS procedure should consult the reference cited for Morris and Sashkin before attempting to use this technique.

Semantic Intuition

Developed at the Battelle Institute in Frankfurt (Schaude, 1979), semantic intuition is based on a reversal of the procedure normally used when an invention has been produced. Instead of naming an invention (or idea) after it has been developed, names are developed first and then used to suggest inventions (or ideas). The result is a procedure that produces a moderate amount of problem remoteness that can aid in the generation of unique ideas. The major steps are:

1. Use the principles of classical brainstorming, and generate two lists of words that are related to the problem area.

2. Arbitrarily combine a word from the first list with a word from the second list to produce a new name.
3. Use this name to help prompt ideas.
4. Continue combining words and generating ideas until all possible names have been considered.

Suppose your problem is to consider different ways to make meetings more efficient. Although there is no "correct" way to set up the technique, you might begin by selecting two problem areas such as *meeting* and *room*. Words could be listed for each of these words as follows:

Meeting	Room
Agenda	Table
People	Chairs
Topic	Walls
Process	Lights

Next, after examining different two-word combinations, you might come up with such names as: Agenda-Walls, Agenda-Lights, People-Walls, Topic-Table, and Process-Chairs. After looking over these names, you might generate such ideas as: (1) putting the agenda on a board for all to see (Agenda-Walls), (2) putting a light bulb beside each item on an agenda board and having the bulb light up for the particular item being discussed (this would be a signal that no other items can be considered until the light changes) (Agenda-Lights), (3) having people come early to the meeting and write down their concerns on sheets of paper (attached to the walls) that would be used to guide the meeting and help prevent the introduction of "hidden" agenda items (People-Walls), (4) building into the table a device that contains cards that pop up to reveal the topic under consideration (Topic-Table), and (5) allowing people to speak only in sequence, as determined by seating arrangements (Process-Chairs).

Stimulus Analysis

The stimulus analysis technique, developed at the Battelle Institute in Frankfurt, uses words or objects unrelated to a problem to help stimulate ideas. As with similar methods, it helps provoke ideas by restraining problem solvers temporarily from focusing directly on the problem. The result should be more unique ideas than could be obtained without using an external source of stimulation. According to Schaude (1979), the major steps for using this method are:

1. Using the principles of classical brainstorming, generate a list of ten concrete words or objects that are unrelated to the problem area.

2. Select the first word and list all of its descriptive characteristics (e.g., specific parts, relationships, principles, what it does).
3. Examine each of these characteristics and use each one as a stimulus for suggesting ideas.
4. Select another characteristic and generate ideas using it until all possible ideas have been exhausted. Continue this process with all the characteristics for the word.
5. Select another word and repeat the process described in Steps 2 through 4. Continue selecting words, listing characteristics, and generating ideas until all ten words have been dealt with.
6. Examine all the solutions generated and select the ones with the most potential for solving the problem.

As an example of stimulus analysis, consider a problem of how to improve an artist's paint brush. As the stimulus object, I will use an office telephone. The procedure can then be set up as follows:

Analysis	*Possible Solutions*
Has a plastic shell.	Sell brushes with a reusable plastic cover to keep bristles pliable.
Rings with incoming calls.	Install a buzzer that sounds when bristles begin to fall out, thus indicating the brush should be replaced.
Buttons light up when receiver is picked up.	Attach or build in a small light for painting detail work.
Coiled cord helps prevent tangles.	Attach a lightweight cord to the end of the brush to make it easy to retrieve.

Synectics

Synectics is a relatively complex brainstorming variation that relies on metaphors and analogies to prompt ideas. It was originally developed by William Gordon (1961), who was later joined by George Prince (1968). Together they established Synectics, Inc., and then they parted to found separate organizations, each using a slightly different version of the synectics process. The procedural steps that follow represent a distillation of both approaches (the only major differences lie in the terminology and the use of various mechanisms for stimulating ideas):

1. Problem as given (PAG): Describe the problem to the group as it was presented by the client (the person with the problem).

2. Short analysis of the PAG: Attempt to make the strange familiar by using analogies and metaphors as well as information supplied by the client. The primary purpose of this stage is to gain a better understanding of the problem.

3. Purge: Have the group members verbalize known or trivial solutions. By getting these solutions out into the open, increased understanding of the problem should result. In addition, purging solutions at this point in the process should allow more innovative solutions to emerge later on.

4. Problem as understood (PAU): Using a fantasy analogy or wishful thinking, have the group members describe their understanding of the problem. In consultation with the client, use these problem viewpoints to help you to select a portion of the problem to focus on.

5. Excursion: Ask the group members to "take a vacation" from the problem and shut out all conscious awareness of it. During this stage, the intended outcome is to make the familiar strange, so that new problem perspectives can be achieved. To do this, ask the group members to generate different types of analogies, and then select one for detailed analysis and elaboration. After the analogy has been explored fully, have the group proceed to the next stage.

6. Fantasy force fit (FFF): Have the group members write down a statement describing the relationship between the analogy developed in the excursion stage and the problem as understood. Specifically, instruct the group members to develop a fantasy analogy between the result of the excursion stage and the PAU. The outcome should be a new way of viewing the problem, although no practical solution may be apparent yet.

7. Practical force fit (PFF): Use the fantasy analogy developed in the FFF stage to develop a practical solution to the problem. Instruct the group members to think of practical applications suggested by the fantasy analogy. In other words, the group must force together what is fantasy and what is practical to produce a workable solution.

8. Viewpoint: In this last stage of the process, a new way of looking at the original problem may be produced. Consider this viewpoint tentative if no practical and workable solution was developed in the preceding stage. In this case, a new way of viewing the problem might represent a redefinition of the problem as understood and the group should return to the PAU stage and repeat the process. However, if a problem viewpoint has resulted in development and implementation of a practical solution, the process can be terminated.

Such a brief description of the synectics process does not provide an adequate picture of how the procedure is used in practice. Furthermore, there are many assumptions, principles, and idea-prompting techniques associated with this method that cannot be described adequately in the space available. Interested readers should consult the references listed for Gordon and Prince to obtain a more thorough understanding.

Note also that the role of the leader in the synectics process can be critical to its success. In addition to the in-depth knowledge of synectics required of the leader, the leader must also have certain skills and behaviors to facilitate a synectics group effectively. Just reading about synectics probably will not be sufficient. The best way to learn about this method is to attend a synectics training session. Interested readers should write to Synectics, Inc., 17 Dunster Street, Cambridge, Massachusetts 02138, for more information.

Visual Synectics

Visual synectics was developed at the Battelle Institute in Frankfurt (Schaude, 1979) to assist groups in developing analogies during a synectics session. However, it also works quite well by itself as an idea-generation method. Somewhat similar in process to stimulus analysis, visual synectics relies on direct viewing of pictures to stimulate ideas. In using this technique, the group leader should:

1. Write down a problem statement on a chalkboard or flip chart and read it aloud to the group.
2. Show the group a picture that is unrelated to the problem (individual pictures can be distributed to each group member, or slides or transparencies can be projected onto a screen).
3. Have the group members describe out loud what they see in the picture.
4. As the descriptions are verbalized, write down each one on a chalkboard or flip chart.
5. Point to each description and ask the group members for any ideas that are suggested for dealing with the problem.
6. After all descriptions have been examined and all ideas have been generated, show another picture and repeat the process (use no more than ten pictures during any one session).

When selecting pictures for this technique, be sure to use pictures that are unrelated to the problem area. Such pictures, are likely to produce more unique ideas. In general, pictures that are abstract, likely to provoke negative emotional reactions, or feature people prominently should be avoided. Pictures that depict or imply different types of motion, are in color (although one or two black-and-white photographs could be useful), and contain a variety of elements will work best. Pictures found in *National Geographic* and similar magazines work very well for this method.

Although initially some people have trouble using this technique, they can usually be drawn out by the group leader. In particular, you should push group members to describe from a picture as many different features, concepts, principles, and relationships as they can. Then you can suggest ways of relating these descriptions to the problem, by giving specific examples.

Nominal Brainwriting Techniques

Nominal Group Technique

Delbecq and Van de Ven (1971) developed the nominal group technique (NGT) as an efficient procedure for helping groups make program planning decisions. Although this technique provides some opportunity for group discussion, its primary idea-generation component features silent, written generation of ideas. As a result, it does not accommodate social interaction needs to a great degree, but it does ensure that ideas will be developed in a timely fashion without any unnecessary discussions. In addition, NGT incorporates a procedure for idea evaluation and selection, so that group members can leave an NGT meeting with a sense of closure on the problem. The major steps in this procedure are:

1. Silent generation of ideas in writing: Read a problem statement aloud. Then ask group members to write down their ideas without engaging in any discussion with other group members. Allow only five or ten minutes for this activity.
2. Round-robin recording of ideas: Ask the group members to read their ideas aloud, in turn. As each idea is read, assign a number to it and record it on a chalkboard or flip chart visible to all group members. Do not permit discussion of the ideas during this stage.
3. Serial discussion for clarification: Point to each idea listed and encourage the group members to ask questions or make comments about the idea's importance, clarity, meaning, or underlying logic. During this activity, control the discussion to avoid heated debates. And make it clear that individuals who suggested an idea do not need to comment on it if they don't want to.
4. Preliminary vote on item importance: Have each group member select a few of the best ideas out of the total and write each one down on a 3" × 5" card. (The group leader should determine the number of ideas to be chosen—for example, 10 percent of the total. A number of ideas

between five and nine usually works well.) The idea number from the master list should be recorded in the upper left-hand corner of each card. Next, have the group members silently read over all the ideas they selected and rank each one by assigning a 5 (assuming only five ideas were selected) to the most important one, a 4 to the next most important idea, and so forth, until all ideas have been ranked. The ranks for each idea should be recorded on the lower right-hand corner of each card. Next, record all the ranked scores on a flip card or chalkboard so that the rank numbers correspond with each idea number. Finally, count all the vote tallies and note the idea with the most votes (i.e., the idea with the highest score). If there is a clear-cut idea winner at this point, the process can be terminated; if there is no clear-cut winner or there are inconsistencies in votes for the highest-ranked ideas, two additional steps can be added to the process.

5. Discussion of the preliminary vote: In this step, the group examines any peculiar voting patterns. If such patterns occur (e.g., an idea receives four 5 votes and three 1 votes), have the group discuss the ideas in question to clarify the meanings and logic behind the ideas. During this step, do not permit group members to try to influence the votes of others.

6. Final vote: After the clarifying discussion has ended, ask the group members to vote on the ideas again, using the ranking procedure described for the preliminary vote (Step 4). At the conclusion of this activity, the process can be terminated.

Although this method has several advantages, it should be noted that the lack of external sources of stimulation and the lack of any sharing of ideas could result in ideas that are relatively low in quality. NGT is an extremely efficient method, but it may not be capable of producing the unique ideas possible with other methods.

Crawford Slip Writing

Crawford slip writing is similar to NGT in the basic procedure used to generate ideas, but it differs greatly in the overall complexity of the steps involved. Crawford slip writing was developed by C. C. Crawford (Whiting, 1958) and has been popularized by Clark (1978) as a method for soliciting ideas from very large groups (up to 5,000 people). However, it is also appropriate for much smaller groups. The major steps are:

1. Give each participant at least twenty-five 3" × 5" slips of paper.
2. Read a problem statement aloud to the group.

3. Instruct the group members to write down one idea on each slip of paper and to defer all judgment while doing so. If desired, various graphics can be used to help prompt ideas.
4. After five to ten minutes, tell the group members to stop writing and turn in their idea slips.
5. Dismiss the group members, and appoint an evaluation task force to sort the idea slips into predetermined categories. The best ideas can then be developed into workable solutions.

In comparing Crawford slip writing and NGT, it should be apparent that NGT provides for more group member participation and produces a greater sense of closure. Like NGT, Crawford slip writing does not involve sharing of ideas to help prompt new ideas. However, unlike NGT, Crawford slip writing uses external stimulation aids. For example, Clark (1978) describes how graphics with different arrangements of dots can be used to prompt ideas pertaining to problems in organizations.

Interacting Brainwriting Techniques

Gallery Method

Developed at the Battelle Institute in Frankfurt, the gallery method reverses the procedure used in most interacting brainwriting methods: Instead of ideas circulating among people, people circulate among ideas. The name of the method was derived from what can be observed in an art gallery, where people walk around and look at different works of art. In the gallery method, people walk around looking at the ideas of other group members. This technique has the following steps (Geschka, 1980):

1. Attach sheets of flip-chart paper to stands or to the walls of a room. Assign each group member to one of the sheets of paper.
2. Write down a problem statement in a visible location in the room and read it aloud.
3. Have the group members discuss the statement to make sure it is clearly understood.
4. Have the group members silently write down ideas on their sheets of paper for 20 to 30 minutes.
5. Instruct the group members to take a 10- or 15-minute break and walk around the room, studying the ideas written down by the other group members.
6. Have the group members return to their own sheets after the break and

continue writing ideas, using the other group members' ideas as sources of stimulation. Encourage the group to build on or improve the ideas they looked at.

7. After 20 to 30 minutes of writing, ask the group to stop and consider the solution potential of all the ideas generated by each member.

Pin Cards

With the pin cards technique, a large number of ideas can be generated and evaluated in a relatively short time. In addition, the sharing of ideas provided by this method serves as a source of stimulation similar to that found in the gallery method. According to Geschka (1980), using pin cards involves the following steps:

1. Write down a problem statement in a location visible to all group members (who are seated around a small table). Read the statement aloud, and ask the group members to discuss it to clarify their understanding of it.
2. Distribute at least 50 blank computer cards (or large index cards) to each group member.
3. Instruct the group members to silently write down one idea on each card and pass the card to the person on the right.
4. Tell the group members to read the card given to them by the person on their left, write down on a blank card any new ideas stimulated (or modifications), and pass the new idea card on to the person on the right. The stimulation card may be retained temporarily to use for suggesting additional ideas, or it may be passed along with the new card. However, encourage the group members to keep the cards circulating as much as possible.
5. After 20 to 30 minutes of this activity, collect all the cards and have the group members pin them onto a large bulletin board (or tape them to a wall). The cards should be arranged into columns according to different categories of ideas, with a title card placed above each column.
6. Instruct the group to read over all the cards to eliminate duplicates and rearrange categories if needed.
7. Point to each card and ask for general comments or questions to help clarify the logic or meaning of each idea.
8. Evaluate the ideas by appointing an evaluation task force or by having the group members vote on the ideas. Voting can be facilitated by having group members initial a specified percentage of the ideas they

favor or by having them place a certain number of self-sticking paper dots on their preferred ideas. For example, if there are 100 ideas, each group member might be given 10 dots and told to allocate them in any manner desired, placing them all on one idea, one each on ten ideas, or any other combination.

Combination Brainstorming-Brainwriting Techniques

Battelle Bildmappen Brainwriting

The major process involved in generating ideas with Battelle bildmappen brainwriting (BBB) is similar to that used for visual synectics. Developed at the Battelle Institute in Frankfurt, BBB (Warfield, Geschka, and Hamilton, 1975) uses picture portfolios (the bildmappen) as the primary means for stimulating ideas. The following steps are used:

1. Read aloud a problem statement and ask the group to brainstorm (verbally) known or trivial solutions.
2. Give each group member a folder containing eight to ten pictures that are not related to the problem area (information on how to select these pictures can be found in the description of visual synectics beginning on p. 180).
3. Instruct the group members to examine each picture and silently write down any new ideas or modifications of previous ideas suggested by the pictures.
4. After a designated period, ask the group members to read their ideas aloud.
5. As each idea is read, ask the group members to discuss it and try to develop new ideas or modifications. Record all new ideas as they are suggested.
6. Collect the ideas and evaluate them at another time.

When there are fewer picture portfolios than there are group members, a group can use one portfolio if the members follow some of the steps for using visual synectics. But instead of having the group members verbalize their ideas after examining the pictures (as is done in visual synectics), have them follow the BBB method, beginning with Step 3. Of course, other procedural variations can also be used, since "correctness" of procedure is not as important as the outcome of any given procedure.

SIL Method

When translated from the German, the acronym SIL stands for successive integration of problem elements. Developed at the Battelle Institute in Frankfurt, the SIL method uses the principles of forced relationships and free association to generate ideas. The following steps are used (Warfield, Geschka, and Hamilton, 1975):

1. Have the group members individually generate ideas (silently and in writing) in reference to a problem statement previously read aloud to them.
2. Ask two members to read aloud one idea each.
3. Instruct the other group members to develop ways of integrating the two ideas to produce just one idea (all the group members help select the final integrated idea).
4. Ask a third group member to read one of his or her ideas, and instruct the rest of the group to integrate this idea with one just produced.
5. Continue this process of reading ideas and integrating them with previous ideas until a workable problem solution is suggested.

Before using this technique, note that the convergent idea-generation procedure used in the SIL method may inhibit idea quality. By considering only ideas resulting from previously integrated ideas, a group may overlook many potentially valuable solutions. If an idea is forced together with another idea without examining its potential to be modified, its possible value in producing a workable solution will be weakened through its combination with another idea. However, the structured nature of the SIL method ensures that all ideas will be considered equally, even though some spontaneity may be lost in the process.

Summary

Although often used interchangeably, the concepts of ideas and solutions are not synonymous when examined as elements of the idea-generation process. Ideas usually precede solutions and are the raw material that may be transformed into solutions. Ideas are general conceptions about how a problem might be solved; solutions are methods that specify or imply how problems can be solved.

Because of the tentative, often fleeting, nature of ideas, it is important that group members withhold judgment when generating ideas. Otherwise, the potential of ideas to be developed into workable solutions will not be exploited fully. And premature judgment of ideas is likely to lead to low-quality solutions.

Group idea-generation techniques can be classified according to their use of brainstorming, brainwriting, or combination procedures. Brainstorming techniques are either structured or unstructured. Structured brainstorming can be distinguished from unstructured brainstorming by its use of an agreed-upon idea-generation procedure. Brainwriting techniques can be classified as using either nominal or interacting procedures. Nominal procedures rely on the silent, written generation of ideas without any sharing of the ideas among the group members; interacting procedures rely on the silent, written generation of ideas that are shared among the group members.

At least nine criteria can be used to select group idea-generation techniques: idea quantity, idea quality, time/money costs, interpersonal conflict potential, accommodation of social interaction needs, contribution to group cohesiveness, pressure to conform, task orientation, and skill/experience requirements. The importance of any one criterion will vary across individual groups. However, most selection decisions will involve certain tradeoffs, depending on the particular criterion emphasized. For example, the desire to accommodate social interaction needs will limit the choice to brainstorming techniques. Many of the tradeoffs involved in technique selection can be avoided by using combination brainstorming-brainwriting techniques.

Fifteen group idea-generation techniques were presented in this chapter. Nine of the techniques were classified as structured brainstorming procedures (e.g., classical brainstorming, semantic intuition, synectics), and two each as normal brainwriting (NGT and Crawford slip writing), interacting brainwriting (gallery method and pin cards), and combination brainstorming-brainwriting (Battelle bildmappen brainwriting and the SIL method).

10

Evaluating and Selecting Ideas

The generation of ideas is a necessary, but not sufficient, condition of creative problem solving. Creativity involves more than producing ideas for resolving a problem. The ideas somehow must be reduced in number, assessed, and further narrowed down so that one or more potential solutions can be implemented. This task of examining a pool of generated ideas is known as idea evaluation and selection.

In this chapter, a conceptual distinction will be made between the processes of evaluation and selection. Then some basic guidelines will be presented for managing these processes. Finally, eight evaluation and selection techniques will be described and discussed briefly.

Evaluation Versus Selection

The process of idea evaluation precedes that of idea selection. Before you can make a choice, you first must develop some basis for the choice. Then, once you have applied this basis, the selection process will fall into place, with very little difficulty involved in how final choices are made. At least this is what should happen.

What often does happen is that ideas are selected with very little consideration given to the basis for the choice. People often select ideas without any conscious awareness of what criteria they used to guide their selections. Although such intuitive decision making can work out quite well for many types of problem situations, it can be a severe liability when high-quality solutions are sought. To increase the odds of choosing high-quality solutions (i.e., solutions with the greatest probability of resolving a problem), everyone involved in the decision-making process should be aware of the specific criteria being used.

In most group decision situations (as well as in individual situations), the criteria used to guide idea selection will be implicit, explicit, or some combination of the two. The use of implicit criteria occurs when ideas are assessed for their potential to solve a problem without formally acknowledging the specific criteria used to assess each idea. In groups, this means that each member individually applies his or her own criteria without sharing the criteria with other members. Frequently, this lack of sharing occurs when members have not agreed on a need to share criteria or when individual members are not aware of the criteria they are using. When explicit criteria are used, the group members will have formally acknowledged and agreed on the standards they will use in evaluating each idea. It also is possible that the criteria may be both implicit and explicit. For example, a group may agree to use certain criteria, but individual members may consciously or unconsciously apply their own criteria in conjunction with the agreed-upon criteria.

Because creative problem solving is typically used when unique, high-quality solutions are desired, the use of explicit criteria is an absolute necessity. However, there will be instances in which criteria cannot be fully explored and developed. For example, if time is a critical factor, voting procedures (that use no formal, explicit criteria) may be required. This consideration and others will be discussed further in the next two sections. Nevertheless, explicit criteria should be used whenever possible.

Basic Guidelines

As with most of the other problem-solving modules, idea evaluation and selection will proceed more smoothly when basic guidelines are available to help structure the processes involved. Such guidelines are especially important when high-quality solutions are needed. If careful attention is not given to idea evaluation and selection, the odds will be diminished for transforming any ideas into workable problem solutions. The best ideas in the world will be of little value if they are not first screened and evaluated, so that the cream of the crop can be selected for possible implementation.

The use of guidelines also involves another advantage. By helping to structure a process that often involves little structure, the use of guidelines increases greatly the group members' commitment to the ideas. Even though formal techniques may be used, the outcome is more likely to result in higher member satisfaction with the process when a systematic process is followed.

Although not chiseled in stone, the guidelines that follow should help any group approach the evaluation and selection process with more confidence and enthusiasm. Many groups view idea generation as the most interesting and stimulating aspect of the creative problem-solving process. And it may be that it is. However, idea evaluation and selection can at least be interesting if the group approaches its task in an orderly fashion.

1. *Assess participation needs.* Even though the emphasis in this book is on group problem solving, knowing when groups should be used during different modules is an important consideration that should not be overlooked. As with any of the other modules, it may be better for you to evaluate and select ideas alone instead of involving the group; in some situations, it may be better for the group to participate; and in other situations, both individual and group decision making may be better. In order of importance, the major variables that need to be assessed when making such decisions are: (1) the amount of time available, (2) the importance of selecting a high-quality solution, (3) the need for group members to accept the solution selected, and (4) the need for group members to experience the evaluation and selection process for their own personal and professional development.

You should select ideas alone when there is little time available, the importance of selecting a high-quality solution is relatively low, and the group members do not need to accept the solution or experience the process. Conversely, the group should participate when time is available, a high-quality solution is important, successful implementation of a solution depends on group member acceptance of the solution, and the group members would benefit from experiencing the process.

However, many participation decisions cannot be made in an either-or manner. In some situations, it may be necessary for you to make some selection decisions alone and allow the group members to make the remaining decisions. For example, if time is in relatively short supply, but not enough to justify excluding the group, you might select a final pool of ideas, turn these ideas over to the group, and have the group develop a final solution. Such a procedure would be especially useful when it is important for the members to accept a solution. *

Since this book emphasizes group problem solving, the remaining guidelines are based on the assumption that group evaluation and selection procedures will be used. Nevertheless, these guidelines are also equally applicable to individual evaluation and selection of ideas.

2. *Agree on a procedure to use.* The group will need to agree on a procedure for evaluation and selection. The group may decide to follow the guidelines presented here, to use some other procedure, or to proceed directly to the

---

* The reader interested in a more refined approach to making group participation decisions should consult *Leadership and Decision Making* by Vroom and Yetton (1973).

evaluation and selection techniques. If the group decides to ignore the guidelines described here, you should still stress the need to consider developing evaluation criteria. The group will also have to decide how to narrow down the pool of generated ideas to a more manageable number. Beyond these considerations, the group probably will be on safe ground no matter what procedure it elects to follow. The important concern is that the group agree on some procedure and avoid the temptation to proceed in a haphazard manner.

3. *Preselect ideas.* If a group has generated a large number of potential ideas (e.g., 50 or more), it will need to reduce this number to a more workable size. Some of the techniques described in the next section can be used for this purpose, or the group can decide to use other methods.

Whatever method is used, two major variables to consider are the amount of time available and the importance of the problem. If there is plenty of time and the problem is important (i.e., the consequences will be serious if it is not solved), the group should devote considerable effort to this activity, assuming the members are motivated to do so. If there is little time, the problem is not very important, and group motivation is low, some shortcuts will have to be taken.

An initial step that a group can take to narrow down an idea pool is to examine all the ideas with the goal of developing combinations. When two similar ideas are joined together, the overall number is reduced. The group should also be encouraged to consider combining dissimilar ideas. Such combinations can often lead to higher-quality solutions than could be obtained from implementing two individual ideas.

When your group has developed all possible combinations, you should check for understanding on the part of the group members. Determine whether all group members understand the logic, meaning, and purpose of all the ideas. Then poll the group members to see whether they are comfortable with the idea list. (Examination of an idea pool will often stimulate new ideas that might be added to the list or combined with others. If this occurs, add the new ideas to the pool.)

When the group has agreed on a final list, it will have to choose the best procedure for further reducing the number of ideas. If time is inadequate for a thorough evaluation of each idea, two actions can be taken, either alone or in sequence. The group can organize all the ideas into logical categories according to some criterion such as problem type or potential effectiveness. Then it can eliminate those categories of ideas that appear to have the lowest potential as high-quality solutions. A second action would be to give each member a certain number of votes. For example, if there are 100 ideas, each member could be given 10 votes (10 percent of the idea pool) to allocate as desired. An even better procedure might be to use idea categories and votes together. This could be done by voting on categories or by voting on ideas within categories.

These procedures can also be used if time is not a major concern. However, if the problem is very important, the group can use a slightly different method of reducing the ideas, either by itself or in combination with categories and voting. This procedure involves establishing a minimally acceptable criterion and then eliminating every idea that fails to satisfy this criterion. For example, the group might decide to eliminate every idea that would cost more than a certain sum of money to implement. (If time permits, more than one criterion could be used.)

A decision to use this approach, however, must be made with some caution. If an inappropriate or relatively trivial criterion is selected, many potentially valuable ideas could be eliminated prematurely. Moreover, what appears to be an obstacle to implementing an idea can often be overcome with a little additional problem solving. For instance, it may appear that an idea will cost too much to implement, but minor modifications may make it more workable.

Regardless of which approach the group uses to narrow down the number of ideas, it must come up with a final list of ideas that are ready for evaluation and selection. The group can consider this list tentative, depending on the particular technique or techniques used for final selection. It may be, for example, that the group finds itself with too many ideas to screen, even after preselecting ideas from the initial pool. Or the amount of available time may decrease suddenly. In such cases, the group could recycle the idea list through the preselection phase and produce a shorter list.

With your group, check the list to be used for final evaluation and selection for clarity and understanding of the meaning and logic underlying all the ideas. When the group understands and accepts the list, it can start the next step in the process.

4. *Develop and select evaluation criteria.* Although many of the evaluation and selection methods described in this chapter use explicit evaluation criteria, there are some that do not. As discussed earlier, the quality of ideas selected without explicit criteria may be lower than the quality of ideas selected with such criteria. As a result, the group should attempt to make explicit all the criteria it will be using, whether or not a technique requires such explicitness. For example, a voting procedure that relies on implicit criteria will be used by the group to greater advantage if the group takes some time to discuss and agree on criteria that might be used in assigning votes.

In developing criteria, the group should try to generate as many criteria as possible. As with idea generation, quantity is likely to result in quality. The more criteria the group thinks of, the greater will be the odds that the group will select a high-quality solution. And just as it is important to defer judgment when generating ideas, it is important to defer judgment when generating criteria. Encourage the group members to stretch their minds and think of as many criteria as possible without regard to their initial value or relevance.

After the group has generated a list of criteria, it must select the criteria to be used in evaluating and selecting the ideas. The actual number of criteria selected will depend on the same variables used in preselecting ideas: available time and importance of the problem. When time is available and the problem is important, the group should select as many criteria as possible to use in evaluating the ideas. When little time is available and the problem is not important, the group can select a minimal number of criteria. However, if only a few criteria are used, it is imperative that the group choose relevant, important criteria that will be most likely to result in selection of a high-quality solution.

5. *Choose techniques.* The choice of evaluation and selection techniques can be as easy or as difficult and complex as you want. As with choosing idea-generation techniques, many variables can be considered when choosing evaluation and selection techniques. However, in this instance, the choice really narrows down to one among voting procedures, evaluation procedures, and some combination of each. Beyond these considerations, the only other real issue is the amount of time available. Voting obviously will consume less time than group evaluation, even if the group agrees on voting criteria prior to actually voting.

Of the eight techniques described in this chapter, three use "pure" voting methods, three use a criteria-based evaluation procedure that results in selection of an idea without the need for voting, and two use "pure" evaluation procedures with no built-in voting mechanism or explicit criteria. There are four major criteria that can be used when selecting from among these techniques: the ability of a technique to screen a large number of ideas, the provision for use of explicit evaluation criteria, the use of weightings for each of these criteria, and the relative time requirements for using each technique.

A partial matrix weighting procedure (one of the selection methods) can be used to illustrate how the selection techniques might be evaluated. The eight techniques and four selection criteria just discussed are presented in the matrix weighting chart shown in Figure 10-1.

In this figure, a scale of 1 to 7 points has been used to rate each technique against each criterion. A rating of 7 indicates that a technique fully satisfies a criterion; a 1 indicates that a technique satisfies a criterion only a little or not at all. Numbers 2 through 6 represent differing degrees of satisfaction between

Figure 10-1. Using a modified matrix weighting method to choose evaluation and selection techniques.

Criteria	Screens large number of ideas	Uses explicit criteria	Uses weighted criteria	Requires little time	Total Scores
Criterion weightings					
Advantage-disadvantage	7	7	1	5	20
Battelle method	5	7	7	2	21
Electronic voting	5	1	1	7	14
Idea advocate	1	1	1	1	4
Matrix weighting	3	7	7	4	21
Nominal group technique	7	1	1	6	15
Reverse brainstorming	1	1	1	1	4
Sticking dots	5	1	1	7	14

Techniques (row label on left side)

these extremes. For example, the advantage-disadvantage technique has been given a 7 for its ability to screen a large number of ideas but only a 1 for "uses weighted criteria," due to its lack of any weighted criteria.

The matrix weighting procedure shown in Figure 10-1 is a slight modification of the way it is normally used. Specifically, the criteria have not been assigned weights to reflect different degrees of importance. The weights assigned to each criterion should be based on judgments of the individuals in a particular group, since no two groups will view a situation in the same way. For example, members of one group may believe that time is very important, while members of another group may view time as relatively unimportant. As a result, the total scores shown in Figure 10-1 may be misleading. Without assigning weights to include the preferences and needs of your group, you may end up using a procedure that will be inappropriate for your particular situation. If you decide that weighted criteria are important, consult the description of the matrix weighting technique (pp. 204–206).

Note also that the four criteria used in Figure 10-1 may be too limiting for your group. If this is the case, you should consider generating additional criteria and then selecting those that are most important to you. Furthermore, you may want to dispense with any formal selection procedure and base your decisions, instead, on the information contained in the technique descriptions, as well as any experience you may have in using the techniques.

6. *Evaluate and select ideas.* At this point in the process, the group should apply one or more techniques to help it evaluate and select the ideas. On the basis of the number of ideas being evaluated, the amount of time available, and the perceived problem importance, the group should select one or more ideas for possible implementation.

If the group selects more than one idea, it should examine possible ways of combining the ideas to produce a higher-quality solution. If the ideas cannot be combined easily (or logically) and the ideas are judged to be equal in quality, the group should consider implementing all the ideas, either in sequence or all at the same time. If the group decides that there are too many ideas to implement, it can assign implementation priorities to the ideas and implement as many as possible in the time available. Or it can screen the ideas again by using an evaluation and selection technique, but with more stringent criteria this time, in order to reduce the idea total. Regardless of what procedure the group chooses for dealing with the remaining ideas, it should constantly be aware of its ultimate objective of selecting a high-quality solution.

The group will, of course, determine the quality of the ideas before it selects any ideas for implementation. In judging idea quality, note that rating of the ideas, as used in many of the selection techniques, will result in a quality evaluation for each idea. Thus quality will have already been considered at this point in the process. The group will need to evaluate again any ideas that survive these ratings, however, in order to ensure that it has selected the idea with the greatest probability of resolving the problem. The group may have overlooked important criteria, or new information may have become available that could affect the previously determined quality ratings of the ideas.

Thus the last step in the evaluation and selection process is to conduct a final check on the ideas that have survived the screening process. To do this, each group member could rate each idea (on a 7-point scale) with respect to its likelihood of resolving the problem. The group could then average the ratings or discuss them, with the purpose of achieving consensus. If the group judges none of these ideas to be of high quality, it could re-review ideas that initially failed to survive the screening process, but were rated high, and evaluate them with respect to their quality.

An alternative to this procedure is to proceed to the product module, where idea quality can be examined more thoroughly. As described in Chapter 12, product module activities emphasize evaluating ideas against general quality standards, revising ideas when necessary, and transforming these revisions into workable solutions. Note, however, that this module is optional and should be analyzed only when there is a question about the quality of ideas selected in the process module.

Technique Descriptions

In this section, the eight evaluation and selection techniques mentioned earlier will be described. Each description includes a step-by-step procedure for using the technique as well as any relevant information about the technique's strengths and weaknesses. As with all such techniques, modifications should be made to suit a group's particular preferences or needs.

Advantage-Disadvantage

There are several variations of the advantage-disadvantage technique, but only two will be described here (VanGundy, 1981). The first variation relies on implicit criteria and uses a listing of each idea's advantages and disadvantages. The second variation uses explicit, unweighted criteria that serve as direct measures of advantages and disadvantages.

Follow these steps to implement the first variation:

1. For each idea, develop separate lists of its advantages and disadvantages.
2. Select the ideas that have the most advantages and the fewest disadvantages.

The second variation uses these steps:

1. Develop a list of criteria to use in evaluating the ideas.
2. Write the criteria across the top of a sheet of paper.
3. To the left of the criteria, list the ideas in a single column down the side of the paper.
4. For each idea, make a check beside each criterion that is an advantage.
5. Add up the number of checkmarks for each idea and select the ideas with the most checkmarks.

These two variations can be illustrated using a problem on how to improve communications between two departments in an organization. For this problem, suppose that a few of the ideas generated are to:

1. Install computer terminals in each department.
2. Hold weekly meetings to discuss job-related problems.
3. Assign one person the role of interdepartmental project coordinator.
4. Have members of both departments attend a workshop on improving communication skills.
5. Have both departments meet to identify specific communication problems and generate possible solutions.

For the first variation of the advantage-disadvantage technique, you might evaluate these ideas using the format that follows. For purposes of illustration, only two ideas will be used.

Idea 1: Install computer terminals in each department.

Advantages	*Disadvantages*
1. Provides rapid communication.	1. Would be fairly expensive to install.
2. Makes it easy to store and retrieve information.	2. Requires training to use.
3. Would be convenient.	3. Would take up space.
4. Would be fun for people who like using computers.	4. Many workers would not be motivated enough to receive training.
	5. Reduces the social satisfactions provided by face-to-face interactions.
	6. Can be used by only one person at a time.

Idea 2: Hold weekly meetings to discuss job-related problems.

Advantages	*Disadvantages*
1. Provides for social interaction needs.	1. Time-consuming.
2. Allows people to better understand the motives of others.	2. Conflict may arise and make some people uncomfortable.
3. Specific problems can be dealt with by everyone involved.	3. Some individuals may dominate the discussions.
4. Other people's ideas can be built on to improve solution quality.	

On the basis of the advantages and disadvantages, the idea of using weekly meetings to discuss job-related problems would be selected because it has four advantages and three disadvantages. The first idea, of installing computer terminals, would not be selected because although it has four advantages, it has six disadvantages. Note, however, that had all the ideas been considered together, it is possible that several of the ideas would have been selected.

Using the same problem, but with all the ideas, the second variation could be set up as follows:

| | Criteria | | | | |
	Little Time	Low Financial Cost	Provides for Social Needs	Convenience	Total
Idea 1	X			X	2
Idea 2		X	X		2
Idea 3	X	X		X	3
Idea 4			X		1
Idea 5		X	X		2

On the basis of the results of this analysis, the idea of one person functioning as an interdepartmental project coordinator would be selected because this idea has the most advantages.

Both these variations have their own advantages and disadvantages. The first variation considers advantages and disadvantages that may be unique to each idea. However, it is relatively time-consuming to use, makes comparisons difficult due to the lack of standard criteria, does not use weighted criteria, and is subject to manipulation by its users. That is, it would be quite easy to adjust the outcomes so that one idea would be a clear winner over another. The second variation has strengths in its ability to screen a larger number of ideas in less time than the first variation, in its use of standardized criteria, and in the fact that its outcomes are less subject to manipulation when compared to the first variation. However, the second variation has disadvantages as well: it requires that an either-or decision be made in rating each idea, and, like the first variation, it lacks a provision for weighted criteria.

In choosing between these two variations, you may want to use the first one when you are concerned primarily with conducting a thorough evaluation of each idea and you have the time to do so. The second variation would be more suitable when you have relatively little time and/or you wish to narrow down a large number of ideas for preselection purposes. It would also be appropriate for making final selections, but it is limited by the lack of rating range and especially by its consideration of all criteria as equal in importance. Using both variations would be another alternative to consider; this would be acceptable as long as the weaknesses of each are taken into account.

Battelle Method

Developed at the Battelle Institute in Columbus, Ohio, for screening business development opportunities (Hamilton, 1974; VanGundy, 1981), the Battelle method uses three levels of screens to evaluate ideas. Each level uses criteria that are progressively higher in cost. In the Battelle method, cost refers to the resource investments required to obtain information needed to evaluate an idea. Thus ideas are evaluated first using information that is relatively easy to obtain, then using information that is more difficult to obtain, and finally using information that is the most difficult to obtain. The funnel effect produced by using such screens makes it possible to reduce a moderate amount of ideas to only a few. The major steps for using the Battelle method are:

1. Develop lost-cost screens (or culling criteria) phrased in questions that can be answered with a yes or a no.
2. Establish a minimally acceptable passing score.
3. Develop medium-cost screens (rating criteria) phrased in questions that can be answered with a yes or a no.
4. Establish a minimally acceptable passing score.
5. Develop high-cost screens (scoring criteria) presented in the form of different value ranges (e.g., poor, fair, good).
6. Assign a weight to each criterion.
7. Establish a minimally acceptable passing score.
8. Compare each idea with each of the culling criteria questions.
9. Eliminate any idea that receives a no response.
10. Using the remaining ideas, compare each one with each of the rating criteria questions.
11. Eliminate any idea that falls below the minimally acceptable passing score for the rating criteria.
12. Using the ideas that survive, numerically rate each one against each

scoring criterion and multiply that rating by the weight established for the criterion.
13. Add up the products obtained in Step 12, and compare each one with the minimally acceptable passing score for the scoring criteria.
14. Eliminate the ideas that fall below the minimally acceptable passing score.
15. If more than one idea remains, attempt to combine some of the ideas or subject them to more intensive analysis.

This procedure can be illustrated more vividly if we look again at the problem of improving interdepartmental communications. Using the idea of holding weekly meetings to discuss job-related problems, the Battelle method can be set up as follows:

Culling Screens

	Yes	No
1. Provides for social interaction needs?	X	
2. Involves members from all departments?	X	
3. Requires no new equipment purchases?	X	
Total:	3	0

Minimum yes score is 3

Pass?   Yes X   No ____

Rating Screens

	Yes	No
1. No special training required to implement?	X	
2. No more than 20 hours required to implement?		X
3. Will cost no more than $2,000 to implement?	X	
Total:	2	1

Minimum yes score is 2

Pass?   Yes X   No ____

Scoring Screens

	Poor	Fair	Good	Weight*	Total
1. Projected return on invest-ment?	1	2	③	2	6
2. Likelihood of reducing job errors?	1	②	3	3	6
3. Likelihood of reducing role conflicts?	1	2	③	3	9
				Total:	21

Minimum total score is 18

Pass?   Yes X   No ____

---

* A 3-point weighting scale is used here, although a greater range of weights would also have been appropriate.

According to the outcome illustrated, this idea survives all the screens and could be selected for implementation, combined with other surviving ideas, or retained for additional analysis. Note that the idea of installing computer terminals would have been rejected by the culling screens, because it involves a new equipment purchase (assuming computers are not available from any other source).

Early rejection of an idea in this manner is a strength of this technique because it makes idea screening more efficient. Some ideas are quickly eliminated at the outset, so the group can use its time more wisely for evaluating the remaining ideas. However, early rejection of ideas could also be a weakness. Answering questions with a yes or a no at the first stage may result in overlooking ways to circumvent any apparent obstacles. For example, computer terminals might be donated, especially if the organization is nonprofit. Thus the wording of the questions must be considered carefully.

Perhaps the most important consideration is how the criteria are grouped together. What constitutes a low- or high-cost screen, for example, can be very difficult to determine, especially when the criteria are highly subjective. To overcome this weakness, Hamilton suggests grouping the criteria into cost-homogeneous units within screens. Of course, the number of criteria has to be large enough to do this. Another alternative is to use relatively low minimal passing scores, at least during the first pass through the screens. Should a large number of ideas survive all three screens on their first pass, the minimal passing scores could then be raised in small increments and successive passes conducted through the screens until the desired number of ideas is achieved.

On the positive side, the Battelle method provides a relatively efficient means for systematically screening ideas. The involvement of the group in developing criteria for the screens also should increase group commitment to the final ideas selected. Finally, the use of weighted criteria in the scoring screens ensures that all criteria are not assumed to be of equal importance.

Electronic Voting

For groups that can afford it and like to jazz things up a little bit, electronic voting may be an attractive choice. However, it has no provision for discussing the value of potential solutions. Nonetheless, when time is short or the group has already spent time in evaluating ideas, electronic voting can be used quite appropriately. As used at the Battelle Institute in Frankfurt (Geschka, 1979; VanGundy, 1981), the major steps for this technique are:

1. Give each group member a seven- or nine-button console connected to a screen visible to all group members.
2. Instruct the group members to rate each idea by pushing the button that corresponds to the value they would place on the idea. For example, if there are seven buttons, the first button would be used to signify little or no value to the idea, while the seventh button would be used to signify a very high value (the remaining buttons would be used to rate ideas in between these two extremes).
3. Have the group look at the vote tallies for each idea displayed on the screen.
4. Ask the group members to examine the vote tallies and comment on any apparent inconsistencies. For instance, the group may note that an idea has been given a 7 by three members and a 1 by four members. In such cases, the inconsistency should be analyzed to help clarify why it occurred.
5. After discussing and clarifying all inconsistencies, have the group vote again and note the vote tallies that result. If no inconsistencies are observed with the second round of voting, terminate the process by selecting the highest-rated idea (or ideas); if inconsistencies are observed, repeat the procedure of clarifying and voting until no inconsistencies appear or a preestablished time limit has been reached.

The electronic voting method is very similar to the nominal group technique. However, electronic voting has three major advantages over NGT's voting procedure. First, votes can be tabulated almost instantaneously with electronic voting; considerable time can be consumed doing the same thing with NGT. Thus quick feedback is provided to the group members. Second, the speed with which voting is conducted and the results tabulated makes it possible to process a large number of ideas more efficiently. Finally, using a memory bank with electronic voting permits rapid retrieval of vote tallies should a future examination of the votes be required.

Idea Advocate

In contrast to electronic voting, the idea advocate method emphasizes evaluation over selection. The group carefully analyzes the positive aspects of each idea to ensure that no potential solutions are overlooked. The group then selects the ideas on the basis of the outcome of these analyses. Four steps are involved in using this method (Geschka, 1979; VanGundy, 1981):

1. Give each group member a list of previously generated ideas.
2. Assign each group member to play the role of advocate for one or more of the ideas. These assignments can be made according to whether or not a group member would be responsible for implementing an idea, was the original proposer of the idea, or simply has a strong preference for an idea.
3. Read the first idea aloud and have that idea's advocate discuss why it would be the best choice. Repeat this procedure for the remaining ideas.
4. When all the ideas have been discussed, have the group review the ideas and select the idea (or combination of ideas) that seems most capable of resolving the problem.

An obvious disadvantage of this technique is that it is not suitable for screening a large number of ideas. It will simply be too time-consuming for most groups to use for processing a large pool of ideas. The technique also may not work well if status differences exist within a group or if there are dominant personalities. Under such circumstances, all ideas are not likely to receive a fair hearing. Furthermore, the technique's focus on only the positive features of an idea may result in a distorted picture of an idea's value. If time permits, it may prove useful to incorporate some negative comments to provide a more balanced picture.

In spite of these disadvantages, the idea advocate technique can be appropriate when used in conjunction with more structured selection procedures. And it is especially appropriate when a large pool of ideas has been narrowed down to a more manageable number (e.g., no more than two or three ideas for each member of a group). When only a few ideas are dealt with, each one is more likely to receive a fair hearing and a more in-depth analysis (assuming, of course, that status differences among the group members are minimal or can be controlled and that dominant personalities are not a factor).

Matrix Weighting

In contrast to the advantage-disadvantage technique, which assumes all criteria are equal in weight, the matrix weighting technique uses criteria that have been weighted according to their relative importance. As a result, the quality of ideas selected is likely to be higher.

Matrix weighting is identical to the scoring screens used in the Battelle method. Only the basic format used in setting up the technique is different. The steps (VanGundy, 1981) are:

1. Construct a matrix table as shown in Figure 10-2. List the ideas down the left side of the matrix and the criteria across the top. (Note that in Figure 10-2, the evaluation and selection techniques are being used as examples of ideas to be weighed and evaluated.) In the row above the ideas column, include spaces for criterion weightings. Draw a diagonal line (as shown in the figure) within each square in the ideas rows.
2. Using a 7-point scale (with 1 being low importance and 7 being high importance), rate the importance of each criterion. Use the criterion weightings row to do this.
3. Using the same rating scale, rate each idea (independent of the others) against each criterion. For example, if an idea is seen as involving little time, it might be given a 7 (higher numbers should always indicate a more favorable rating).
4. Record the ratings for each idea in the upper portion of each box (as divided by the diagonal line).
5. Multiply the weighting for each criterion by the rating given to each idea on that criterion. Write the product in the lower portion of the box. For example, if a criterion of low cost was assigned a weighting of 5 and an idea was rated a 2 on this criterion, the product would be 10.
6. Add up the products (numbers below the diagonals in each box) for each idea and write the sum in the boxes in the total scores column.
7. Select the idea with the highest total score.

To illustrate this technique, the matrix weighting used in Figure 10-1 has been revised and is shown in Figure 10-2. In Figure 10-2, hypothetical criterion weightings have been added as well as the diagonals for the appropriate boxes.

Figure 10-2. Example of the matrix weighting technique.

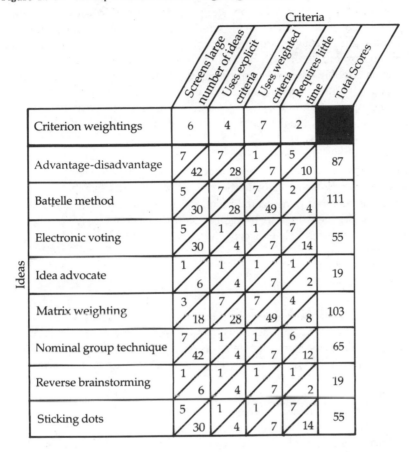

Ideas	Criteria — Screens large number of ideas	Uses explicit criteria	Uses weighted criteria	Requires little time	Total Scores
Criterion weightings	6	4	7	2	
Advantage-disadvantage	7 / 42	7 / 28	1 / 7	5 / 10	87
Battelle method	5 / 30	7 / 28	7 / 49	2 / 4	111
Electronic voting	5 / 30	1 / 4	1 / 7	7 / 14	55
Idea advocate	1 / 6	1 / 4	1 / 7	1 / 2	19
Matrix weighting	3 / 18	7 / 28	7 / 49	4 / 8	103
Nominal group technique	7 / 42	1 / 4	1 / 7	6 / 12	65
Reverse brainstorming	1 / 6	1 / 4	1 / 7	1 / 2	19
Sticking dots	5 / 30	1 / 4	1 / 7	7 / 14	55

For this example, screening a large number of ideas was viewed as important, using explicit criteria was seen as moderately important, using weighted criteria was perceived as very important, and the requirement for little time was rated low in importance. (Note that these ratings are hypothetical and could vary considerably depending on who is doing the ratings.) The criterion weightings are multiplied by the ratings given each technique and the products are summed. The Battelle method receives the highest total score and would be selected for use. However, the matrix weighting technique is a fairly close second and also might be selected.

There are several cautions to observe when using the matrix weighting procedure. First, it is a moderately time-consuming technique. It will be most useful after a large number of ideas have been preselected. Second, the idea receiving the highest score may not always "feel" right to the group members. In some cases, group members may express dissatisfaction with the highest-rated idea but be unable to provide a rationale. When this occurs, additional criteria might be sought and the process repeated, or the ratings themselves might be examind to see whether any changes should be made. Finally, disagreement may arise among the group members over the ratings to be used. When disagreement occurs and cannot be resolved within the time available, voting can be used and the averages used for the ratings. Or if you have the authority, you could make the final ratings after considering the preferences of the group members.

On the whole, the matrix weighting technique is a popular procedure with many groups because of its systematic way of processing ideas for selection. In addition, the discussions about the criteria and ratings can help to clarify each group member's understanding about the ideas and what is required to ensure development of a high-quality solution. Consequently, group members are often more likely to accept the idea selected and be committed to its implementation.

Nominal Group Technique

The steps involved in using NGT have already been discussed in Chapter 9. The voting procedure is described again here because it contains the steps that deal with the selection process. As described by Delbecq, Van de Ven, and Gustafson (1975), NGT uses the following steps to vote on ideas:

1. Discuss each idea in turn to clarify the logic and meaning behind it. During this time, make it clear to the group members that the purpose of this step is to clarify their understanding of ideas and not to debate the ideas' merits. In this regard, you should pace the discussion to avoid spending too much time on any one idea and to avoid heated debates.
2. Conduct a preliminary vote on the importance of each idea.
   a. Have each group member select a few of the best ideas out of the total. (The group leader should determine the number of ideas to be chosen—for example, 10 percent of the total. A number of ideas between five and nine usually works well.)
   b. Instruct the group members to write each idea on a separate 3" × 5" card and to record the number of the idea in the upper left-hand corner of the card.
   c. Have the group members silently read the ideas they have selected and rank them by assigning a 5 (assuming five ideas were selected) to the best idea, a 1 to the worst idea, and so forth, until all the ideas

have been ranked. The rankings for each idea should then be written in the lower right-hand corner of each card and underlined three times (to prevent confusion with the idea number).

d. Collect the cards, shuffle them, and construct a ballot sheet. Record the idea number in a column on the left side of the sheet, and record the rank numbers given to each idea next to the idea numbers. For example, if idea 1 was given rank votes of 5, 2, and 3, this would be recorded as: 1.   5-2-3.

e. Count the vote tallies and note which idea received the most votes (the highest total score).

f. Terminate the selection process if a clear preference has emerged. If no clear preference is evident, go on to the next step.

3. Discuss the results of the preliminary vote by examining inconsistencies and rediscussing ideas seen as receiving too many or too few votes. For instance, if an idea received four votes of 5 and three votes of 1, the meaning behind the idea might be discussed to see whether there were differences in how the idea was perceived. Emphasize that the purpose of this discussion is to clarify perceptions and not to persuade any members to alter their original votes.

4. Conduct a final vote using the procedures outlined for the preliminary vote (Step 2).

The idea-selection portion of the NGT procedure has major strengths in ensuring equality of participation and in eliminating status differences and the harmful effects of a dominant personality. The procedure also provides a highly efficient means for processing a large number of ideas. Furthermore, NGT voting concentrates disagreements on ideas instead of individuals.

On the minus side, NGT does not use explicit evaluation criteria. The rankings are produced by group members using their own criteria, which may or may not be shared by other group members. For this reason, the NGT voting procedure might be improved by asking group members to consider a general set of criteria that all will use in ranking their ideas. If this procedure is added, there may be fewer inconsistencies in the final vote tally and less need to repeatedly discuss ideas for clarification.

Reverse Brainstorming

The classical brainstorming technique described in Chapter 9 is designed to generate a large number of ideas. Reverse brainstorming is also concerned with generating ideas but not for solving a problem. Instead, the ideas are couched in terms of criticisms of previously generated ideas. Thus this technique uses a procedure opposite that of the idea advocate method: Negative rather than positive features of ideas are sought. As described by Whiting (1958), the major steps of reverse brainstorming are:

1. Give each group member a list of previously generated ideas (or write the ideas on a chalkboard or flip chart).
2. Ask the group members to raise their hands if they have a criticism of the first idea (or each member can be systematically given a chance to offer a criticism).
3. When all the criticisms for the first idea have been brought out, ask the group to criticize the second idea. Continue this activity until all the ideas have been criticized.
4. Instruct the group to develop possible solutions for overcoming the weaknesses of each idea.
5. Select the idea (or ideas) with the fewest weaknesses that cannot be overcome or circumvented.

As with the idea advocate method, reverse brainstorming can be extremely time-consuming if a large number of ideas are being processed. As a result, it is best to use it when the original idea pool has been narrowed down some. Perhaps the major weakness of this technique, however, is its emphasis on the negative. Stressing what is wrong with every idea may lead to development of a negative climate that is not conducive to creativity. Although a climate conducive to creativity is more important during idea generation, the lack of such a climate during evaluation can make it difficult for the group to combine or elaborate on ideas (in a positive manner) before making the final selection.

The major strengths of reverse brainstorming are the amount of discussion devoted to each idea and the provision for developing ways of overcoming idea weaknesses. While analyzing each idea, possible implementation obstacles may be suggested and dealt with, which can ensure more successful implementation. Looking at ways to overcome idea weaknesses may reduce the negative atmosphere that often develops in a group after it spends so much time criticizing the ideas. Furthermore, looking at ways to overcome weaknesses should also increase the probability of implementation success.

Although reverse brainstorming does have advantages, it probably could be used more effectively in combination with the idea advocate technique. This would provide a more balanced evaluation of each idea and not be as likely to result in a negative climate. Of course, the decision to add another technique has to be weighed against the increased amount of time that will be required.

Sticking Dots

This technique, described by Geschka (1980), is one of the simplest and most time-efficient voting methods available. Members each receive a fixed number of self-sticking paper dots with which they can indicate their idea preferences with minimal time and effort. The steps involved are:

1. Display a previously generated list of ideas on a flip chart or on cards attached to a bulletin board.
2. Give each group member a sheet of self-sticking colored dots. Each member should receive a different color, and the number of dots should equal about 10 percent of the ideas to be evaluated.
3. Ask the group members to vote for ideas by placing dots next to the ideas they prefer. They may allocate their dots in any way they wish. Thus all of one member's dots may be placed next to one idea, one dot may be placed next to one idea, half the dots may be placed on one idea and the other half on another idea, and so forth.
4. Count the votes received by each idea, and select the idea with the most votes.

In addition to the relatively small amount of time required to use this method is the advantage of the sense of equal participation that it affords the group members. Placing dots next to ideas is an activity in which all members have an opportunity to participate on an equal basis. Furthermore, should questions arise about the voting distribution, the color coding of the dots makes it relatively easy to ask people why they voted the way they did.

There are, however, several disadvantages associated with this technique. First, and perhaps most significant, the lack of anonymity may result in a certain degree of voting conformity. By seeing how the vote clusters develop, some members may feel pressured to vote in a similar manner. Second, no discussion is conducted on criteria to use in making voting decisions. Finally, there is no built-in mechanism for clarifying the meaning and logic underlying the ideas and for examining voting inconsistencies. This technique could be improved by giving all members dots of the same color, conducting a discussion on criteria to be used, and providing time to clarify ideas and examine inconsistencies in the voting patterns. However, the problem of voting conformity would remain.

Summary

Ideas must be evaluated before they can be selected. An important aspect of evaluation involves developing and selecting criteria for judging ideas. Most criteria used during the evaluation and selection process are implicit, explicit, or some combination of the two. Whenever possible, a group should attempt to use explicit criteria that are acknowledged and accepted by all group members. In doing so, the odds of selecting a high-quality solution will be increased.

Development of high-quality solutions and group member commitment to their implementation can be achieved best by following basic evaluation and selection guidelines. Examples of such guidelines are: (1) Assess participation needs—consider time available, problem importance, need for members to accept a solution, and need for members to benefit personally by their participation. (2) Agree on a procedure to use—avoid haphazard approaches to evaluation and selection. (3) Preselect ideas—reduce in size a large pool of ideas by combining some ideas, by grouping the ideas into logical categories, or by voting. (4) Develop and select evaluation criteria—deferring all judgment, generate as many criteria as possible and select those that are most relevant and important. (5) Select techniques—guide your choices by using explicit criteria and any previous experience acquired from using the techniques. (6) Evaluate and select ideas—select one or more ideas for possible implementation and reassess idea quality using subjective ratings or the product module.

Eight evaluation and selection techniques that can be used by groups are advantage-disadvantage, Battelle method, electronic voting, idea advocate, matrix weighting, nominal group technique, reverse brainstorming, and sticking dots. Of these techniques, electronic voting, the nominal group technique, and sticking dots are primarily voting procedures; idea advocate and reverse brainstorming are primarily evaluation procedures; and advantage-disadvantage, the Battelle method, and matrix weighting use explicit criteria to both evaluate and select ideas.

11
Implementing Ideas

Importance and Nature of Implementation

Next to redefining the problem, this last component of the process module is often the most critical. A high-quality idea that appears to have a high probability of resolving a problem will be of little value if it is not implemented properly. Although this statement may seem obvious, it is extremely important when you consider that it is only by taking action that a problem can be resolved. However, this action must be of the right type; an inappropriate action may magnify a problem—rendering the chosen solution obsolete—or it may create entirely new problems. The key to avoiding both of these outcomes is effective implementation planning.

However, there may be group resistance to taking the time to plan for implementation. Many groups become impatient and lazy after they have gone through the three preceding process module components. Having already devoted considerable time to dealing with a problem, group members often are eager to terminate all problem-solving activities once they have selected a final solution. In addition, they usually have exerted so much effort in the previous stages that they begin looking for easy ways to avoid further dealings with the problem. "Let's just get it over with" is frequently heard at this point in the process. Moreover, the amount of time left to deal with the problem may have been reduced, resulting in increased pressure to get the problem resolved. Consequently, the attitude often is to do something, but to leave out consideration of the consequences involved.

Although it may be normal for group members to experience such feelings, becoming impatient or looking for shortcuts at this stage could jeopardize the problem's resolution. Creative problem solving is a cumulative process, with each step building on the preceding one. If this is disregarded and the solution is not implemented properly, all previous efforts may have been in vain. As much planning and care should be devoted to implementation as were devoted to the previous stages. Remember Murphy's law: "If anything can go wrong, it will."

At its most basic level, implementation is a creative problem-solving process. A gap exists between what is and what should be, and actions are required to close this gap. In this case, the "what is" is the potential solution selected for resolving the focal problem and the "what should be" is the application of this solution to the focal problem. All the actions taken to apply the potential solution to the problem then constitute the implementation process.

From this perspective, a specific implementation task is a problem only if the original, focal problem is still perceived as a problem. Problems and our perceptions of them often change over time. While a group was working on the problem, the characteristics of the problem may have changed over time. As a result, the solution developed by the group may no longer be adequate. Or the original problem may have changed so much that it is no longer a problem. In either of these instances, implementation would not be a problem. If the original problem has changed or disappeared, there is no reason for a group to bother with implementation.

Although this may appear obvious, it does highlight the need for groups to check on their problem perceptions periodically. Such a check is especially important immediately prior to implementation; otherwise, considerable resources may be expended unnecessarily. If it appears that the problem has changed, the group must either redefine the problem or modify the solution before implementing it. The choice will depend on the extent to which the problem has changed. Nevertheless, deciding whether a solution should be implemented can be just as important as determining how it should be implemented; if the wrong decision is made, then the wrong problem may be solved. However, assuming that the original problem still exists and the chosen solution appears to be appropriate, the group can proceed with implementation.

Change and Implementation

One of the first considerations in implementing solutions is the general concept of change. Most people fear change. Or, at least, they view it with dislike and try to resist it. "Don't rock the boat" is an expression frequently heard when any type of change is proposed.

In organizations, the issue of change is especially complex because many parts of the organization are interrelated. A change introduced into one part may have a direct or indirect effect on one or more other parts. For example, if workers in department A have their jobs enriched in an attempt to increase their productivity and workers in department B do not have their jobs enriched, the change may backfire. Although the productivity of workers in department A may increase, the workers in department B may resent not being included and retaliate by lowering their productivity. The result might be a net loss in productivity.

Related considerations involved in implementing changes are the degree of employee involvement in the change, the extent to which employees are affected, the magnitude of the change, whether or not the change was requested, the amount of resistance to the change, and the effects of the change on employee attitudes. Because implementing ideas involves a change, either directly or indirectly, the group must be aware of all these considerations when planning for implementation.

If other people have a need to be involved in implementing an idea, they should be included in the planning process. Inclusion of others is especially important when they will be affected significantly by implementation of an idea. Broad changes that are likely to affect many people also will require input from others. Furthermore, involvement of others is necessary whenever a change is not requested, since unrequested changes are more likely to meet with resistance and have a negative impact on employee attitudes and morale.

To overcome resistance to change when implementing ideas, follow these general rules of thumb:

1. Involve other people in the entire problem-solving process, including implementation, whenever: (a) they have a need to be involved, (b) they will be affected directly by the idea, (c) the change is broad in scope, and (d) the change is not requested. Of course, not everyone affected by a change will want to be involved, and time or logistical considerations may not permit a great degree of involvement. Nevertheless, an attempt should be made to involve as many other people as needed.

2. Be as specific as possible about the amount and type of change likely to result from implementing an idea. Nothing is more likely to engender resistance than ambiguous messages about a change. Most people fear the unknown. Providing vague information about a change is a sure way to reduce the chances for successfully implementing an idea.

3. When planning for the implementation of a change-producing idea that will affect others, stress the personal benefits to be obtained if the idea is implemented. If people can see some personal gain from an idea, the path to implementation will be smoothed considerably.

4. Whenever possible, create shared perceptions within groups about the need for a change. If the need for a change develops from within a group, it is more likely to be supported.

5. Identify key opinion leaders within the larger organization and convince

them to support the change. It is much easier to convince a small number of individuals about the need for a change than it is to convince an entire organization. Once the opinion leaders are convinced of the need for a change, they can help convince others. These opinion leaders need not be in formal positions of authority, however. Change may receive broader support if informal leaders are perceived as supporting the change.

Implementation Guidelines

The change guidelines just discussed are general considerations involved in implementing ideas. Although they are useful by themselves, successful implementation requires a more specific approach. The implementation planning process is more likely to result in a resolved problem if a group uses more structuring than is provided by broad change principles.

Very often, an idea must be "sold" before it can be implemented. In highly centralized organizations, where lines of authority are drawn clearly, most new ideas must receive higher approval. In such organizations, all proposed changes must go through channels. And in order to move through the channels, an idea must be sold at each level. But not all ideas must be sold to an authority structure. In many cases, ideas must be sold laterally in an organization or to groups or individuals outside an organization. The process involved in selling ideas laterally or vertically is essentially the same. The only difference is the level at which the ideas must be sold.

The activities involved in selling an idea usually precede the actual implementation of the idea. Of course, not all ideas need to be sold. Depending on the degree of involvement in formulating an idea, the amount of trust placed in the idea formulators, and the perceived impact of the problem on others, an idea may encounter little opposition. However, not all ideas will be widely accepted, and steps will have to be taken to gain acceptance.

Gaining acceptance for an idea by attempting to sell it is just as important to implementation as applying a solution to a problem. If the necessary acceptance is not gained, the idea cannot be implemented and the problem will not be solved. Thus a group must devote some attention to developing a strategy for selling its ideas.

In general, such a strategy should go hand in hand with the overall implementation strategy. Because gaining acceptance of an idea is an integral part of implementation, the activities involved in selling an idea should flow together with those involved in applying the idea to the problem. If these activities do not flow together smoothly, the idea may not solve the problem.

Selling and implementing ideas are complementary activities that must be considered simultaneously.

In addition to the obvious need to sell an idea before it can be implemented, there are two reasons why selling an idea is important to implementation. First, the feedback that a group often receives while attempting to sell an idea can provide information relevant to implementation. People may offer many suggestions that the group can use to smooth an idea's implementation. Or someone to whom an idea is being sold may be able to provide resources to help ensure successful implementation. The second reason is the psychological support and commitment that often results from selling an idea. If an idea is sold, those who "bought" it will be more likely to support it through the rest of the implementation process. Just knowing that significant others support and are committed to an idea can help ease the task of those responsible for implementation.

The following implementation guidelines will help you and your group develop an overall strategy. If you decide that an idea does not need to be sold, you can omit the steps concerned with making an idea presentation.

1. *Develop and evaluate goal statements.* The first task of the group is to develop goal statements that accurately reflect the purposes of the implementation process. Although group members often assume that their implementation goals are understood by others, this is not always the case. Thus it is important that these goals be made explicit at the outset and be clearly understood by all group members.

These statements should be specific, clear, and realistic, and they should include a time schedule. Sweeping generalizations, ambiguous wording, unrealistic assessments of resources, and omitted time schedules should be avoided. For example, the following statement for selling an idea would not satisfy these criteria:

> To convince the board of directors that our piece-rate plan is the best and most inexpensive idea for improving worker productivity.

A better goal statement would be:

> By the end of this quarter, we will meet with the board of directors to gain approval for a piece-rate plan that is projected to increase worker productivity by 5 percent and to cost no more than $20,000 to implement.

Similarly, this statement for applying an idea would be inappropriate:

> To train workers to use personal computers.

A better statement of this goal would be:

> By March 15, workers in departments A and B will be trained to use personal computers to transmit production data to each other. The training will take place in conference room C from 9:00 A.M. to 4:00 P.M. every Friday between now and March 15.

Frequently, a group will need to make several attempts at developing these statements. When the group selects the final statements (one for idea selling, if needed, and one for applying the idea), it should evaluate them to ensure that they satisfy all the criteria. Furthermore, the leader should make certain that all group members clearly understand the statements.

2. *Assess your resources.* Implementation resources are the means used to accomplish the goal statements. Whatever is needed to sell an idea and apply it to a problem is a resource. Such things as information, time, people, and physical considerations are categories of resources that need to be assessed. The nature of these resources and the means for evaluating them have already been discussed in Chapter 5. No additional discussion will be presented here other than to note that the problem input analysis form in Figure 5-2 should be especially useful for assessing implementation resources.

3. *Assess the needs of the people to be influenced.* If an idea needs to be sold, the group should consider the needs of the people who must buy the idea before it develops a sales presentation. Most people will respond favorably to an idea if they believe that it will satisfy one or more of their basic needs. If you can determine what these needs are, you will increase the chances of getting your idea accepted.

Examples of needs you should consider are:

Power and control	Being liked
Security	Recognition
Affiliation	Impressing others
Personal growth and development	Being seen as creative or intelligent
Helping others	Task accomplishment and comple-
Freedom	tion
Dominance	Avoiding crisis situations

Of course, these needs are only representative of the many needs we all have. Take time to consider what other needs might be important to the person (or persons) you and your group want to influence.

Assessing these needs can be a difficult task, since it usually is not possible to administer a psychological test of needs. Even if you could administer such a test, you would still need to interpret it in a valid manner—a task that would require professional assistance. How, then, might you assess needs without administering a psychological test? The answer lies in your powers of observation. Although certainly not as valid and reliable as a scientifically tested instrument, observational data can provide some clues.

The first thing you should observe is how the decision maker behaves. What patterns of behavior seem to characterize this person over time? For example, in group meetings, is the decision maker the one doing most of the talking? Does he or she tend to discount the opinions of others? If so, this person may be exhibiting signs of a need to control or dominate others. Another thing to observe is how the decision maker behaves during stressful situations (e.g., crisis situations). During times of intense stress, primary motives are more likely to appear. Identify these motives and you may have another clue to the decision maker's needs. Two additional things to observe are personal possessions and hobbies. An individual's car, house, books, clothes, and other possessions can indicate the types of things he or she values. If the decision maker drives a 1967 Ford pickup truck, he or she is communicating values different from those of someone who drives the latest model Buick sedan. Hobbies can reveal needs in a somewhat similar manner. A person who spends a lot of free time collecting, categorizing, and organizing radio knobs, for example, is likely to value detail work and have an inquisitive mind. (The fact that the person collects something like radio knobs should also reveal something!)

A slightly different way to assess the needs of a decision maker is to consider that all people have problems they would like to solve. What problems of the decision maker could your idea solve? What problem gaps (between the "what is" and the "what should be") could your idea help close? If you can identify these problems and structure your idea presentation around some of them, you should find the decision maker highly receptive.

4. *Assess your implementation strengths and weaknesses.* You have strengths and weaknesses that can either help or hinder implementation of ideas. To implement an idea successfully, you first must acknowledge that you have strengths and weaknesses. Assuming that you have just strengths or just weaknesses can lead to self-defeating behavior. Once you acknowledge that you have both strengths and weaknesses, you must become aware of what they are. The only way you can have any measure of control over the implementation process is to acknowledge that some things about you will help and some things will hinder implementation. Identifying these things and assessing their contribution to implementation is the key to many successfully solved problems.

In group settings, the net effect of all the members' strengths and weaknesses must be evaluated. For example, if most members are proficient at planning and only one or two are proficient at carrying out plans, an imbalance may exist. However, if only one or two members are needed to carry out a plan, then there may actually be a functional balance, since the imbalance of strengths and weaknesses will not prevent successful implementation. Each group must determine whether specific imbalances will be helpful or harmful, functional or dysfunctional.

To assess a group's implementation strengths and weaknesses, you should first make a list of all activities that will need to be performed. Next, have each group member list which activity is a strength or a weakness that he or she possesses. Encourage the members to be realistic. Many people tend to overrate their strengths and weaknesses. As the leader, you will have to make the final determination. Finally, match people with activities based on their ability to perform those activities.

Although this approach may seem obvious, it is often overlooked because of other considerations. For example, group leaders often assign some tasks on the basis of favoritism or to repay a previous contribution made by a member. Assigning implementation tasks in this way will not only jeopardize implementaton, but will also create ill feelings among the other group members.

Of course, all this assumes that a group will be involved in implementation. Often, this will not be the case, either because there is not enough time or because the task simply does not require the efforts of more than one or two people. Selling an idea, for instance, is usually handled by the leader and possibly one or two others. In this regard, the leader and any others involved will need to assess their idea-selling strengths and weaknesses. Note that selling strengths and weaknesses may differ considerably from implementation strengths and weaknesses. As a result, separate assessments will need to be conducted for these two activities.

5. *Analyze idea benefits.* Assuming that an idea must be sold before it can be applied, you will need to make an analysis of its major benefits. Not only will such an analysis help produce a more convincing presentation, but also it will help the idea presenters in their understanding of the idea. This understanding can prompt suggestions for eventual implementation. In addition, while the group analyzes an idea's benefits, some last-minute modifications to improve the idea's quality may be suggested.

Analyzing benefits is a divergent process similar to generating ideas. The first step is to list all the major features of an idea while withholding all evaluation. Next, generate a list of benefits for each feature listed. The list of criteria used to select the idea may help the group in doing this. Then select the benefits most likely to persuade the decision maker of the idea's worth. If any idea modifications are suggested during this activity, decide whether you want to include them, and then reassess the idea's benefits.

As an illustration of benefit assessment, suppose that your idea for keeping drunk drivers off the highways involves mandatory installation of a breathalyzer in every car. The assessment might be set up as follows:

Features	Benefits
Compact size.	Takes up little space.
Few mechanical parts.	Requires little maintenance; unlikely to break down very often.
Ignition system hookup automatically prevents car from starting when driver's alcohol content exceeds legal limits.	Drunks cannot drive.
Alarm sounds when driver's alcohol content exceeds legal limit.	Police will be alerted.

6. *Prepare for the presentation.* If you must make a formal or informal presentation of your idea, you should spend some time preparing for it. Nothing can doom a proposed idea more quickly than a poorly conducted presentation (except, perhaps, a poor-quality idea). Thus any investment in preparation should result in high returns.

Some of the elements involved in preparing for a presentation are:

Time. Avoid Mondays and Fridays; try to schedule the presentation for midmorning or midafternoon, but not too close to the lunch hour.

Location. A pleasant, comfortable physical environment is best; if possible, try to use a location away from the regular work environment.

Length. Set a time limit and build the presentation around it; keep it as short as possible.

Presenter. Select the person with the best presentation skills; however, make sure that this person is not viewed unfavorably by the decision maker.

Support. If possible, cultivate advocates for your idea before the presentation. For presentations to a group, this would mean contacting the group members in advance; for presentations to one person, you could try to gain support from others who are close to this person.

Receptivity. Try to anticipate how receptive the decision maker is likely to be to your idea. If nothing else, you may be motivated by knowing you will be entering a hostile climate.

Funding. Obtain any funds needed for the presentation; review any funding required for your idea; develop alternative approaches to funding your idea.

Materials and equipment. Inventory all materials and equipment needed for the presentation; obtain missing materials and equipment.

Compromising. Decide which and how many features of your idea you would be willing to give up in order to gain acceptance. Or if you are willing to give up your idea, determine what other idea might be acceptable.

Data. If relevant, gather any data that might reinforce or support the value of your idea (e.g., testimonials, statistics, observations, experts).

7. *Conduct the presentation.* If you have done a thorough job of preparing, the presentation itself should be a relatively simple task. All you—or the chosen presenter—need to do now is to apply the insights you have gained from assessing your resources, strengths and weaknesses, the needs of the decision makers, the idea benefits, and the presentation considerations. However, the manner in which you apply these insights will determine how successful you will be. Part of what is involved is style and part is substance. That is, how you present your idea can be just as important as what you present.

Before you conduct your presentation, consider the following tips:

a. Try to adapt yourself to your audience. If your audience is highly analytical and skeptical, structure your proposal accordingly. If your audience is more intuitive and visually oriented, make sure that you use visual aids and emphasize wholes rather than parts.

b. Start on time. Failure to start on time may upset your audience unnecessarily and create negative attitudes at the outset. Being prompt won't help your presentation, but starting late will certainly hurt it.

c. Avoid memorizing your presentation. If you speak naturally (guided only by a memorized outline), you will seem knowledgeable and be much more convincing than if you deliver a memorized talk.

d. Be yourself. Never try to emulate someone else's presentation style. Instead, focus on your idea and worry about how it looks, not how you look.

e. At the outset, describe what you hope to accomplish and how you will do it. The more straightforward you are, the more credible your idea will appear.

f. Avoid clichés and jargon. Unless both you and your audience use clichés and jargon on a regular basis, avoid them. If you use them inappropriately, you may come across as being more concerned with impressing others than with selling your idea.

g. Keep loose. Try not to be overly serious, especially when referring to yourself. Use humor when appropriate, and stay open to all comments and questions.

h. Keep your eyes on your audience. If you don't maintain eye contact, your audience may think you have something to hide.

i. Avoid repetitious statements. Although you should restate your major points to get them across, try not to repeat yourself frequently. Don't linger too long in discussing any one point.

j. Try to avoid distracting mannerisms. Continually pulling at your shirt collar or other obvious mannerisms may shift attention from your idea to you.

k. Don't criticize competing ideas. Try to be objective and nonjudgmental. Both you and your idea will be seen as more credible if your presentation is balanced and fair.

l. Listen effectively. Try to understand the content and feeling of what is being said to you; practice using reflective feedback. For example, "As I understand it, you think that . . ."

m. Don't exaggerate. Never make unsubstantiated claims about the worth of your idea. Let the idea sell itself.

n. Respond directly to all questions. Be as specific as possible in your answers, and be sure you deal with every question you are asked. Avoid generalities or shifting the focus of a question. You don't want to appear to be evasive.

o. Try not to "oversell" your idea. Once it appears that you have been successful, conclude your presentation. Otherwise, it may appear that you are not very confident about your own idea.

p. Finish on time. End your presentation when you said you would. Finishing a couple of minutes over your allotted time is seldom a problem, especially if the audience shows a lot of interest. However, exceeding your time by very much is likely to upset the audience members, most of whom probably consider their time valuable.

8. *Develop an implementation strategy.* You and your group should have already thought out the basics of your implementation strategy, and you may have included them in your presentation. For some ideas, how they are to be implemented may be just as important to your audience as the nature of the ideas themselves. However, if you have not already developed an implementation strategy, now is the time to do it. Or if you have developed a sketchy outline of a strategy, it now should be filled in and developed. You must have a plan to guide implementation.

Most of the techniques described in the next section can be used for this purpose. However, the group leader will have an important decision to make on the way these techniques are used. Specifically, you will need to decide whether the other group members should be involved. If there is sufficient time, the acceptance of others is critical to effective implementation, and the others are likely to benefit either personally or professionally, you should involve the other group members. Of course, if these conditions do not exist, you must consider implementing the idea by yourself.

9. *Implement the idea.* The last step in the implementation process is to apply the idea to the problem. If the preparation and planning have been conducted thoroughly, the problem should be resolved with little difficulty. Of course, not all implementation obstacles can be anticipated, and the problem may not be resolved as expected. When this occurs, you may need to review the implementation process and devise new plans. Note, however, that one of the techniques to be described, potential problem analysis, can avert many implementation problems. Whenever possible, use this technique before using any of the other implementation methods.

Implementation Techniques

With the exception of potential problem analysis, the techniques described in this section represent variations of strategies that can be used to implement ideas. Some are more complex than others, but all are capable of providing the structuring needed for implementation activities.

In selecting from among these techniques, there is one major factor that must be considered: the complexity of the idea. When an idea has multiple facets (in terms of time and activities) that you must deal with, you will need to use more complex techniques. For these types of problems, PERT is most appropriate; for moderately complex ideas, flow charts are appropriate; and for relatively simple ideas, the five Ws and time/task analysis are appropriate (the appropriateness of the copy cat technique will depend on the particular method being copied).

Of course, the decision to use any of these methods also depends on the group's needs and preferences in addition to many other variables. For example, even though PERT should be used to implement a complex idea, there may not be sufficient time to do so. The group might have to use another technique instead. Or the group might decide to modify the way the procedure is used to reduce the amount of time required.

Potential Problem Analysis (PPA)

Originally developed by Kepner and Tregoe (1965) and later modified by Woods and Davies (1973), PPA serves as a bridge between implementation planning and actual implementation of an idea. In contrast to the other implementation techniques, PPA is designed specifically to anticipate possible implementation problems and develop countermeasures. As a result, you should use PPA before using any other implementation method. Based on earlier versions and with some modifications by me, the major steps for conducting a potential problem analysis are:

1. Develop a list of potential problems. Withhold all evaluation, and think of everything that could possibly prevent the idea from being implemented successfully.
2. Determine possible causes of each problem listed.
3. Using a 7-point scale, estimate the probability of occurrence and the seriousness of each cause (1 = low probability or seriousness; 7 = high probability or seriousness).
4. Multiply each probability rating by each seriousness rating, and record the products. These products are known as the probability-times-seriousness scores.
5. Develop preventive actions for each cause. Think of what could be done to eliminate or minimize the effect of each cause.
6. Using a 7-point scale, estimate the probability that a cause will be problematic after a preventive action is taken (1 = low probability; 7 = high probability). This estimate is known as the residual probability. For example, if the likelihood that a cause will occur is originally estimated to be a 6, taking a preventive action might reduce this likelihood to, say, a 2 (depending on the circumstances).
7. Multiply each probability-times-seriousness score (obtained in Step 4) by the corresponding residual probability rating, and record the products.
8. For each product obtained in Step 7, develop as many contingency plans as your time and resources permit.

Figure 11-1 illustrates how PPA might be applied. In this figure the idea being implemented involves conducting an in-house workshop on using the modular approach. For this idea, five potential problems have been identified and two possible causes have been listed for each problem. After all the ratings and preventive actions were determined, contingency plans were developed for the four highest scores in the PS × RP column. Of these plans, the most important ones appear to deal with the potential problem of the participants' losing interest.

The usefulness of PPA is exemplified best by the maxim: "An ounce of prevention is worth a pound of cure." The amount of resources consumed in the systematic anticipation of potential problems and development of countermeasures will be well justified if the idea is successfully implemented. For relatively important implementation tasks, the short-run costs of using

Figure 11-1. Using potential problem analysis (PPA) to anticipate problems with a workshop.

Problems/causes	P	S	PS	Preventive Actions	RP	PS × RP	Contingency Plans
A. Memo not understood:							
1. Written illegibly	1	7	7	Type memo	1	7	Have several people read the memo
2. Ambiguous wording	3	7	21	Have someone else read it	2	42	
B. Memo not received:							
1. Not mailed	1	7	7	Mail personally	1	7	
2. Got lost	2	7	14	Hand deliver	1	14	
C. Equipment not available:							
1. Already reserved	4	3	12	Reserve well in advance	2	24	
2. Costs too much	3	5	15	Lease equipment	1	15	
D. Location not available:							
1. Already reserved	3	5	15	Reserve well in advance	2	30	Reserve backup locations
2. Not large enough	2	6	12	Specify size needed in advance	1	12	
E. Participants lose interest:							
1. Boring lectures	7	7	49	Use visual aids	4	196	Use participant exercises
2. Material not relevant	4	7	28	Use relevant examples	2	56	Ask participants to check the relevancy of the material before the workshop

PPA will be offset, in most cases, by the long-run benefits. Another major advantage of PPA is that it can be used easily by both individuals and groups. Furthermore, the ratings can be obtained in groups quite efficiently by using averages whenever time is not available to achieve consensus.

A disadvantage of PPA is that it is not always possible to identify all the potential problems and likely causes. Leaving out just one major problem or cause could doom implementation success. As a result, considerable care must be used to generate as many potential problems and causes as possible. A second disadvantage of this method concerns the amount of time expended relative to problem importance. Spending time to do a PPA must be weighed against the costs of not solving the problem. If a group decides to use PPA, it will need to balance the amount of time spent against both the need to solve the problem and the likelihood of encountering major obstacles. It would make little sense to spend several days on an implementation task that involves a relatively unimportant problem and comparatively few major obstacles.

Copy Cat

If your idea is similar to one that has been implemented before by other groups or individuals, you can be a "copy cat." Instead of trying to reinvent the wheel, you can borrow someone else's implementation strategy. However, before you do this, make sure that the strategy you borrow will work with your idea. Even a relatively minor difference between your idea and another one could preclude using a borrowed strategy. Nonetheless, there will be many situations in which only a few modifications will be required, and thus considerable savings in time and effort will result.

Five Ws

In addition to being useful for redefining problems, the five Ws technique can be very useful for implementing ideas. For relatively simple implementation tasks, this method provides an efficient and orderly means for seeing that an idea is applied to a problem. (It can also be used quite easily in conjunction with other methods.) The major steps are:

1. Ask who, what, where, and when in regard to implementation tasks. For example, you might ask: Who will implement the idea? What will they do? Where will they implement the idea? And when will they implement the idea? Then answer each of these questions, being as specific as possible.
2. Ask why for each of the preceding questions and answer each question.

For example: Why should these people implement the idea? Why should they do what they are going to do? and so forth. (By asking why, you provide a rationale for each implementation action and ensure that no major activities are overlooked.

3. If asking why reveals any overlooked implementation activities, revise the implementation strategy.
4. Implement the idea.

Flow Charts

When a sequence of activities is required to implement an idea, flow charts can be used to guide the process. Similar to the diagrams computer programmers use to depict the operations needed to carry out a program, flow charts provide an efficient means for structuring implementation activities. The basic elements of a flow chart are activities, decision points, and arrows or activity indicators. Using these elements, a flow chart can be constructed as follows:

1. State the objectives to be achieved, including the desired end result.
2. Generate a list of all activities needed to implement the idea.
3. Put the activities in the order in which they must be performed.
4. Examine each activity and decide whether any questions must be asked before the next activity can be completed.
5. Write the first activity at the top of a sheet of paper and draw a box around it. Draw an arrow from this box to the next activity or decision point (draw a diamond shape around questions at decision points).
6. Continue listing each activity and decision point in sequence until the terminal activity has been reached.
7. Using the flow chart as a guide, implement the idea.

Examples of flow charts can be found in Chapter 4 in the figures used to illustrate the modular process. The best way to learn how to make flow charts is to practice using them. Always make a rough sketch first and don't be afraid to add your own modifications. For instance, many people find it helpful to add time estimates for each activity.

PERT

The PERT method (program evaluation and review technique) was developed by the military in the 1950s to facilitate development of a new missile project. It is a relatively complex implementation procedure and requires use of a computer for large projects. However, it can be adapted for smaller implementation projects and set up without any computer assistance.

The basic steps are similar to those used to construct flow charts, except that time estimates are an essential part of the PERT method. In addition, the terminology differs somewhat. With PERT, activities are work efforts that consume resources. Activities are represented by arrows. Those places where activities begin and end are known as events and are represented by circles. Dummies are activities of zero duration that consume zero resources and are used only to maintain the logic between events and activities. Dashed-line arrows are used to represent dummies.

To construct a relatively simple PERT network, use the following steps:

1. Define the implementation objectives, including an end product.
2. Generate a list of all activities needed to implement the idea. Whenever possible, list subactivities as well.
3. Put the activities in the order in which they must be performed, and assign numbers to them to indicate their order. If two or more activities need to be performed at the same time, assign each of these activities the same number.
4. Construct the basic PERT network by connecting the events and activities. Place event numbers in the event circles. Write activities above the arrows.
5. Review the network and make any modifications needed to ensure that the network is complete.
6. Estimate the amount of time needed to complete each activity (in hours, days, weeks, months, years) and write these estimates below each activity arrow.
7. Review the network as close as possible to the implementation target date (the time of the first event). Update the network if any new information has become available that requires changes.
8. Implement the idea, using the PERT network as a guide.

The actual construction of a PERT network should be guided by certain rules. The most important of these rules are:

1. A previous activity must be completed before a new event can begin.
2. Only a single event can be used to begin and end a network.
3. All activity arrows must be used to implement an idea.
4. Any two events can be connected with only one activity. When more than one activity connects two events, a dummy activity is required.
5. A previous event must occur before a new activity can begin.

A PERT network is presented in Figure 11-2 to illustrate how PERT might be applied to the workshop example used for PPA. The activities involved and their assigned event numbers are:

1. Develop the workshop.
2. Write a memo describing the workshop.
3. Send the memo to the participants.
4. Reserve required equipment.
4. Request snacks for breaks.
5. Conduct the workshop.
6. Evaluate the workshop.
7. Terminate the evaluation.

These event numbers and descriptions of the activities are shown in Figure 11-2. A time estimate (in minutes) for completing each activity can be found below each activity arrow. Because reserving equipment and requesting snacks are seen as activities to be performed at about the same time, a dummy activity has been included to preserve the network's logic.

Note that Figure 11-2 presents only a very elementary PERT network. Implementing ideas that require more precise time estimates and that are more complex than the one represented here involves using much more sophisticated networks. For example, there are a variety of methods for calculating time estimates for individual activities to increase the accuracy of the time estimate for the entire process. The reader interested in these more advanced PERT procedures should consult the numerous books available on this topic.

Time/Task Analysis

One of the simplest implementation techniques is time/task analysis (T/TA), also known as Gantt charts. Similar in purpose to PERT, T/TA is used by relating time requirements to implementation tasks and constructing a graph to depict the flow of events. The major steps for conducting a T/TA are:

1. List every task that must be completed to implement the idea. Be as specific as possible and try not to leave anything out—even relatively simple tasks may be critical for implementation success.
2. Estimate the amount of time available to implement the idea. Make this estimate as realistic and accurate as possible.
3. Determine how much time will be needed to complete each task.

Figure 11-2. Using PERT to implement a workshop.

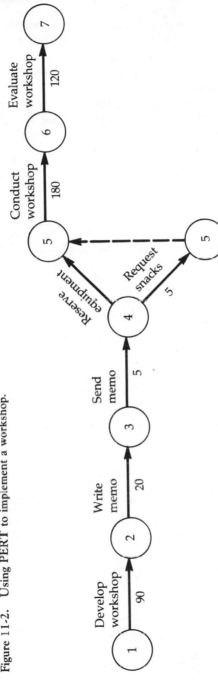

Again, try to be realistic and avoid underestimating the time required. Make sure that the time required for completing all the tasks does not exceed the total amount of time available. As a rough rule of thumb, remember that most tasks take longer to complete than people originally think they will.

4. Construct a graph showing the relationship between each task and its time estimate. Plot the tasks on the vertical axis and the time on the horizontal axis.
5. Implement the idea, using the T/TA as a guide.

Suppose, for example, that your idea involves recruiting minority personnel to fill various engineering positions in your company. To implement this idea, you could develop a chart such as the one shown in Figure 11-3. With this chart, it is easy to see which tasks overlap each other, which ones must be done after the previous one has been completed, and the relative amount of time required for each one.

Summary

The importance of implementation should not be underestimated. The best idea in the world will be of little use if it is not implemented properly. Consequently, groups should avoid any temptation to skimp on implementation and, instead, set aside time to develop an effective implementation strategy.

In its basic form, implementation is a creative problem-solving activity involving the attempted resolution of an ill-structured problem. However, any one implementation activity will be problematic only as long as the original problem is still perceived to be a problem. Problem perceptions change over time, and implementation may become unnecessary or inappropriate if the original problem disappears or changes. Thus never assume that an idea must be implemented just because it has been selected as a potential solution.

Many implementation efforts involve some elements of change. Because people often resist change, overcoming their resistance is a prerequisite to effective implementation. Tactics for overcoming resistance to change include involving people who are affected by a change, being as specific as possible about the nature of a proposed change, emphasizing personal benefits likely to be associated with a change, creating shared perceptions within groups about the need for a change, and identifying key opinion leaders within the larger organization and attempting to enlist their support for a change.

Figure 11-3. Using time/task analysis to select an engineering candidate.

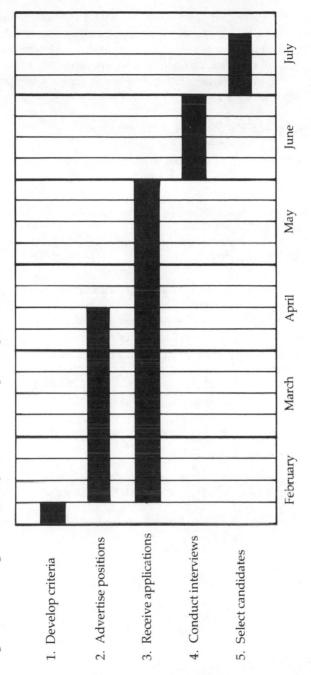

	February	March	April	May	June	July
1. Develop criteria						
2. Advertise positions						
3. Receive applications						
4. Conduct interviews						
5. Select candidates						

In many instances, an idea must be sold to others before it can be implemented. In the process of gaining acceptance for an idea, increasing support and commitment as well as suggestions on how to implement the idea are obtained, all of which can help implementation.

Some of the major guidelines for developing an implementation strategy and selling an idea are to:

1. Develop and evaluate goal statements.
2. Assess your resources.
3. Assess the needs of the people to be influenced.
4. Assess your implementation strengths and weaknesses.
5. Analyze idea benefits.
6. Prepare for the presentation.
7. Conduct the presentation.
8. Develop the implementation strategy.
9. Implement the idea.

Among the formal techniques available for implementing ideas are PPA, copy cat, five Ws, flow charts, PERT, and time/task analysis. Potential problem analysis differs from the other methods in that it is more appropriate for anticipating implementation obstacles and developing means for overcoming these obstacles. As a result, this technique should be used before any of the other techniques are used.

12

Product

Overview of the Product Module

Products are ideas that have been generated as potential solutions. As noted previously, these ideas can be judged according to their quality. A high-quality idea is one that has a high probability of resolving a problem; a low-quality idea has a low probability of resolving a problem.

Whenever a group judges an idea to be of high quality, it can skip the product module and proceed directly to implementation. However, if a group judges an idea to be of low quality, it should subject the idea to more analysis than was provided during idea evaluation and selection. Thus, if a group is dissatisfied with the idea selected, it should devote some time to upgrading it. (Of course, if additional time is not available, the group will have to go with the idea selected and forgo analysis of the product module.)

There are three other times to consider using the product module. The first is when the slightest doubt exists about the quality of an idea. Decisions about quality are not always of an either-or nature. Group members often question an idea's ability to resolve a problem. When this occurs, the group should use the product module if time permits. The second occurs when a group has difficulty achieving consensus during idea evaluation and selection. The analyses required during the product module frequently can clarify differences of opinion as well as lead to improvements in idea quality. The third is when it is a good idea to provide the group members with training and experience in product analysis. Even ideas judged to be of high quality can be used to provide this training and experience. In fact, using this module for a high-quality idea may reveal that the quality of the idea is not as high as originally thought. Moreover, practice with this module should strengthen the quality of future judgments made during idea evaluation and selection.

When you decide to use the product module, you should review the basic procedure involved with your group. The first step is to review the general criteria to be used in analyzing the idea. (These criteria are discussed in the next section.) If these criteria are not clearly understood by the group members, you should provide training to increase their understanding. The objective of this training is to ensure that every group member has a working knowledge of each criterion. Once the group understands the criteria, it should analyze the idea using the criteria. From this analysis, the group will determine that the idea either is satisfactory as it is or needs to be revised or modified. If the idea needs revising, the group should discuss possibilities and make changes using the criteria as guides (the discussion of the specific steps for doing this begins on p. 242).

When following this process, remember that the primary purpose of product analysis is to improve idea quality. Many ideas are solutions in the rough that require polishing to attain the brilliance needed to resolve a problem situation. If an idea's major strengths are not brought out or weaknesses compensated for through modifications, the odds of solving the problem will be diminished. Thus analysis of the product must be conducted with some care.

Conducting this analysis requires the use of general criteria that will correlate with idea quality. Although the criteria used during idea evaluation and selection serve as screens for idea quality, their primary purpose is to differentiate quality among a larger pool of ideas. That is, the quality of several ideas is compared to help the group select the one idea with the highest relative quality. Product analysis emphasizes another level of relative idea quality: the ability of an idea to solve a problem. It is possible that a selected idea may be high in quality relative to other ideas considered at the same time but not be high enough in quality to solve the problem. For this reason, product analysis applies broader criteria in an attempt to increase an idea's quality relative to the problem.

Description of Product Criteria

The use of broad idea criteria has been the subject of some controversy for many years. Such criteria as originality, novelty, and appropriateness are among those most often proposed. However, these criteria and others have never been systematically investigated. Furthermore, and perhaps most important, there is no universal set of agreed-upon criteria that can be applied broadly.

Some preliminary research has been conducted in an attempt to remedy this situation. In a seminal article, Besemer and Treffinger (1981) reviewed 125 criteria, which they grouped into 14 general categories. They then organized these categories into three broad dimensions of novelty, resolution, and elaboration and synthesis. The novelty dimension includes the criteria: germinal, original, and transformational. Resolution includes five criteria: adequate, appropriate, logical, useful, and valuable. Elaboration and synthesis, the third dimension, contains six criteria: attractive, complex, elegant, expressive, organic, and well crafted. Although not empirically derived, these dimensions provide a useful framework for making rough estimates of product quality.

Novelty

A novel idea is one that represents newness inside and outside a field. Part of the concept of novelty is an idea's potential influence on the generation of future ideas.

The germinal qualities of an idea refer to its ability to stimulate different uses and prompt development of future ideas.

Originality refers to the infrequency with which an idea occurs among the ideas produced by people in similar fields. For example, if a production manager generates an idea not commonly produced by other production managers, the idea would be rated high in originality—even if the idea would be found commonly among people in other fields.

Transformational refers to the potential of an idea to lead to a new way of looking at things, an ability to produce fresh perspectives. To be transformational, an idea must be capable of causing a shift in the way people have typically viewed resolution of a problem situation. Minor modifications of previous ideas would not qualify as being transformational. The invention of the printing press is a transformational idea; the invention of a slightly modified printing press, however, would not be transformational.

Resolution

The criteria in this dimension are all similar in that they pertain to the ability of an idea to satisfy the requirements of a problem situation. An idea possesses the general quality of resolution if it appears capable of doing what it is supposed to do.

The first resolution criterion is adequacy—the extent to which an idea satisfies the minimum number of problem requirements. In general, the adequacy of an idea is relative, since it will vary with such factors as problem difficulty, problem complexity, and the success rate of previously attempted solutions. Thus an idea may be adequate for one problem situation but not for another.

The second resolution criterion is appropriateness, which refers to the suitability of an idea for solving a problem. If an idea appears to "fit" a problem, it would be rated high in appropriateness. In contrast to adequacy, which deals with how well an idea fits a problem, an idea needs only to fit a problem to be appropriate.

The degree to which an idea is logical is the third resolution criterion. To be logical, an idea should be consistent with accepted facts and appear to follow the "rules of the game." However, being logical is not sufficient for an idea to merit a rating as creative. A logical idea must also possess a quality of newness to set it apart from other logical ideas.

Usefulness, the fourth resolution criterion, refers to the extent that an idea has clear implications for some practical application. What is practical, of course, may be a matter of opinion. A work of art, for example, might not be judged to be practical by some people. Nevertheless, as long as a case can be made for some type of usefulness, an idea should be rated high on this dimension. Thus, if a work of art is judged to have social or aesthetic usefulness, it should be rated high in practicality.

The last resolution criterion is value—the worth of an idea for fulfilling a particular need. This is one of the most subjective criteria, because an idea's value can be open to considerable variance in interpretation. When a group judges an idea's value, it is important that it do the judging in relation to a specific context and specific factors. For example, an idea's effect on employee satisfaction should be viewed in terms of specific aspects of satisfaction, such as satisfaction with pay or working conditions. Moreover, other factors such as long-term versus short-term satisfaction and supervisor versus nonsupervisor satisfaction need to be considered.

Elaboration and Synthesis

This dimension includes criteria that pertain to style. The six criteria in this category reflect aesthetic idea qualities. In judging ideas on elaboration and synthesis, note that the high degree of subjectivity involved requires the existence of a common language between the creator and the judges. If a group judges its own ideas on this dimension, there should be no problem in this regard. However, if the group members do not possess the expertise needed, expert judgments should be sought.

The first criterion in this dimension is attractiveness. An idea that commands attention by its appearance or brings out feelings of surprise, enjoyment, or humor would be rated high in attractiveness.

The second criterion, complexity, is the extent to which an idea contains many different elements, all of which might exist at different levels. For instance, an idea might be viewed as complex at the technical or ideational level. A painting, for example, might be viewed as high in ideational complexity but low in technical complexity.

To the extent that an idea can be expressed in a refined and understated manner, it will be rated high in elegance—the third criterion. Using the simple to represent the complex in an economical way would indicate an elegant idea.

The fourth criterion in this dimension is expressiveness. If an idea has been communicated in an understandable way, it is expressive. To have meaning to people other than the creators, an idea must be expressed in a manner that can be understood clearly by an interested observer; otherwise, the idea will be of little value to anyone except its creators.

The organic aspects of an idea make up the fifth criterion. An idea is organic if it conveys a sense of completeness or wholeness. An idea that appears to "hang together" with a quality of comprehensiveness and organizational unity will be judged high on this criterion.

The sixth and last criterion in the resolution and synthesis dimension pertains to the extent that an idea is well crafted. Ideas that are high on this criterion give the appearance of having been polished and reworked to obtain their greatest potential. If it is apparent that considerable effort and care have gone into a creative product, it should be judged as well crafted.

These 14 criteria provide a comprehensive framework for evaluating creative products. The breadth of the criteria represented makes it possible for a group to consider a wide range of elements in evaluating an idea. Moreover, this breadth allows evaluators to analyze many different types of ideas. Thus there is no need to develop a new set of criteria for each idea.

However, note again that these broad criteria should be used only for a final analysis of idea quality. Although a group might find many or all of these criteria useful when selecting from among the initial pool of ideas, it is important that the criteria used for that purpose pertain specifically to the particular problem at hand. Using only broad criteria for initial idea selection reduces the likelihood of the group's making fine discriminations among the ideas. If possible, save most of the broad criteria for product analysis.

Assessing Idea Quality*

Once group members have a rough understanding of the broad product criteria, they can apply their understanding by assessing an idea's quality. Although a group could conduct this assessment by discussing each criterion in relation to the idea, it can make a higher-quality assessment by using a more systematic procedure. In particular, if the group uses a quantifiable instrument, assessment should proceed more smoothly.

* This section was written in collaboration with Susan P. Besemer.

To date, no scientifically validated instrument exists for assessing ideas using the 14 product criteria. However, Besemer (1983) has recently developed an unvalidated checklist, similar to the type used to evaluate creativity in people. This instrument, the CPAM Adjective Checklist (CPAM stands for creative product analysis matrix), has the potential to provide a relatively quick and easy indication of product quality.

No data exist to verify that this instrument actually measures product quality. In addition, no data exist supporting this instrument's ability to produce consistent results among different judges or across different products. It is merely a gross indicator of the way that evaluators feel about the product being evaluated. You will have to consider this instrument on its face value and not on its scientific value. Thus considerable caution should be used in interpreting the results.

Nonetheless, if you and your group use this checklist to evaluate ideas against each criterion, the evaluation process should proceed more efficiently. It is also more likely that each criterion will receive equal consideration. As a result, your final evaluation of an idea's quality should be more accurate than it might be from utilizing a more unstructured discussion. Furthermore, specific adjectives will help the group to stay focused on the evaluation task and, in most cases, will lead to greater satisfaction with the outcome.

To use the CPAM Adjective Checklist in Figure 12-1, first have each group member individually evaluate the idea and compute a total score. Then have the group members discuss the evaluations, paying particular attention to why they evaluated the idea the way they did. Finally, the group should try to develop a group evaluation based on consensus. Avoid averaging individual scores unless there is little time available.

Figure   12-1. CPAM Adjective Checklist.

Instructions: Quickly read over all the adjectives listed. Next, read through the list more slowly and place a checkmark beside each adjective that seems to describe the product being evaluated. Do not spend too much time thinking about any one adjective. Because the adjectives are designed to apply to a wide range of product types, many of the adjectives will not be appropriate for the product you are evaluating. Check only as many adjectives as seem to be appropriate to you in describing this product. Then, review all the adjectives you have checked and select the 20 that seem to best describe the product. Once you have selected the list of 20 adjectives, you will be ready to score the product.

__Adequate	__Effective	__Messy	__Startling
__Amazing	__Elegant	__Murky	__Subtle
__Appropriate	__Facile	__Novel	__Surprising
__Attractive	__Feasible	__Obvious	__Transparent
__Balanced	__Flimsy	__Old hat	__Unattractive
__Banal	__Fluent	__Operable	__Unbalanced
__Beautiful	__Functional	__Ordinary	__Unclear
__Boring	__Garbled	__Organic	__Unfeasible
__Busy	__Goes nowhere	__Original	__Unfocused
__Careful	__Harmonious	__Out of kilter	__Unified
__Charming	__Humorous	__Overused	__Unimaginative
__Clashing	__Illogical	__Pedantic	__Unimportant
__Clear	__Inadequate	__Plain	__Uninteresting
__Coarse	__Inappropriate	__Playful	__Unique
__Commonplace	__Incomplete	__Predictable	__Unusual
__Complete	__Incorrect	__Radical	__Unworkable
__Complicated	__Ineffective	__Redundant	__Usable
__Confused	__Inept	__Refined	__Useful
__Correct	__Influential	__Relevant	__Useless
__Crude	__Ingenious	__Restful	__Usual
__Deep	__Inoperable	__Revolutionary	__Valuable
__Deft	__Interesting	__Rough	__Warmed-over
__Deliberate	__Irrelevant	__Seminal	__Well-made
__Delightful	__Just right	__Senseless	__Well-crafted
__Disjointed	__Labored	__Shallow	__Workable
__Dull	__Limited	__Simple	__Worthless
__Durable	__Logical	__Sloppy	
__Economical	__Makes sense	__Spontaneous	

Scoring and Interpretation: The group members can calculate separate scores for the three dimensions by consulting the scoring values shown in Table 12-1 (Novelty), Table 12-2 (Resolution), and Table 12-3 (Elaboration and Synthesis). Simply add up the values within each dimension that apply to the 20 adjectives you checked. (Hint: Add up positive values first and then subtract the sum of the negative values from this figure.) These three totals will represent the product quality scores for each dimension. A total score can be computed by adding together the scores for each of the three dimensions.

According to Besemer (1983), a combined score of zero can be considered average, with possible scores ranging from −50 to +50. Any product that receives a score greater than zero can be considered to be above average in product quality; a score of 10 or more indicates a promising product that might benefit from improving some of its elements; a score of 20 or above suggests a quite good product requiring only a little refinement; and a score of 30 or more indicates a superior product that requires very few adjustments. Any scores below zero indicate that the product is low in quality and that major adjustments are needed.

Table 12-1. Scoring values for novelty adjectives.

Amazing	3	Overused	−3
Banal	−3	Predictable	−3
Commonplace	−3	Radical	3
Influential	3	Revolutionary	3
Ingenious	3	Seminal	3
Limited	−3	Unimaginative	−3
Novel	3	Unique	3
Old hat	−3	Unusual	3
Ordinary	−3	Usual	−3
Original	3	Warmed-over	−3

Table 12-2. Scoring values for resolution adjectives.

Adequate	2	Irrelevant	−2
Appropriate	2	Logical	2
Correct	2	Makes sense	2
Durable	2	Operable	2
Effective	2	Relevant	2
Feasible	2	Senseless	−2
Flimsy	−2	Unfeasible	−2
Functional	2	Unimportant	−2
Illogical	−2	Unworkable	−2
Inadequate	−2	Usable	2
Inappropriate	−2	Useful	2
Incomplete	−2	Useless	−2
Incorrect	−2	Valuable	2
Ineffective	−2	Workable	2
Inoperable	−2	Worthless	−2

To illustrate this procedure, suppose that you checked the following 20 adjectives while evaluating a proposal for using a team approach to increase sales performance:

1. Attractive	11. Limited
2. Balanced	12. Makes sense
3. Correct	13. Murky
4. Deft	14. Novel
5. Feasible	15. Radical
6. Functional	16. Rough
7. Harmonious	17. Simple
8. Inadequate	18. Unique
9. Incomplete	19. Usable
10. Ineffective	20. Valuable

Table 12-3. Scoring values for elaboration and synthesis adjectives.

Attractive	1	Economical	1	Redundant	1
Balanced	1	Elegant	1	Refined	1
Beautiful	1	Facile	1	Restful	1
Boring	−1	Fluent	1	Rough	−1
Busy	−1	Garbled	−1	Shallow	−1
Careful	1	Goes nowhere	−1	Simple	1
Charming	1	Harmonious	1	Sloppy	−1
Clashing	−1	Humorous	1	Spontaneous	1
Clear	1	Inept	−1	Startling	1
Coarse	−1	Interesting	1	Subtle	1
Complete	1	Just right	1	Surprising	1
Complicated	−1	Labored	−1	Transparent	−1
Confused	−1	Messy	−1	Unattractive	−1
Crude	−1	Murky	−1	Unbalanced	−1
Deep	1	Obvious	−1	Unclear	−1
Deft	1	Organic	1	Unfocused	−1
Deliberate	1	Out of kilter	−1	Unified	1
Delightful	1	Pedantic	−1	Uninteresting	−1
Disjointed	−1	Plain	−1	Well-made	1
Dull	−1	Playful	1	Well-crafted	1

The novelty score for these adjectives would be +6 (from Table 12-1), the resolution score would be +6 (from Table 12-2), and the elaboration and synthesis score would be +3 (from Table 12-3). Added together, the total score for this proposal is +15.

In this illustration, the proposal could be rated above average in product quality (based on the total score of +15). This product was rated moderately low on novelty and resolution and low on elaboration and synthesis. Major refinements for this idea should be focused on elaboration and synthesis, followed by resolution and then novelty.

In reviewing the adjectives that were scored negatively in evaluating this product, "murky" and "rough" apply to the elaboration and synthesis dimension; "inadequate," "incomplete," and "ineffective" apply to resolution; and "limited" applies to novelty. From these adjectives, it appears that this idea lacks too many details to be considered for immediate implementation. Instead, the idea probably should be taken back to the drawing board so that more specific features can be added. For example, specific sales areas or functions of the team members might be added to the idea to improve its quality.

Although this approach to increasing idea quality may be all that is needed, there may be occasions where a more elaborate approach will be needed. For instance, an idea may be evaluated as being below average in quality or the need for a high-quality idea may be extremely important. In both cases, the group may want to rework the idea. Some suggestions for doing this are described in the next section.

Using Product Criteria to Increase Idea Quality

Before deciding to try to increase an idea's quality by using the CPAM Adjective checklist, the group should consider three alternative actions: Accept the idea as it is, and implement it as originally planned. Reject the idea, and select another one to evaluate for quality through the use of the CPAM checklist. Or attempt to modify the idea without using the CPAM checklist. Selection of the first alternative is usually due to a severe time constraint. There simply may not be enough time to alter the idea, and the group will have to trust its luck and hope that the idea can have some positive effect on the problem. If the group selects the second alternative of evaluating another idea, adequate time will be needed to conduct a second evaluation. Selection of the third alternative represents a compromise that should be undertaken only if there is not enough time available to use the CPAM checklist, but there is enough time to perform a cursory evaluation.

If the group decides to attempt to increase the idea's quality, it must be aware that such attempts are not always successful or easy. The process of transforming an idea into a workable solution can involve many subtle actions that are not easily determined or carried out. Furthermore, knowing how to change an idea can be just as important as knowing what to change. The group must take care to ensure that the quality is not reduced as a result of its attempt to increase it.

Using the product criteria (more specifically, the adjectives from the CPAM Adjective Checklist) can help increase the likelihood that quality will not be affected adversely as a result of the transformational process. By looking at specific aspects of quality that need improving, the group can conduct a more systematic transformation. Furthermore, the group is more likely to be satisfied with the process if it uses explicit criteria to guide and structure it.

To use the adjectives to increase an idea's quality rating, the following procedure is suggested:

1. Review the criteria and check for understanding.
2. Classify the idea as below or above average in quality. If the idea is classified as below average, consider the alternatives discussed earlier; if the idea is classified as above average, proceed to the next step.
3. Identify the adjectives that received negative values within each dimension.

4. Using the dimension with the lowest subtotal score, select adjectives to use in upgrading the idea's quality. Try to select only those adjectives with the highest potential and feasibility for upgrading idea quality.
5. Decide on the approach to be used. Two possible approaches are:
   a. Have the group brainstorm or brainwrite ways to increase quality, using each adjective selected.
   b. Use a modified creative problem-solving process, with such stages as fact finding, problem finding, idea finding, solution finding, and acceptance finding. For example, develop a problem statement such as, "In what ways might we increase the originality of this idea?" Now use the five Ws method to gather information about an adjective (in relation to the idea), develop possible redefinitions, select a redefinition, generate ways of solving the problem redefinition selected, choose the best idea, and develop ways to integrate it with the original idea.
6. If time permits, select adjectives from the next highest-rated dimension and repeat Step 5.
7. After attempting to upgrade as many criteria as possible, use the CPAM Adjective Checklist to reassess the idea's quality. This assessment will help you determine how successful your upgrading efforts have been. However, caution the group members to be as objective as possible in conducting this reassessment. Being involved in an extensive revision of an idea can lead to bias due to a certain amount of ownership that often accompanies this process.

As an illustration of increasing idea quality, consider the problem, "In what ways might the personnel department save money interviewing job applicants?" For this problem, an idea might be selected that involves having each department manager conduct interviews. This idea might save money in the personnel department by reducing the time needed to interview applicants and also by making it possible to reduce the number of interviewers needed in the personnel department.

After using the checklist to judge the quality of this idea, the adjective "inappropriate" might be selected for use in the revision process. A group might then decide to use the problem-solving stages of fact finding, problem finding, and idea finding to increase the appropriateness of this idea. The problem in this case would be "In what ways might we increase the appropriateness of this idea?"

For the fact-finding stage, the five Ws method could be used as follows:

Who will view this idea as appropriate? Department managers, staff in the personnel office, and job applicants.
What is appropriate about this idea? It saves time, cuts costs, enables

applicants to view the actual job setting, and will involve more people in the interviewing process, which would give those people insight into the problems faced by personnel staff.

Where will this idea be appropriate? Where skill requirements can be judged best by department managers and where department managers possess basic interviewing skills and some knowledge of personnel administration.

When will this idea be appropriate? When costs exceed the benefits likely to be derived from having the personnel department do all the interviewing (e.g., when there are large numbers of applicants and not enough time or staff to interview them).

Why is this idea inappropriate? Managers may not possess the interviewing skills that are needed, and managers will need to devote time to interviewing that they would normally be able to spend on their other activities.

On the basis of the responses to the fact-finding questions, redefinitions might be developed during the problem-finding stage. Five possible redefinitions in this case might be:

1. IWWM (In what ways might) time be saved doing interviews?
2. IWWM more people be involved in the personnel function?
3. IWWM the benefits of this idea be accepted by more people?
4. IWWM department managers acquire interviewing skills?
5. IWWM department managers use their time more efficiently?

The group members should select the redefinition that best captures their needs in relation to the idea's appropriateness. In this instance, we will assume that the group has selected the fourth redefinition.

Using the fourth redefinition—"IWWM department managers acquire interviewing skills?"—the next step is to begin idea finding. For this stage, a variety of techniques can be used. However, assume that brainstorming is selected and produces some of the following ideas:

1. Conduct formal or informal training programs.
2. Use role playing.
3. Collect video and audio tape recordings of managers conducting interviews, and discuss the outcomes with the managers, providing them with feedback.
4. Use case studies.
5. Have managers observe skilled interviewers conduct job interviews
6. Use combinations of the preceding ideas.

These ideas are then used to increase the appropriateness of the original idea of having department managers (instead of the personnel department) conduct interviews. In this case, implementation of the idea is contingent on the department managers' receiving training in conducting interviews. Inclusion of a training component should enhance the overall quality of the idea. If the group gives the same amount of attention to other adjectives with negative ratings, the cumulative effect on quality should be considerable.

Summary

The product module is concerned with increasing the quality of the ideas (products) selected for implementation. Because many ideas will be judged to be of high quality at the time they are selected, this module may not be required. However, if there is any doubt about an idea's quality and time is available, this module should be used. Other times when this module would be appropriate are: when groups experience difficulty achieving consensus on quality and when group members might benefit from the experience of using the module.

Using the product module involves the following general steps: (1) Review the criteria to be used in analyzing the idea. (2) Provide training to increase understanding of the criteria, if necessary. (3) Analyze the idea, using the criteria. (4) Decide whether the idea should be revised or modified to increase its quality. And (5) modify the idea, if necessary.

Most ideas are selected through the use of criteria related directly to the problem, rather than through the use of broad criteria. Moreover, the ideas usually are selected on the basis of their quality relative to the other ideas under consideration. As a result, the overall quality of the final idea selected may not be as high as desired. Using broad criteria for the specific purpose of increasing quality can help a group to transform an idea into a more workable solution.

On the basis of some preliminary research on product criteria, three dimensions containing 14 criteria have been identified. These dimensions (and their respective criteria) are: (1) novelty (germinal, original, transformational), (2) resolution (adequate, appropriate, logical, useful, valuable), and (3) elaboration and synthesis (attractive, complex, elegant, expressive, organic, well crafted).

With these criteria, it is possible to analyze a wide range of creative products. Using the CPAM Adjective Checklist as a guide, a group score can be obtained (using consensus) to help determine which aspects (criteria) of an idea should receive attention. In general, ideas that receive below-average ratings on the dimensions should be considered prime candidates for increasing quality.

The steps involved in increasing an idea's quality are:

1. Review the criteria and check for understanding.
2. Classify the idea as below or above average in quality.
3. Identify adjectives receiving negative values.
4. Select adjectives with the highest potential for increasing idea quality.
5. Use either brainstorming or a modified creative problem-solving process to increase idea quality.
6. Use the CPAM Adjective Checklist to reevaluate idea quality.

13

Outcomes

Nature and Types of Outcomes

Outcomes are results or consequences of previous actions or events. Whenever an action or event stimulates the development of subsequent actions or events, an outcome will be the product. What causes an action or event to result in an outcome is as unpredictable as the nature of the outcome itself. Depending on the type of action or event, the timing involved, the people involved, and a variety of situational and environmental factors, any one action or event could lead to a number of different types of outcomes.

With respect to the concepts of general systems theory, an outcome can occur whenever awareness exists about a product. According to general systems theory, changes in a subsystem of a larger system can produce changes in one or more other subsystems. Because many of the subsystems within a larger system are interdependent, the products of a subsystem may lead to outcomes within other subsystems—if awareness exists about the products. If the members of a subsystem do not notice a product from another subsystem, outcomes may not develop.

Outcomes can also occur within subsystems (e.g., groups). In a group, the products produced may lead to both internal and external outcomes. For example, if a group in a service-oriented company produced a solution for processing client claims more efficiently, many types of internal and external outcomes might result. To give just two examples, group members may be satisfied or dissatisfied with the solution (an internal outcome), and clients may receive faster or slower service when submitting their claims (an external outcome).

Outcomes can also have a generative effect. Outcomes resulting from one product can generate other outcomes, which, in turn, can generate other outcomes, and so forth. In the example of processing claims, a change in the rate of service was one possible outcome. Once such a change is perceived,

247

another outcome might be produced, such as satisfaction with the change. A slower rate might lead to dissatisfaction with the outcome, while a faster rate might produce satisfaction. Satisfaction or dissatisfaction might then lead to other outcomes, such as a reduction or an increase in the number of claims filed or a change to another claims-servicing agency.

With regard to group creative problem solving, two basic types of outcomes will be dealt with, both of which are internal to groups. These two types of outcomes are outcomes pertaining to the problem and outcomes affecting group member satisfaction and group development.

Outcomes pertaining to the problem refer to any effect—whether intended or unintended—that an implemented idea has on a problem. Once a solution has been implemented, it may affect the problem in a variety of ways. If everything goes according to plan, the primary effect will be positive and the problem will be resolved. However, an applied solution often results in unintended outcomes that can produce additional problems. These additional problems might affect resolution of the original problem, or they might have no effect. If the original problem is affected, resources may have to be diverted to deal with these problems, and depending on how much urgency is involved, the original problem may be only partially resolved.

The second category of outcomes pertains to effects on group member satisfaction and group development. In most cases, these outcomes are not considered by groups—especially groups with a high task orientation. With pressure to "get the job done" and solve the problem, many groups simply do not have the time or motivation to weigh the effects of the problem-solving process on such people-oriented issues as satisfaction and group development. Furthermore, such outcomes usually are more subtle and difficult to pinpoint than are outcomes that pertain directly to the problem.

In general, satisfaction outcomes involve perceptions about the adequacy of the process used and the degree of satisfaction with the resolution of the problem. Group development outcomes pertain to perceptions about the group's progress in such areas as interpersonal trust, support, communication, and conflict resolution. Satisfaction and group development outcomes are interrelated, with one capable of influencing the other.

Importance of Outcomes

The importance of outcomes pertaining to the problem should be evident. The resolution of a problem cannot be determined unless the effect of a solution can be observed. Without such observations, a problem will continue to be a problem, whether the outcome is negative or positive.

In the claims-processing example cited earlier, inefficiency will continue as a problem until the effect of the solution can be determined. If a negative outcome is observed, the problem will still exist; if a positive outcome is observed, the problem will no longer exist—at least not in its original state. However, complete lack of knowledge about outcomes deprives a group of the feedback needed to make adjustments or to terminate the problem-solving process. Thus it is easy to make a case for the importance of outcomes pertaining to a problem's resolution.

The case for outcomes related to intrapersonal and interpersonal aspects of group functioning is a little more difficult to make. Nevertheless, this category of outcomes shares equal importance with problem resolution outcomes. Very often, the extent to which a problem is resolved depends on the level of group member satisfaction and group development. As discussed in earlier chapters, the task and the interpersonal elements of group problem solving go hand in hand. One cannot be dealt with adequately unless the other one also is considered.

In the short run, group member satisfaction and growth and development are important because of their contribution to problem resolution. The human relations aspects of a group represent resources needed to accomplish a task. If a group overlooks these resources, task accomplishment will be much more difficult. Consequently, a group's failure to analyze the contribution made by these resources is likely to result in decreased problem-solving effectiveness.

Perhaps more important, however, are the long-run consequences of group member satisfaction and growth and development. Over time, most groups with a stable membership are transformed interpersonally in addition to gaining increased skill in using the problem-solving process. Through their interaction over time, group members learn about working together and how this ability to work together affects their satisfaction and their ability to grow and develop as a group. Being aware of the current state of satisfaction and growth and development is essential for any group's well-being.

It is easy for a group to overlook outcomes that are not directly related to a problem's resolution. However, a group's success as a problem-solving unit requires that it devote some effort to periodically analyzing all the outcomes associated with problem solving. The group should then make adjustments to increase its ability to deal with future problems.

Analyzing Outcomes

The sequence of activities involved in analyzing outcomes has been described in Chapter 4. As shown in Figure 4-8, there are specific actions that can be taken to facilitate outcome analysis. These actions are:

1. *Assess the level of group member satisfaction and growth and development.* If the outcomes in these areas are judged to be positive, proceed to the next activity. If the outcomes are seen as negative (i.e., the members are

dissatisfied, and growth and development are not evident), the group should hold a discussion to identify possible sources of dissatisfaction and develop plans to increase satisfaction and growth and development.

2. *Determine whether the solution had a positive or a negative effect on the problem.* If the effect was positive, terminate the process. If the effect was negative, evaluate the possibility of making adjustments. For example, if the group decides that a solution failed to resolve a problem because of insufficient funding, it might seek additional funds. Of course, such adjustments will not always be possible, and the entire process may need to be reviewed and analyzed to determine what might have led to the implementation of a low-quality solution. If this review and analysis fail to identify process deficiencies, consider starting the process again.

3. *If the group has attempted to make adjustments to the solution after observing a negative outcome, determine whether the adjustments resulted in creation of a new problem (or problems).* For instance, if additional funds were obtained to strengthen a solution's quality, was a funding shortage created in another area—an entirely new problem? If new problems are perceived to exist, the group should return to Figure 4-2 and start the process over (assuming, of course, that the group has problem ownership and time is available); if no new problems have been created, the modular process can be terminated.

In conducting an analysis of outcomes, the group might find the questionnaires presented here helpful. The first questionnaire (Figure 13-1) deals with group satisfaction; the second (Figure 13-2) deals with group growth and development; and the third (Figure 13-3) deals with the extent of problem resolution. These questionnaires are not scientific, so do not place too much emphasis on any results obtained from using them. It is probably better to view these questionnaires as rough guides for analyzing outcomes, rather than as precise measuring instruments.

Individual members should complete the questionnaires first, without consulting with anyone else. Then the group should discuss the individual results and attempt to achieve consensus. Finally, the results should be used to help guide decisions for future actions—both short-term and long-term.

Figure 13-1. Satisfaction outcome questionnaire.

Instructions: For each of the following questions, place an X above the one response that best describes your degree of satisfaction.

How satisfied are you with the outcome of the modular process?

1. Very dissatisfied	2. Dissatisfied	3. Satisfied	4. Very satisfied

How satisfied are you with the process used to achieve this outcome?

_____ _____ _____ _____

1. Very dissatisfied   2. Dissatisfied   3. Satisfied   4. Very satisfied

How satisfied are you with the interactions you had with the other group members while working on the problem?

_____ _____ _____ _____

1. Very dissatisfied   2. Dissatisfied   3. Satisfied   4. Very satisfied

Scoring and Interpretation: Convert each of your responses to the numerical value next to each response and add up the results. Possible scores range from 3 to 12. For individuals, a score between 9 and 12 indicates satisfaction; a score between 3 and 8 indicates dissatisfaction. Group scores can be interpreted in a similar manner by simply adding up all the scores and averaging them.

Figure 13-2. Growth and development outcome questionnaire.

Instructions: For each of the following questions, place an X above the one response that best describes the extent to which the group now uses the behavior described as compared to how it behaved when it first began the modular approach.

To what extent:

Do group members seem to be more trusting and supportive of one another?

_____ _____ _____ _____

1. Not at all   2. Somewhat   3. A lot   4. Completely

Do group members seem to deal more openly with interpersonal problems?

_____ _____ _____ _____

1. Not at all   2. Somewhat   3. A lot   4. Completely

Do group members appear more willing to assume greater responsibility for their actions?

_____ _____ _____ _____

1. Not at all   2. Somewhat   3. A lot   4. Completely

Do group members seem to be capable of working together more efficiently and effectively?

_____ _____ _____ _____

1. Not at all   2. Somewhat   3. A lot   4. Completely

Are group members better able to use the modular approach?

_____   _____   _____   _____
1. Not at all   2. Somewhat   3. A lot   4. Completely

Scoring and Interpretation: Convert each of your responses to the numerical value next to each response and add up the results. Possible scores range from 5 to 20. A score between 15 and 20 indicates that the group has grown and developed; a score between 5 and 14 suggests very little or no growth. Keep in mind that if the group was proficient in using the approach initially, not much improvement would be expected.

Figure 13-3. Problem resolution outcome questionnaire.

Instructions: For each of the following questions, place an X above the one response that best describes your perceptions.

To what extent has the problem been resolved?

_____   _____   _____   _____
1. Not at all   2. Somewhat   3. A lot   4. Completely

Compared to your initial perceptions about the problem, to what extent is the problem clear to you now?

_____   _____   _____   _____
1. Not at all   2. Somewhat   3. A lot   4. Completely

To what extent is it likely that this problem will occur again and affect your group?

_____   _____   _____   _____
1. Not at all   2. Somewhat   3. A lot   4. Completely

Scoring and Interpretation: Convert each of your responses to the numerical value next to each response and add up the results. For this questionnaire, possible scores range between 3 and 12. The problem is perceived as resolved if an individual's or the group's averaged score is between 9 and 12; a score between 3 and 8 indicates that there still is some question about the degree to which the problem has been resolved. A low score on this questionnaire suggests the need to consider making adjustments in the solution and reapplying it or to start the process (or a portion of it) over again.

After completing these questionnaires and discussing the results, the group should construct separate lists of (1) concerns about process satisfaction, (2) concerns about group growth and development, and (3) concerns about the degree of problem resolution. The group should rank-order the concerns in each list by assigning a 1 to the most important concern, a 2 to the second most important concern, and so forth. Next, categorize each concern as either a short- or a long-term issue. That is, should (or can) the concern be dealt with immediately, or should (or can) it be dealt with later on? Finally, develop action plans to specify who will do each needed task, where the person will do it, and when it will be completed.

Although development of such action plans is important, the follow-up needed to ensure that the plans are carried out is even more important. If a follow-up is not conducted, the outcome analysis will not be complete. And group members will not be as likely to learn about themselves and make any needed adjustments the next time the modular approach is used. Therefore, it is essential that someone be assigned the task of riding herd over all the action plans and assisting the group in processing what it has learned and in clarifying the nature of future adjustments.

As an illustration of how a follow-up activity might be used, assume that members of a group decide they are not satisfied with the equality of participation during group discussions. They might agree to assign someone the task of monitoring discussions to help with this problem. For example, after a discussion, such a monitor could note the amount of participation that existed or help facilitate participation during discussion. Over time, this role could be rotated among the group members to help develop equal participation as a group norm.

Having someone observe only one discussion and then discussing the observations once is too limited an approach. Extended follow-up on participation is critical to success. Group members should work on their outcome learnings continually and evaluate their progress regularly over an extended period of time. Otherwise, no learning will take place and old, dysfunctional behavior norms will continue to impede the group's ability to work together.

Summary

Outcomes are the results or consequences of previous actions or events. An outcome will not exist unless there is awareness about a product. From a systems perspective, groups in organizations may be aware of some products produced by other groups, but they may be totally unaware of other products.

When a product is produced, it may result in outcomes that are either internal or external to the group that produced the product. For example, a product may lead to satisfaction among the group members and have a positive impact on a service offered to clients. Moreover, outcomes from one product can generate other outcomes, which can generate still more outcomes, in a continuing cycle of outcomes.

In the area of creative problem solving in groups, outcomes pertain to effects on group member satisfaction, growth and development, and problem resolution. Since most groups are concerned with problem resolution outcomes, member satisfactions and growth and development are frequently overlooked.

The importance of outcomes is evident. It is necessary to know about the effects of a solution on a problem in order to take corrective actions. Without such knowledge, the group might continue the problem-solving process indefinitely. Outcomes pertaining to satisfaction and growth and development are equally important because human resources are needed to solve problems. Groups tend to learn from their experiences and interactions, which can, in turn, affect their task performance. Thus groups should assess both task and maintenance outcomes periodically.

Analyzing outcomes involves a series of activities described in Chapter 4. Included among these activities are (1) assessing group member satisfaction and growth development, (2) discussing possible sources of dissatisfaction and lack of growth and development, (3) determining whether the solution had a positive or a negative effect on the problem, (4) terminating the process if the effect was positive or making adjustments if the effect was negative, and (5) starting the modular approach over again if new problems have been created.

Questionnaires can be used to help guide discussion of the outcomes. Following analysis of questionnaire results, group members should select priority concerns to work on, categorize the concerns as being either short- or long-term, and develop action plans for dealing with activities suggested to strengthen group efforts.

Finally, the group should conduct a follow-up assessment on all actions taken. Specific follow-up roles should be assigned to people to make observations about group functioning and to help the members process what they have learned. Furthermore, all follow-up activities should be conducted over an extended period of time to ensure that new learnings are fully integrated into group behaviors.

14

A Minimodular Approach

Rationale

The material presented in this book is based on a rational approach to managing group creativity. Such an approach assumes that people who use the modular concept are guided by reason and logic. That is, once people have been presented with the "facts," they will change their behavior and adopt the prescribed procedures.

Unfortunately, not all of us are quite that rational. Most of us tend to be guided more by our emotions. Although we know what we should do, we do not always do it. And quite often, we are unable to do what we think we should do. Various constraints, such as time, money, and information, frequently preclude rational actions. Instead, we must "make do" and settle for the best possible course of action, given the pressures and limitations under which we must operate.

For these reasons, it must be reemphasized that the complete version of the modular approach will not be practical in all situations. Of course, a major advantage of the modular approach is its adaptability to a wide range of preferences, needs, and situations. For example, if time is a major constraint, a group can decide to eliminate some modules and modify others to best suit its needs.

Although this flexibility represents a major strength of the modular approach, it can also be a weakness. Too much flexibility can be just as much a liability as little or no flexibility. Without some structure to guide a group's selection of modules and help it use them, less than satisfactory outcomes may result. Because some of the modules are more important than others, relatively less time and effort should be expended on the less important modules. In some situations, a group might be better off using an unstructured approach. Thus the flexibility of the modular approach does not mean that it is appropriate to every problem situation.

It is entirely possible that a group can construct its own version of a minimodular approach and succeed quite well in resolving its problems. However, a group may not have the time or the motivation to undertake an analysis of the best combination of modules and how they might be used for optimal effectiveness. Such a group might want an approach that will require a minimal amount of time and effort but that will be capable of achieving its problem-solving objectives. For such groups, the minimodular approach that follows might serve as a general model around which they can construct their own approach.

The approach that follows is essentially a condensed version of the modular approach described in the preceding chapters. It is not intended, however, to serve as a rigid model for managing group creativity and problem solving. Instead, it is a basic framework from which a group can develop many alternative approaches. Each group will have to decide on the exact format that will work best for a particular situation.

Guidelines and Suggestions

An overriding rule of thumb to follow in using the minimodular approach is: If the costs of using a module (or a portion of it) are likely to outweigh the probable benefits, do not use the module. In other words, if a particular module is not likely to be a clear-cut asset in solving your problem, eliminate the module. This decision may have to be weighed every time you begin work on a problem, depending on any changes in composition of the group, the amount of time available, the motivation of the group members, and a variety of other factors that may be unique to a particular problem situation. In any event, you want to construct an approach that is economical, yet will still provide the structure and guidance needed to produce a high-quality solution.

In using the approach that follows, you may have little difficulty in analyzing each of the modules you have chosen. However, in some instances, you may find some modules more difficult to analyze than others. When such situations occur, consider referring to the assessment questionnaires described earlier. Very often, harmful group conflict can be avoided and time can be used more wisely if you take the time to use a more structured analytical approach. Thus, if you cannot decide as a group on how to analyze a module, use a questionnaire and then abide by the averaged responses. Although this is not as desirable as reaching a consensus, it is better for the group members to devote more of their energy and time to actual problem-solving activities.

One final suggestion: When using any problem-solving model, try to avoid becoming too attached to one particular format. Although it may be important to use the same framework when solving a problem (e.g., the same basic stages), the use of identical techniques and processes within the framework may be dysfunctional in the long run. Don't let your group fall into a rut from using the same monotonous routine. Vary the way you use the modules. In doing so, there is less chance of spontaneous and unique ideas being lost. A group can easily become stale without some variety.

Assessing the Group Climate

Group creative problem solving is likely to be most successful when a group's climate is conducive to creative thinking. If creative thinking is stifled by forces within a group or a larger system, creative solutions will not be generated easily—if at all.

If group membership remains relatively stable and a creative climate has been established, there will be little need to assess the group climate each time the creative problem-solving process is begun. However, if group membership is relatively unstable, the group is relatively new, or the creative climate has never been fully evaluated, some type of assessment will be needed. In conducting this assessment, consider the following factors:

1. The openness of expression of new ideas.
2. The receptivity of other group members to new ideas.
3. The amount of risk taking observed.
4. The explicit recognition of worthy ideas.
5. The closeness of supervision.
6. The willingness of group members to test assumptions.
7. The tendency of group members to defer judgment when new ideas are proposed.
8. The use of humor during problem solving.
9. The amount of confidence shown toward other group members.
10. An overall spirit of cooperation to get the job done.

Analyzing the Inputs

This module deals with the analysis of four elements: problems, time, people resources, and physical resources. Generally speaking, you need to analyze all these elements every time you deal with a new problem. However, the degree of analysis required for each element may vary quite a bit. Problems and time usually will require the most attention, people resources may require a moderate amount of attention, and physical resources often will require very little attention. Thus this module should probably never be excluded from analysis, although the amount of attention given to it may vary.

Problems

Collect all information that pertains to the problem. Include all pertinent information, no matter how remote or unrelated it may seem at the time. Using this information, develop a tentative definition of the problem. Next, determine whether the problem is ill structured. In general, an ill-structured problem is characterized by a lack of information about what the problem situation is, what the problem situation should be, or how to close the gap between what is and what should be. Only ill-structured (or semistructured) problems are appropriate for creative problem solving. If the problem is relatively structured, routine procedures can usually be used.

Time

Determine how much time is available to resolve the problem. If the time available appears to be totally inadequate, consider ways of increasing it. If necessary, redefine the problem in such a way that more time will be perceived to exist for dealing with the problem.

People Resources

If group membership has remained relatively constant over time and each member's strengths and weaknesses are known and integrated into the group's processes, there will be little need to analyze the people resources. However, if the opposite conditions exist, these resources will need to be analyzed—at least on a superficial level. Among the factors to look at are skills, knowledge, experience, values, motivation, and expectations.

Physical Resources

Review any special needs for equipment, supplies and materials, and physical facilities. Also included in this category is money, which is often needed to obtain the other physical resources.

When analyzing the four input resources, consider using the four criteria of adequacy, availability, applicability, and importance. That is, determine the extent to which each input "can get the job done," is ready for use, is usable and relevant, and is required for problem resolution. If any input does not satisfy the criteria, make appropriate modifications or obtain new resources, if feasible.

Analyzing the Content

This module contains four major variables: group composition, role clarity, task clarity, and environmental conduciveness. If the group membership has been relatively stable and the group seems to be functioning with no major problems, you can eliminate this module. However, if there is any doubt about the content variables or the group is new, give this module at least a cursory analysis.

Group Composition

If it is possible to exert any control over group composition, select members for creative problem solving on the basis of their ability to: (1) tolerate ambiguity, (2) use their intelligence effectively, (3) develop different problem perspectives, (4) generate many different types of ideas, (5) be expressive rather than repressive or suppressive, (6) use both convergent and divergent thinking, (7) use both intuitive and analytic thinking, (8) produce original ideas, (9) believe in themselves as the primary determinant of what happens to them in life, (10) persevere when working on a problem, (11) have confidence in their abilities, (12) take calculated risks, (13) generate large numbers of ideas in a relatively short period of time, (14) add detail to their ideas and the ideas of others, (15) express themselves aesthetically, and (16) think independently.

In addition to these individual abilities, the ideal creative problem-solving group would be composed of (1) members of the same sex (especially for brainstorming groups), (2) diverse personalities, (3) members who can cooperate with one another, (4) members whose needs can be mutually satisfied and whose personalities complement each other rather than clash, (5) members with fewer than two years of experience working together, and (6) no more than five members.

Role Clarity

Determine whether group members are clear about what is expected of them during the creative problem-solving process. If specific roles have been assigned, ask each group member to describe how he or she perceives the roles of the other group members. If these group descriptions do not match the perceptions of the person whose role has been described, discuss the perceptual differences in some detail and attempt to achieve a consensus on role perceptions.

Task Clarity

Determine whether group members understand how to do what is expected of them. If there is low clarity, provide structure to increase understanding.

Environmental Conduciveness

Evaluate the possible effects on group functioning of concrete aspects (rooms, color, lighting, temperature, and noise), territoriality, personal space (particularly role invasion), and spatial arrangements. For example, consider whether different rooms should be used, how the group deals with territoriality and personal space in interacting with one another, and how seating arrangements affect leadership issues and conflict resolution.

Conducting Process Activities

This module forms the core of the modular approach and should be used whenever you undertake a creative problem-solving task. However, the extent to which you give attention to different stages may vary somewhat, depending on the amount of time available, the experience level of the group members in using the process, and other factors specific to individual groups. The basic process activities are redefining the problem, generating ideas, evaluating and selecting ideas, and implementing ideas.

Redefining the Problem

Using such techniques as analogies, boundary examinations, the five Ws, reversals, and the why method, generate a variety of problem redefinitions. Some guidelines to follow when generating redefinitions are: Withhold all judgment; avoid searching for "correct" redefinitions; consider all redefinitions tentative; and make certain that all group members understand the meaning and intent of each redefinition. After all possible redefinitions have been generated, select the one that best describes the problem situation as understood by the group members (or an outside client).

Generating Ideas

Decide whether to use brainstorming, brainwriting, or a combination of brainstorming and brainwriting to generate ideas. Next, select specific brainstorming or brainwriting techniques. Criteria to use in selecting these techniques might include such factors as (1) amount of time available, (2) potential for interpersonal conflict to arise, (3) accommodation of social interaction needs, (4) group cohesiveness requirements, (5) status differences among group members, and (6) skill and experience in using the various techniques. Withholding all judgment, generate as many ideas as possible.

Evaluating and Selecting Ideas

Determine whether group members should participate in the evaluation and selection process (time available? need for group members to accept a final solution?). If the group is to participate, agree on an overall strategy to use. Next, if the number of generated ideas is relatively large, preselect a final idea pool by combining ideas, by grouping ideas into logical categories, or by voting. Deferring all judgment, generate as many evaluation criteria as possible. Choose evaluation and selection techniques, and select one or more ideas for implementation. If the quality of the final solution is in doubt, use the product module.

Implementing Ideas

Begin by assessing the state of the original problem in relation to the solution selected. If the problem has changed substantially, revise the solution or develop a new one. Next, determine whether the solution represents a change that is likely to result in resistance from others. If resistance is likely, develop a strategy for overcoming this resistance. For example, involve the people likely to be affected by the solution, be as specific as possible about positive and negative consequences of the solution, emphasize personal benefits likely to result from implementing the solution, and attempt to enlist the support of key opinion leaders within the organization. If the solution must be "sold" to others before implementation, develop an implementation strategy, using the following actions: (1) Develop and evaluate goal statements. (2) Assess available resources. (3) Assess the needs of the people to be sold. (4) Assess the implementation strengths and weaknesses of the group members. (5) Analyze the solution benefits. (6) Prepare for the solution presentation to others. (7) Conduct the presentation. (8) Devise the final implementation strategy (including selection of formal implementation techniques). And (9) implement the solution.

Analyzing the Product

This module is optional, depending on the perceived quality of the solution selected for implementation, whether or not the group has trouble achieving consensus when selecting a solution, and whether or not there is a need for the group to receive training and experience in analyzing products.

Criteria

Determine whether the group members understand the major product dimensions of novelty, resolution, and elaboration and synthesis, as well as the specific criteria associated with each. If the criteria are not understood, provide training; if the criteria are understood, use the CPAM Adjective Checklist to analyze the selected solution. After conducting this analysis, decide whether you want to accept the solution and implement it, reject the solution and select another one, attempt to increase the solution's quality through the use of the CPAM checklist, or attempt to make modifications or revisions that increase the solution's quality without using the CPAM checklist.

Increasing Solution Quality

If you decide to attempt to increase the solution's quality, the following procedure can be used: (1) Review the criteria and check for understanding. (2) Classify the solution as below or above average in quality. (3) Identify the adjectives that received negative values within each dimension. (4) Using the dimension with the lowest subtotal score, select adjectives to use in increasing the solution's quality. (5) Decide on the approach to use (e.g., use brainstorming, brainwriting, or a modified creative problem-solving process). (6) If time permits, repeat Step 5, using adjectives from the next highest-rated dimension. And (7) use the CPAM Adjective Checklist to reevaluate the quality of the upgraded solution.

Analyzing the Outcomes

Delete this module only if there is not enough time or motivation to warrant using it. The major activities involved in this module are to: (1) determine how satisfied the group members are with working with one another and with using the modular approach, (2) determine the extent to which the group was able to grow and develop while using the modular approach, and (3) determine whether the implemented solution had a positive or a negative effect on the problem.

If the group members are dissatisfied with working with one another and with their growth and development, conduct a discussion to identify and eliminate the sources of dissatisfaction. If the solution had a positive effect on the problem, terminate the process; if the solution had a negative effect, determine whether any solution adjustments are possible, and if they are, make the required adjustments. Finally, determine whether any new problems were created by implementing the solution. Terminate the process if no new problems were created, or begin the modular approach again if new problems were created.

Summary

The modular approach is based on a rational view of managing group creativity. However, because most people are not completely rational, flexibility is required to apply the modular approach. Given such constraints as time, motivation, and resource availability and adequacy, groups must decide which modules they will need to deal with a problem. Moreover, the modular approach will not be appropriate to every situation.

Although a group can develop its own minimodular approach to best suit its needs, it is more efficient to work from a structured format, modifying and adapting it. The minimodular approach presented in this chapter is structured in this way; it can and should be used as a basic framework that groups develop as they wish.

When you use the minimodular approach, certain guidelines should be followed. For example, do not use any module that will not be a clear-cut asset for dealing with a particular problem situation, refer to the assessment questionnaires (described in earlier chapters) whenever you have trouble analyzing a module, and vary the problem-solving activities slightly every time you deal with a problem to avoid falling into a rut.

Basic minimodular activities include:

1. Assess the conduciveness of the group climate to creative thinking.
2. Analyze the inputs. Pay the most attention to problems and time, followed by people resources, and then physical resources.
3. Analyze the content. If any doubt exists about the appropriateness of a group's content, analyze group composition, role clarity, task clarity, and environmental conduciveness to creative problem solving.
4. Conduct process activities. Redefine the problem, generate ideas, evaluate and select ideas, and implement the selected idea(s). This module forms the core of the modular approach and should be used without exception to resolve ill-structured problems.
5. Analyze the product. Use this module whenever you decide that the quality of a selected idea may be suspect, if the group has trouble achieving a consensus about idea quality, or if you simply wish to provide the group with experience and training in product analysis. If time permits, use the CPAM Adjective Checklist to evaluate the

chosen solution. If you decide the solution is low in quality, use the CPAM Adjective Checklist to help increase solution quality.

6. Analyze the outcomes. Evaluate group member satisfaction in working with each other and with the minimodular approach, the extent to which group growth and development occurred, and the extent to which the implemented solution had a positive or negative effect on the problem. After you have conducted this evaluation, make any needed adjustments by discussing problem areas with the group, modifying the solution, or restarting or terminating the process, depending on whether or not any new problems were created.

Bibliography and References

Altman, I., and Haythorn, W. W. The effects of social isolation and group composition on performance. *Human Relations*, 1967, *20*, 313–340.

Asch, S. E. Effects of group pressure upon the modification and distortion of judgments. In H. Guetzkow (ed.), *Groups, Leadership and Men*. Pittsburgh: Carnegie Press, 1951.

Back, K. W. Influence through social communication. *Journal of Abnormal and Social Psychology*, 1951, *46*, 9–23.

Bales, R. F., Strodtbeck, F. L., Mills, T. M., and Roseborough, M. E. Channels of communication in small groups. *American Sociological Review*, 1951, *16*, 461–468.

Barnlund, D. C. A comparative study of individual, majority, and group judgment. *Journal of Abnormal and Social Psychology*, 1959, *58*, 55–60.

Bell, C. R. *Influencing: Marketing the Ideas That Matter*. Austin, Texas: Learning Concepts, 1982.

Benne, K. D., and Sheats, P. Functional roles of group members. *Journal of Social Issues*, 1948, *4*, 41–49.

Berkowitz, L. Group standards, cohesiveness, and productivity. *Human Relations*, 1954, *7*, 509–519.

Besemer, S. P. Letter to author, May 3, 1983.

Besemer, S. P., and Treffinger, D. J. Analysis of creative products: Review and synthesis. *Journal of Creative Behavior*, 1981, *15*, 159–178.

Bouchard, T. J., Jr. Personality, problem-solving procedure, and performance in small groups. *Journal of Applied Psychology Monograph*, 1969, *53*, 1–29.

————. A comparison of two group brainstorming procedures. *Journal of Applied Psychology*, 1972a, *56*, 418–421.

————. Training, motivation, and personality as determinants of the effectiveness of brainstorming groups and individuals. *Journal of Applied Psychology*, 1972b, *56*, 324–331.

Brightman, H. J., and Urban, T. F. Problem solving and managerial performance. *Atlanta Economic Review*, July–August 1978, 23–26.

Campbell, J. P. Individual versus group problem solving in an industrial sample. *Journal of Applied Psychology*, 1968, *52*, 205–210.

Carey, R. G. Correlates of satisfaction in the priesthood. *Administrative Science Quarterly*, 1972, *17*, 185–195.

Carlston, D. E. Effects of polling order on social influence in decision-making groups. *Sociometry*, 1977, *40*, 115–123.

Cheyne, J. A., and Efran, M. G. The effects of spatial and interpersonal variables on the invasion of group controlled territories. *Sociometry*, 1972, *35*, 477–489.

Clark, C. H. *The Crawford Slip Writing Method*. Kent, Ohio: Charles H. Clark, 1978.

Clement, D. E., and Schiereck, J. J., Jr. Sex composition and group performance in a visual signal detection task. *Memory and Cognition*, 1973, *1*, 251–255.

Coch, L., and French, J. Overcoming resistance to change. *Human Relations*, 1948, *1*, 512–532.

Cohen, D. J., Whitmyre, J. W., and Funk, W. H. Effect of group cohesiveness and training upon group thinking. *Journal of Applied Psychology*, 1960, *44*, 319–322.

Davis, J. H. *Group Performance*. Reading, Mass.: Addison-Wesley, 1969.

Delbecq, A. L., and Van de Ven, A. H. A group process model for problem identification and program planning. *Journal of Applied Behavioral Science*, 1971, *7*, 466–492.

Delbecq, A. L., Van de Ven, A. H., and Gustafson, D. H. *Group Techniques for Program Planning*. Glenview, Ill.: Scott, Foresman, 1975.

Dunnette, M. D., Campbell, J., and Jaastad, K. The effects of group participation on brainstorming effectiveness for two industrial samples. *Journal of Applied Psychology*, 1963, *47*, 10–37.

Exline, R. V. Group climate as a factor in the relevance and accuracy of social perception. *Journal of Abnormal and Social Psychology*, 1957, *55*, 382–388.

Finch, F. E., Jones, J. R., and Litterer, J. A. *Managing for Organizational Effectiveness: An Experiential Approach*. New York: McGraw-Hill, 1976.

Frank, F., and Anderson, L. R. Effects of task and group size upon group productivity and member satisfaction. *Sociometry*, 1971, *34*, 135–149.

French, J. R. P., Jr. The disruption and cohesion of groups. *Journal of Abnormal and Social Psychology*. 1941, *36*, 361–377.

Fry, C. L. Personality and acquisition factors in the development of coordination strategy. *Journal of Personality and Social Psychology*, 1965, *2*, 403–407.

Gergen, K. J., and Bauer, R. A. Interactive effects of self-esteem and task difficulty on social conformity. *Journal of Personality and Social Psychology*, 1967, 6, 16–22.

Gerard, H. B., Wilhelmy, R. A., and Conolley, E. S. Conformity and group size. *Journal of Personality and Social Psychology*, 1968, 8, 79–82.

Geschka, H. Methods and organization of idea generation. Paper presented at Creativity Development Week II. Greensboro, N.C.: Center for Creative Leadership, September 1979.

————. Perspectives on using various creativity techniques. In S. S. Gryskiewicz (ed.), *Creativity Week II, 1979 Proceedings*. Greensboro, N.C.: Center for Creative Leadership, 1980.

Glass, D. C., Singer, J. E., and Friedman, L. N. Psychic cost of adaptation to an environmental stressor. *Journal of Personality and Social Psychology*, 1969, 12, 200–210.

Good, K. J. Social facilitation: Effects of performance anticipation, evaluation, and response competition on free associations. *Journal of Personality and Social Psychology*, 1973, 28, 270–275.

Goodacre, D. M., III. The use of a sociometric test as a predictor of combat unit effectiveness. *Sociometry*, 1951, 14, 148–152.

Gordon, W. J. J. *Synectics*. New York: Harper & Row, 1961.

Gross, E. Primary functions of a small group. *American Journal of Sociology*, 1954, 60, 24–30.

Guilford, J. P. Creativity. *American Psychologist*, 1950, 5, 444–454.

Hackman, J. R., and Morris, C. G. Group tasks, group interaction and group performance effectiveness. In L. Berkowitz (ed.), *Advances in Experimental Social Psychology*, Vol. 8. New York: Academic Press, 1975.

Hamilton, R. Screening business development opportunities. *Business Horizons*, August 1974, 13–24.

Harari, D., and Graham, W. K. Task and task consequences as factors in individual and group brainstorming. *Journal of Social Psychology*, 1975, 95, 61–65.

Haythorn, W. W., Couch, A., Haefner, D., Langham, P., and Carter, L. F. The behavior of authoritarian and equalitarian personalities in groups. *Human Relations*, 1956, 9, 57–74.

Henrickson, P. R. Non-verbal manipulation and creativeness in art. *Studies in Art Education*, 1963, 5, 60–70.

Hermann, W. E. *The Hermann Brain Dominance Instrument*. Stamford, Conn.: Applied Creative Services, 1980.

Hochbaum, G. M. The relation between group members' self confidence and their reactions to group pressures to uniformity. *American Sociological Review*, 1954, 79, 678–687.

Hoffman, L. R. Homogeneity of member personality and its effect on group problem-solving. *Journal of Abnormal and Social Psychology*, 1959, 58, 27–32.

————. Group problem solving. In L. Berkowitz (ed.), *Advances in Experimental Social Psychology*, Vol. 2. New York: Academic Press, 1965.

————. Applying experimental research on group problem solving to organizations. *Journal of Applied Behavioral Science*, 1979, 15, 375–391.

Hoffman, L. R., and Maier, N. R. F. Quality and acceptance of problem solutions by members of homogeneous and heterogeneous groups. *Journal of Abnormal and Social Psychology*, 1961, 62, 401–407.

Horowitz, M. W., and Newman, J. B. Spoken and written expressions: An experimental analysis. *Journal of Abnormal and Social Psychology*, 1964, 68, 640–647.

House, R. J., and Rizzo, J. R. Role conflict and ambiguity as critical variables in a model of organizational behavior. *Organizational Behavior and Human Performance*, 1972, 7, 467–505.

Huber, G. P. *Managerial Decision Making*. Glenview, Ill.: Scott, Foresman, 1980.

Husband, R. W. Cooperative versus solitary problem solution. *Journal of Social Psychology*, 1940, 11, 405–409.

Huse, E. F. *Organization Development and Change* (2nd ed.). St. Paul, Minn.: West, 1980.

Janis, I. L. *Victims of Groupthink*. Boston: Houghton Mifflin, 1972.

Jewell, L. N., and Reitz, H. J. *Group Effectiveness in Organizations*. Glenview, Ill.: Scott, Foresman, 1981.

Kabanoff, B., and O'Brien, G. E. The effects of task type and cooperation upon group products and performance. *Organizational Behavior and Human Performance*, 1979, 23, 163–181.

Katz, D. Morale and motivation in industry. In W. Dennis (ed.), *Current Trends in Industrial Psychology*. Pittsburgh: University of Pittsburgh Press, 1949.

Katz, D., and Kahn, R. L. *The Social Psychology of Organizations*. New York: John Wiley, 1966.

Kelly, H. H., and Thibaut, J. W. Group problem solving. In G. Lindsey and E. Aronson (eds.), *The Handbook of Social Psychology* (2nd ed.), Vol. 4. Reading, Mass.: Addison-Wesley, 1969.

Kent, R. N., and McGrath, J. E. Task and group characteristics as factors influencing group performance. *Journal of Experimental Social Psychology*, 1969, 5, 429–440.

Kepner, C., and Tregoe, B. *The Rational Manager*. New York: McGraw-Hill, 1965.

Koberg, D., and Bagnall, J. *The Universal Traveller*. Los Altos, Calif.: William Kaufmann, 1976.

Lipman, A. Building design and social interaction. *The Architects Journal*, 1968, *147*, 23–30.

Lott, D. F., and Sommer, R. Seating arrangements and status. *Journal of Personality and Social Psychology*, 1967, *7*, 90–95.

MacKinnon, D. W. *In Search of Human Effectiveness*. Buffalo, N.Y.: Creative Education Foundation, 1978.

Madsen, D. B., and Finger, S. R., Jr. Comparison of a written feedback procedure, group brainstorming, and individual brainstorming. *Journal of Applied Psychology*, 1978, *63*, 120–123.

Maginn, B. K., and Harris, R. J. Effects of anticipated evaluation on individual brainstorming performance. *Journal of Applied Psychology*, 1980, *65*, 219–225.

Maier, N. R. F. *Problem Solving Discussions and Conferences*. New York: McGraw-Hill, 1963.

Martens, R., and Landers, D. M. Evaluation potential as a determinant of coaction effects. *Journal of Experimental Social Psychology*, 1972, *8*, 347–359.

Meadow, A., Parnes, S. J., and Reese, H. Influence of brainstorming instructions and problem sequence on a creative problem solving test. *Journal of Applied Psychology*, 1959, *43*, 413–416.

Mehrabian, A., and Diamond, S. G. Seating arrangement and conversation. *Sociometry*, 1971, *34*, 281–289.

Mintz, N. Effects of esthetic surroundings: II. Prolonged and repeated experience in a "beautiful" and an "ugly" room. *Journal of Psychology*, 1956, *41*, 459–466.

Morris, W. C., and Sashkin, M. *Organizational Behavior in Action, Skill Building Experiences*. St. Paul, Minn.: West, 1976.

O'Dell, J. W. Group size and emotional interaction. *Journal of Personality and Social Psychology*, 1968, *8*, 75–78.

Organ, D. W., and Greene, C. N. Role ambiguity, locus of control, and work satisfaction. *Journal of Applied Psychology*, 1974, *59*, 101–102.

Osborn, A. F. *Applied Imagination* (3rd ed.). New York: Scribner's, 1963.

Parnes, S. J. *Creative Guidebook*. New York: Scribner's, 1967.

Parnes, S. J., and Meadow, A. Development of individual creative talent. In C. W. Taylor and F. Barron (eds.), *Scientific Creativity: Its Recognition and Development*. New York: John Wiley, 1963.

Pelz, D. C., and Andrews, F. M. *Scientists in Organizations*. New York: John Wiley, 1966.

Pepinsky, P., Hemphill, J. K., and Shevitz, R. N. Attempts to lead, group productivity, and morale, under conditions of acceptance and rejection. *Journal of Abnormal and Social Psychology*, 1958, *57*, 47–54.

Phillips, D. J. Report on discussion 66. *Adult Education Journal*, 1948, 7, 181–182.

Powell, R. M., and Schlacter, J. L. Participative management: A panacea? *Academy of Management Journal*, 1971, *14*, 165–173.

Prince, G. M. The operational mechanism of synectics. *Journal of Creative Behavior*, 1968, *2*, 1–13.

Raudsepp, E. *How Creative Are You?* New York: G. P. Putnam's Sons, 1981.

Rawlinson, J. G. *Creative Thinking and Brainstorming*. New York: John Wiley, 1981.

Reitan, H. T., and Shaw, M. E. Group membership, sex-composition of the group, and conformity behavior. *Journal of Social Psychology*, 1964, *64*, 45–51.

Rosenberg, S., Erlick, D. E., and Berkowitz, L. Some effects of varying combinations of group members on group performance measures and leadership behaviors. *Journal of Abnormal and Social Psychology*, 1955, *51*, 195–203.

Rotter, J. B. Generalized expectancies for internal versus external control of reinforcement. *Psychological Monographs*, 1966, *80*, Whole No. 609, 1–28.

Russo, N. F. Connotations of seating arrangements. *Cornell Journal of Social Relations*, 1967, *2*, 37–44.

Schaude, G. R. Methods of idea generation. In S. S. Gryskiewicz (ed.), *Proceedings of Creativity Week I, 1978*. Greensboro, N.C.: Center for Creative Leadership, 1979.

Schutz, W. C. What makes groups productive? *Human Relations*, 1955, *8*, 429–465.

Seghers, C. E. Color in the office. *The Management Review*, 1948, *37*, 452–453.

Shaw, M. E. A comparison of individuals and small groups in the rational solution of complex problems. *American Journal of Psychology*, 1932, *44*, 491–504.

———: *Group Dynamics, The Psychology of Small Group Behavior* (2nd ed.), New York: McGraw-Hill, 1976.

Shaw, M. E., and Shaw, L. M. Some effects of sociometric grouping upon learning in a second grade classroom. *Journal of Social Psychology*, 1962, *57*, 453–458.

Shepard, H. A. Creativity in R/D teams. *Research and Engineering*, October 1956, 10–13.

Shonk, J. H. *Working in Teams*. New York: AMACOM, 1982.

Slater, P. E. Contrasting correlates of group size. *Sociometry*, 1958, *21*, 129–139.

Smelser, W. T. Dominance as a factor in achievement and perception in cooperative problem solving interactions. *Journal of Abnormal and Social Psychology*, 1961, *62*, 535–542.

Sommer, R. *Personal Space: The Behavioral Basis of Design.* Englewood Cliffs, N.J.: Prentice-Hall, 1969.

Stein, M. I. *Stimulating Creativity,* Vol. 2, *Group Procedures.* New York: Academic Press, 1975.

Steinzor, B. The spatial factor in face-to-face discussion groups. *Journal of Abnormal and Social Psychology,* 1950, *45,* 552–555.

Street, W. R. Brainstorming by individuals, coacting and interacting groups. *Journal of Applied Psychology,* 1974, *59,* 433–436.

Strodtbeck, F. L., and Hook, L. H. The social dimensions of a twelve man jury table. *Sociometry,* 1961, *24,* 397–415.

Taylor, D. W., Berry, P. C., and Block, C. H. Does group participation when using brainstorming facilitate or inhibit creative thinking? *Administrative Science Quarterly,* 1958, *3,* 23–47.

Taylor, J. W. *How to Create Ideas.* Englewood Cliffs, N.J.: Prentice-Hall, 1961.

Tinker, M. A. Illumination standards for effective and comfortable vision. *Journal of Consulting Psychology,* 1939, *3,* 11–19.

Torrance, E. P. Highly intelligent and highly creative children in a laboratory school. *Research Memo BER-59-7.* Minneapolis, Minn.: Bureau of Educational Research, University of Minnesota, 1959.

Triandis, H. E., Hall, E. R., and Ewen, R. B. Member heterogeneity and dyadic creativity. *Human Relations,* 1965, *18,* 33–55.

Ulschak, F. L., Nathanson, L., and Gillan, P. G. *Small Group Problem Solving.* Reading, Mass.: Addison-Wesley, 1981.

Van de Ven, A. H., and Delbecq, A. L. The effectiveness of nominal, delphi, and interacting group decision making processes. *Academy of Management Journal,* 1974, *17,* 605 621.

VanGundy, A. B. *Techniques of Structured Problem Solving.* New York: Van Nostrand Reinhold, 1981.

―――. *Training Your Creative Mind.* Englewood Cliffs, N.J.: Prentice-Hall, 1982.

Vroom, V. H., and Yetton, P. W. *Leadership and Decision Making.* Pittsburgh: University of Pittsburgh Press, 1973.

Wallach, M. A., Kogan, N., and Bem, D. J. Group influence or individual risk taking. *Journal of Abnormal and Social Psychology,* 1962, *65,* 75–86.

Warfield, J. N., Geschka, H., and Hamilton, R. *Methods of Idea Management.* Columbus, Ohio: Academy for Contemporary Problems, 1975.

Weiss, H. M., and Knight, P. R. The utility of humility: Self-esteem, information search, and problem-solving efficiency. *Organizational Behavior and Human Performance,* 1980, *25,* 216–223.

Whiting, C. S. *Creative Thinking.* New York: Reinhold, 1958.

Whyte, W. F. The social structure of the restaurant. *American Journal of Sociology,* 1949, *54,* 302–308.

Willis, F. N., Jr. Initial speaking distance as a function of the speaker's relationship. *Psychonomic Science*, 1966, 5, 221–222.

Woods, M. F., and Davies, G. B. Potential problem analysis: A systematic approach to problem predictions and contingency planning—An aid to the smooth exploitation of research. *R & D Management*, 1973, 4, 25–32.

Zajonc, R. B. The requirements and design of a standard group task. *Journal of Experimental Social Psychology*, 1965, 1, 71–88.

Zajonc, R. B., and Sales, S. M. Social facilitation of dominant and subordinate responses. *Journal of Experimental Social Psychology*, 1966, 2, 160–168.

Zander, A. *Motives and Goals in Groups.* New York: Academic Press, 1971.

Ziller, R. C. Group size: A determinant of the quality and stability of group decisions. *Sociometry*, 1957, 20, 165–173.

Index